GOLD ON THE HORIZON

'Pretty well nobody has read all that C. S. Lewis read, and so pretty well everybody will have missed all kinds of echoes and allusions in the Narnia books. Jem Bloomfield continues his journey through the series, opening up the rich hinterland of Lewis's wonderful imagination with enthusiasm and an impressively wide familiarity with Lewis's inner world, from the Classics to the school stories of the nineeenth and twentieth centuries. A real delight, and full of illumination.'

Rowan Williams, former Archbishop of Canterbury

'*Gold on the Horizon* is a compelling exploration of C. S. Lewis's *Prince Caspian* and *The Voyage of the Dawn Treader* as novels burdened with the weight of the past; Jem Bloomfield skilfully shows how Lewis's fiction reflected and refracted troubling questions in twentieth-century history and archaeology.'

Dr Francis Young, historian and folklorist, author of *Twilight of the Gidlings: The Shadowy Beginnings of Britain's Supernatural Beings*

'Following his refreshing study *Paths in the Snow* (2023), in which he discussed literary, cultural and theological references in *The Lion, the Witch and the Wardrobe,* Jem Bloomfield's new book *Gold on the Horizon* turns the focus on *Prince Caspian* and *The Voyage of the Dawn Treader*. Citing influences as diverse as the Sutton Hoo ship burial, and H. Rider Haggard's novel *King Solomon's Mines*, he investigates Lewis's focus on the deep past in *Prince Caspian*; while in *The Voyage of the Dawn Treader* he discovers traces of *The Odyssey*, the Grail legends, and the hope of a New Elizabethan Age inspired by the coronation of young Queen Elizabeth in 1952. As ever, Bloomfield is never less than thoughtful and thought-provoking, and this latest work is bound to fascinate fans of Narnia.'

Katherine Langrish, author of *From Spare Oom to War Drobe: Travels in Narnia with my Nine-Year-Old Self*

GOLD ON THE HORIZON

A literary journey through
PRINCE CASPIAN and
THE VOYAGE OF THE
DAWN TREADER

JEM BLOOMFIELD

DARTON·LONGMAN+TODD
INTELLIGENT ♦ INSPIRATIONAL ♦ INCLUSIVE
SPIRITUAL BOOKS

*For Bean, Fliss, Waz and Mel,
with respectful affection.*

First published in 2024 by
Darton, Longman and Todd Ltd
Unit 1, The Exchange
6 Scarbrook Road
Croydon CR0 1UH

© 2024 Jem Bloomfield

The right of Jem Bloomfield to be identified as the Author of this work has been asserted in accordance with the Copyright, Designs and Patents Act 1988.

ISBN 978-1-915412-81-2

A catalogue record for this book is available from the British Library.

Designed and produced by Judy Linard

Printed and bound in Great Britain by Bell & Bain, Glasgow

CONTENTS

PREFACE　　　　　　　　　　　　　　　　　　　　7

PRINCE CASPIAN　　　　　　　　　　　　　11

INTRODUCTION　　　　　　　　　　　　　　　13
THE CROWN BENEATH THE EARTH

CHAPTER ONE　　　　　　　　　　　　　　　23
MOURNING AND DELVING

CHAPTER TWO　　　　　　　　　　　　　　　49
THE PRINCE UPON THE BATTLEMENTS

CHAPTER THREE　　　　　　　　　　　　　　73
LUCY THE PROPHET

CHAPTER FOUR　　　　　　　　　　　　　　91
THE LOST TRIBES OF NARNIA

CHAPTER FIVE　　　　　　　　　　　　　　　119
THE WISDOM OF THE DOCTOR

CHAPTER SIX　　　　　　　　　　　　　　　　137
LEWIS AMONG THE CLERKS

THE VOYAGE OF THE DAWN TREADER 161

INTRODUCTION
ORIENTED FOR THE JOURNEY 163

CHAPTER ONE
FRESH AIR AND OTHER FADS 175

CHAPTER TWO
NARNIAN BUREAUCRACY 195

CHAPTER THREE
OF DRAGONS AND SOLAR HEROES 219

CHAPTER FOUR
THE QUEEN'S HONOUR 245

CHAPTER FIVE
OF WITCHES, FLEECES AND THE WINE-BRIGHT SEA 263

ENDNOTES 281

PREFACE

This book explores the literary aspects of *Prince Caspian* and *The Voyage of the Dawn Treader*, tracing the way these novels construct the magical world of Narnia. It follows on from *Paths in the Snow*, in which I examined the literary and theological landscape of *The Lion, the Witch and the Wardrobe*. This book takes a slightly different approach, but one which I hope will still enable an enjoyable journey through the novels. For a start, this volume covers two Narnia books, since they are slightly less densely packed with allusions and I do not need to spend as much time explaining the literary approach I am taking. I am also not proceeding as precisely through the books chapter by chapter. Instead, I have focused on some major texts with which *Prince Caspian* and *The Voyage of the Dawn Treader* seem to be entwined. These range from *Hamlet* to *King Solomon's Mines*, and from *The Odyssey* to *Tom Brown's School Days*. I have approached these in roughly chronological order; when a chapter in one of the Narnian tales seems particularly close to another work, I begin by focusing on that scene, before expanding out to connections elsewhere in the novel. When the Narnian prince finds himself on the battlements of a castle being told that his uncle murdered his father, for example, I examine the echoes of *Hamlet* in this scene. When Susan cries over the golden chess piece in the ruins of Cair Paravel and remembers her horse, I consider how she is paralleling the Anglo-Saxon elegies. In both cases, though, there are other resonances from the same text throughout the novel which enrich its meanings and these moments give a chance to range backwards and forwards from the immediate scene. At other times, I concentrate more on a literary theme or a cluster of ideas, such as the way the description of the Scrubb family marks them as a recognisable social stereotype in mid-century Britain, or how the figure of Lucy as a young queen attended by an infatuated (if whiskery) courtier taps into the cultural movement known as 'New Elizabethanism'. As in *Paths in the Snow*, I am interested in both how these literary connections shape the meanings of the Narnian novels, and how they present a theological vision. I ask why it matters that the triumphal romp through Narnia with Aslan borrows from both the Gospels and Ovid's *Metamorphoses*, or what the echoes from *The Faerie Queene* suggest about the meaning of dragons.

This book will best be enjoyed with a copy of the Narnian novels nearby, either to read for the first time, or to refresh the reader's memory (or indeed to flick through energetically in the process of quibbling with my interpretation of a passage). I recap some episodes when discussing their literary elements, but the real shape and meaning of the stories can only be felt properly by reading and rereading. One of the pleasures this book might offer, I hope, is the opportunity to revisit familiar territory and notice new features which had gone unremarked before. I would like to thank some of the people who have helped me in my explorations of the Narnia stories, most particularly whilst working on this book. The priests and people of St John the Baptist's church in Beeston deserve more appreciation than I can give here, for their generosity, patience and curiosity. The members of Narnia Club at the University of Nottingham provided many cheery hours of

PREFACE

discussion and insight, and a special acknowledgement is due to Emily Williams for sharing her thoughts on the *Argonautica*. Rebecca Menmuir was kind enough to expound the more abstruse corners of the world of medieval Ovids to me. I have enjoyed working through Lewis's fiction with the members of the online pod entitled 'Religion and Fantasy Literature', who are always happy to throw ideas around to good effect. Finally, many thanks go to Sheenagh.

PRINCE CASPIAN

INTRODUCTION
THE CROWN BENEATH THE EARTH

Prince Caspian is a novel about the past. Its characters are continually finding themselves confronted with the dangers, the excitements, the problems and the claims of the past – and having to decide how they will respond to it. This is true of the Pevensies, who are suddenly called back into Narnia, where they have to face the result of centuries of time passing. They encounter the past in its vast geological scope, by finding that the area around Cair Paravel, which they knew so well, has had its coastline eroded by the relentless attrition of wind and sea. The landscape with which they were familiar has been remoulded by the passing of the years. When they return to the site of their triumph in Narnia, the great hall where they were crowned as Kings and Queens of the realm, they do not recognise it. The castle has fallen into mere ruins, and the orchard which they themselves ordered to be planted has spread ramblingly inside the precincts of their royal palace. Geology gives way to archaeology, as they piece together the traces of the people who must have lived in this place before it fell into ruins. They deduce the outline of this room, the site of the dais where the royalty must have sat, the imagined crowd who would have filled the space. Then the Pevensies are shocked by a realization: these long-dead people, whose archaeological remains they have been interpreting, are their own selves. It is a fictional trick which has something in common with another crucial moment at the beginning of the previous Narnia novel. When Lucy first finds her way into Narnia – or first stumbles into it – she encounters the faun Mr Tumnus. He is both shocked and amazed to meet her, and asks that puzzling question about whether she is a daughter of Eve, the kind of thing which is called a human girl. *The Lion, the Witch and the Wardrobe* insists from its opening chapters that it is as remarkable (and perhaps more remarkable) to be a human girl as it is to be a wild creature from Classical mythology. In the ruins of Cair Paravel all the Pevensie siblings are confronted with a similar mirror moment: as they scrutinise the remains of a past world, they realize they are encountering themselves. The archaeological imagery becomes even stronger, as they hack their way through a door and descend into the earth in search of the treasure-chamber which they half-deduce and half-remember. They make sure to do so before the sun goes down, since they instinctively feel that the past holds horrors as well as glories, and none of them wants to spend a night sleeping near an open door into the depths of history. Like archaeologists opening an English version of the tomb of Tutankhamun, or like those who uncovered the ship burial at Sutton Hoo, the Pevensies find royal treasures and heroic weaponry in the ground underneath the ruins. It is only after this day of geological trekking, antiquarian deduction and archaeological descent that they realize who they are, and reclaim their Narnian identities.

When the Pevensies learn something more about the reason they have been called to Narnia, after rescuing Trumpkin and being told the story of Prince Caspian, they hear another story about the past. Caspian has grown up in the Telmarine royal family, but as he is approaching young manhood, the past begins to weigh on him in unexpected ways. He talks to his uncle, King Miraz, about the folktales of ancient Narnia which he has heard from his nurse: the stories of talking beasts and walking trees, of fauns and dwarves and the four monarchs. Miraz ridicules these stories, but is also clearly appalled that someone has been telling them to the young prince. He reacts by banishing the woman who brought Caspian up with these

INTRODUCTION

'old wives' tales'. The tutor who replaces the nurse, however, assures Caspian secretly that all those stories were true, and that the 'Old Narnia' still exists. The past Narnia Caspian yearns for exists, and not only in the past. Indeed, Doctor Cornelius embodies that past in himself, as he takes back his hood and shows himself to be a half-dwarf. This intriguing figure, who seems to have stepped out of one of the nurse's stories, tells Caspian something more immediate and more troubling about his own personal past. The uncle who brought Caspian up murdered his father, and Caspian is the true heir to Narnia. This fact puts the prince in immediate and physical danger as soon as the queen has a son, since he is now a very visible threat to Miraz's line continuing to rule the land. The past refuses to stay put, and invades Caspian's life from all directions. Fleeing from the danger which his family history has put him in, and trying to reconcile himself to the idea that he might have a duty to avenge his father's death, Caspian rides out of the world he knows and is thrown (literally, as his horse stumbles) into Old Narnia. He meets creatures who hail him as the rightful king of Narnia, and also those who regard him as responsible for his nation's brutal oppression of the country. If the Pevensies encounter the past in its geological and archaeological forms, Caspian has to desperately grapple with the past in its familial, legendary and colonial forms.

This pervasive theme is highlighted by the other texts which appear to be echoed in *Prince Caspian*. As I will suggest in a later chapter, the novel is deeply engaged with *Hamlet*. Shakespeare's play shows a young man who has discovered something horrific in his own family history, and who is being haunted by a ghost until he does something about it. Rider Haggard's adventure novel *King Solomon's Mines* involves travellers who go seeking the treasure of a king named in the Bible, and who find a 'lost civilization' in the process. *Beowulf* and the elegies of the Anglo-Saxon poets are poems in which the past is mourned, pondered and commemorated. A number of the tales in Ovid's *Metamophoses* present aetiologies; they are stories from the mythical past which explain why the world today is the way it is. Not all the literary connections in *Prince Caspian* are specifically about the past, but they cluster around this topic, infusing this Narnian novel with its risks and excitements.

This concern with the past is part of the theological dimension of *Prince Caspian*, as well as its plot and theme. History was one of the intellectual spaces in which religious controversy occurred in the nineteenth and twentieth centuries. History as a discipline, as the organised study of the past, had been of tremendous interest to both intellectuals and the wider public during the Victorian period. The scholar Richard Schoch has stated that 'the century spanned by the writings of Ranke, Macaulay, Marx and Nietzsche was the golden age of history' and that, during this period, 'the desire to know and possess the past rivalled science as the dominant system of cognition', whilst Robin Gilmour describes the Victorians as 'a parvenu civilization' who were 'fascinated by time because they were conscious of being its victims'.[1] This interest in historical enquiry, and in the traces of the past, expressed itself in academic history, but also in the development of national histories, the rise of the historical novel, and even in the idea that certain tartans were ancestrally linked to particular Scottish clans. The Victorian period is sometimes thought of as a time when scientific principles came to dominate people's approach to the world, but (as Schoch notes) history was an equally powerful force. One can even argue that Charles Darwin's *On the Origin of Species* was a historical, rather than scientific, landmark in the minds of most of the Victorian public. One of the ideas in Darwin which shook people's view of the world was that the animals, birds and fish around them were the result of unimaginably

INTRODUCTION

long processes over time. Rather than having been created in the form which they currently took, they were a moment in an ongoing sequence of developments. From this point of view, the natural world was more difficult to see as a direct gift from the Creator, or for the hand of God to be descried in the creatures. Though it is clearly a scientific theory, much of the imaginative impact of *On the Origin of Species* was bound up with the way it seemed to distance God's work across aeons of time, and to give the forms of nature a 'history' of their own.

The practices of history were also used to further understand aspects of religion itself, through the nineteenth century and into the twentieth. The discovery of new manuscripts of the Bible, and the careful study of existing manuscripts, suggested that the Scriptures themselves had a history. They had apparently not always existed in the complete and collected form which they currently took. (This idea was a commonplace for scholars and theologians, of course, but it increasingly came to prominence in public culture.) It is telling that when Sir Frederick Kenyon published a book in the 1930s entitled *The Story of the Bible*, it did not contain a retelling of the creation, the history of Israel and the events of Jesus' life. Instead it was subtitled *A Popular Account of How It Came To Us*, and discussed the existence of variant manuscripts and the transmission of the Bible across the centuries. Kenyon was a devout Christian, and was convinced that the Scriptures testified in reliable ways to the reality of God's relationship with humanity, especially in the life of Jesus. Nonetheless, for his generation the Bible was a collection which could be investigated with the tools of history, and which would reveal its own history. During the 1940s and 1950s this approach was boosted in the public mind by the sensational discovery of a series of ancient manuscripts in the Qumran Caves. The so-called 'Dead Sea

Scrolls' contained both copies of books which ended up in the orthodox Bible, and other texts which were clearly being treated as scriptural. The Dead Sea Scrolls provided a dramatic physical example of the historical evidence which surrounded the Bible and were discussed widely in the public press. During the same period, various archaeologists were attempting to find locations mentioned in the Bible, with results which generally proved inconclusive. Though plenty of material from ancient sites emerged, it was not possible to map the physical evidence simply across the biblical narratives. Whilst this did not 'disprove' the Bible in religious terms, it certainly added to a general sense that history was a potentially destabilising force in matters of faith.

In this context, *Prince Caspian* looks like a novel engaging with one of the key themes in religious belief and apologetic at the time. The odd detail that Narnia is a fantasy world with a functional system of coastal erosion – and that this is made into a significant plot point – suggests a fictional engagement with temporal processes which could undermine faith as effectively as sea-cliffs. Lewis does not ignore the ways in which the passage of time, and historical discussion, might complicate belief. On the contrary, his characters struggle with precisely these problems on a symbolic level. The Pevensies are lost in their own kingdom because of geological change and the ruining effect of the centuries. Caspian's uncle forbids him from listening to legends told by the country people about the land they live on. The site where Aslan died and rose again is now buried deep underground, beneath a barrow. *Prince Caspian* is a novel about the problems of the past, in the same way that we might say *The Lion, the Witch and the Wardrobe* begins as a novel about the problem of believing in the supernatural, *The Silver Chair* is a novel about the problem of interpreting texts correctly, and *The Last Battle* is a novel about the problem of false religion. But the past, and the

INTRODUCTION

act of exploring it, is not only a problem in *Prince Caspian*. It is also exhilarating and liberating. The Pevensies descend into an ancient treasure chamber and find their true selves waiting for them. In the middle of a barrow Caspian has a nightmarish brawl with a werewolf, but in doing so he proves himself the successor to Peter Wolf's-Bane, and immediately the High King himself walks out of the far past into Caspian's life. Narnia is healed by a joyous procession across the land, by creatures who were supposed to be only folk-tales and legends. Lewis's novel dramatizes the problems of the past for a self-consciously modern world, and also the ecstatic presence of the timeless God within that world.

CHAPTER ONE
MOURNING AND DELVING

If *Prince Caspian* is indeed a novel about the past, then it treats the subject in a dramatic and unusual way. I would like to start with the Pevensies in the ruins of a mysterious castle, and suggest that Susan's reaction to what they find there produces echoes of both schoolgirl fiction and Anglo-Saxon poetry. The action the siblings take, in finding out where they are, and indeed who they are, places *Prince Caspian* amongst a cluster of books which express an 'archaeological imagination' about the British landscape. To begin with, it is worth quoting Susan at some length:

> Shortly after the last apple had been eaten, Susan went out to the well to get another drink. When she came back she was carrying something in her hand.
>
> 'Look,' she said in a rather choking kind of voice. 'I found it by the well.' She handed it to Peter and sat down. The others thought she looked and sounded as if she might be going to cry. Edmund and Lucy eagerly bent forward to see what was in Peter's hand – a little, bright thing that gleamed in the firelight.
>
> ...
>
> All now saw what it was – a little chess-knight, ordinary in size but extraordinarily heavy because it was made of pure gold; and the eyes in the horse's head were two tiny little rubies – or rather one was, for the other had been knocked out.
>
> ...
>
> 'Cheer up, Su,' said Peter to his other sister.
>
> 'I can't help it,' said Susan. 'It brought back – oh, such

lovely times. And I remembered playing chess with fauns and good giants, and the mer-people singing in the sea, and my beautiful horse – and – and—'[2]

HORSE SICKNESS

From one point of view, this is a fairly shrewd piece of psychological realism in Lewis's depiction of Susan. Given the popularity of horses and horse-literature amongst teenage girls, from *National Velvet* in the 1930s up to *The Saddle Club* in the 1990s, it seems reasonable that when Susan looks back at her lost glory as queen in Cair Paravel, what she really misses is having her own horse. The mid-Victorian *Black Beauty* and later *National Velvet* are probably the most famous equine novels in the canon of literature for young readers, but the prolific work of Joanna Cannan and her daughter Christine Pullein-Thompson filled out a much larger genre of reading for (mostly) girls interested in the subject. The titles of a string of Cannan's books in the decades leading up to *Prince Caspian* suggest a fairly straightforward form of literary wish-fulfilment was involved, as well as more sophisticated interests in character and setting: *A Pony For Jean* (1936), *Another Pony for Jean* (1938), *More Ponies for Jean* (1943), *They Bought Her a Pony* (1944), *Hamish: the Story of a Shetland Pony* (1944) and *I Wrote a Pony Book* (1950). This element of genre fiction has, as I mentioned, continued through the twentieth century and into the twenty-first, but at least one literary critic has detected its influence in the flourishing of fantasy literature during the same period. Farah Mendlesohn and Edward James have remarked, with a wicked touch of humour, that the enduring appeal of Anne McCaffrey's dragons and dragon-riders may have something the way it enables a fantastical version of 'the girl fantasy of owning a pony of her very, very own and being able to *talk* to it'.[3]

The horse-mad girl had become a recognisable character

MOURNING AND DELVING

across a range of children's fiction. Enid Blyton's *Malory Towers* series of school stories provides a good example, in the person of Wilhelmina. A freckled tomboy who insists on being called 'Bill' by her friends, she has grown up around her father's racehorses and her family's stables, and arrives dramatically on horseback at the beginning of term. The protagonist of the novels, a girl called Darrell, notices a certain melancholy about the new girl as she begins to settle in:

> All the same, she thought Bill looked a bit serious.
>
> 'Not homesick, are you?' she asked, one morning when she was walking down one of the corridors with Bill.
>
> 'Oh no. I'm horse-sick!' said Bill, surprisingly. 'I keep on and on thinking of all our horses at home that I love so much—Beauty and Star and Blackie and Velvet and Midnight and Miss Muffet and Ladybird and . . .'
>
> 'Good gracious! However do you remember all those names?' said Darrell, in surprise.
>
> 'I couldn't possibly forget them,' said Bill solemnly. 'I'm going to like Malory Towers, I know that, but I simply can't help missing all our horses, and the thunder of their hooves and the way they neigh and nuzzle—oh, you can't understand, Darrell. You'll think me silly, I know. You see, I and three of my brothers used to ride each morning to their tutor—four miles away—and we used to go out and saddle and bridle our horses—and then off we'd go, galloping over the hills.'[4]

Pining, as well as enjoyment, is clearly a central element of the relationship between Bill and her equines. This becomes the focus of her subplot during the novel, as she spends more and more time in the school stables instead of studying or joining in with the class activities. Eventually her form mistress, Miss Peters, disciplines her by forbidding her to see Thunder on days when her work is unsatisfactory. Bill nonetheless sneaks

GOLD ON THE HORIZON

down to the stables to spend time with her horse, whom she worries is becoming ill. Miss Peters suspects something, and catches Bill in the stables. The reader sees the scene from the point of view of Darrell, who has hurried down in an attempt to warn Bill of the form mistress's approach, and who ends up hiding in the stables:

> The door opened wide and Miss Peters came in.
>
> 'Oh! So you are here, Wilhelmina!' she said, angrily. 'I suppose you have been systematically disobeying me the whole week. I am really ashamed of you. You will never settle down at school whilst you have Thunder here, I can quite see that. He will have to be sent back home in a horse-box.'
>
> 'No! Oh no, Miss Peters! Don't, don't do that!' begged Bill, even her freckles going pale with anxiety. 'It's only that Thunder's not well. He really isn't. If he was well I'd obey you. But he needs me when he's not well.'
>
> 'I'm not going to discuss the matter,' said Miss Peters, coldly. 'You have heard what I said. I am not likely to change my mind after such a show of disobedience. Please go back to your common-room, Wilhelmina. I will tell you when I have made arrangements to send Thunder home and you can say good-bye to him till the holidays. It will probably be the day after tomorrow.' Bill stood still, quite petrified. She couldn't make her legs move. Darrell couldn't see her, but she could imagine her very well indeed. Poor, poor Bill. 'Go, Wilhelmina,' said Miss Peters. 'At once please.' And Bill went, her feet dragging. Darrell heard a smothered sob.

Once Bill has left the stables, resigned to this fate worse than death, Darrell witnesses an odd aftermath to the scene:

> But Miss Peters didn't go. She waited till Bill had quite gone. Then she went over to Thunder and spoke to him in such

a gentle voice that Darrell could hardly believe it was Miss Peters'!

'Well, old boy,' said Miss Peters, and Darrell heard the sound of her hand rubbing his coat. 'What's the matter with you? Don't feel well? Shall we get the vet to you? What's the matter with you, Thunder? Beautiful horse, aren't you? Best in the stables. What's up, old boy?' Darrell could hardly believe her ears. She wriggled a little in the straw so that she could get a hole to peep through. Yes, there was Miss Peters, standing close to Thunder, and he was nuzzling her and whinnying in delight. Why, Miss Peters must love him! Of course, she was very fond of horses, Darrell knew that. But this was different somehow. She really seemed to love Thunder as if he was her own horse.[5]

The teacher is revealed to be more or less equally horse-mad as her pupil, though she has learned to stop it taking over her entire life. There is even a hint in the novel that Miss Peters is so strict with Bill because she knows very well how a passion for the equestrian life can dominate your personality and consume your time.

Susan's emotion in this scene taps into an identifiable strand of genre fiction. Though we have not seen long scenes of her galloping over the Narnian countryside, I suspect Bill would easily diagnose her as 'horse-sick'. After all, the Pevensies have been whirled away from the railway station where they were waiting to be taken to school, and Susan is still wearing her school uniform. From one point of view, she is a schoolgirl crying for the horse that she cannot spend time with. She can, however, be seen from another angle in this moment. As with so many scenes in the Narnia novels, there are multiple echoes surrounding the characters, and multiple stories taking place.

GOLD ON THE HORIZON

WHERE IS THE HORSE? WHERE THE RIDER?

Whilst mourning her lost horse, Susan is experiencing one of the classic moods of poetry in Old English, the language spoken by the Anglo-Saxons in the period after the Romans had left Britain. One of the most noticeable, and emotionally powerful, strands in this poetic tradition is a mood of passionate nostalgia, of yearning for a lost and nearly-forgotten past. Scholars have connected this tone to the world-view of many of the Anglo-Saxons, who saw themselves as the inheritors of a heroic past which was rapidly falling away as the end of the world approached. This apocalyptic strain in their culture was surely only strengthened by a Christian belief that the world was waiting for the return of Christ in judgement and the events of the Book of Revelation, as well as the post-Roman landscape which they inhabited. Poems like 'The Ruin', which appears to have been composed by a poet contemplating the remains of a Roman city such as Bath, testify to a sense of passionate melancholy in the face of this combination of ancient greatness and modern decay. It begins thus:

> Wrætlic is þes wealstan, wyrde gebræcon;[6]
> *Wonderful are the wallstones; broken by fate*
> burgstede burston, brosnað enta geweorc.
> *The citadel is smashed; the work of giants decays*
> Hrofas sind gehrorene, hreorge torras,
> *The roofs are fallen, the towers ruined,*
> hrungeat berofen, hrim on lime,
> *The cold gate is riven with frost in the lime*
> scearde scurbeorge scorene, gedrorene,
> *The roofs are chipped and fallen*
> ældo undereotone.
> *Undermined by age*

MOURNING AND DELVING

The sharp-eyed reader may have noticed that the Anglo-Saxon poet refers to the works of these imagined giants as 'enta geweorc'. J. R. R. Tolkien borrowed the word 'ent' for an ancient and mysterious race of creatures, and built it into Middle-Earth in the form of Treebeard and his cohorts. The surviving corpus of Anglo-Saxon literature uses the term 'ents' several times when considering the ruins of great buildings, including a passage from a sermon by the preacher and bishop Aelfric of Eynsham describing the creation and destruction of the Tower of Babel. It is difficult to resist speculating that the combination of the word 'ent' with these repeated images of broken walls and overturned towers was somewhere in the depths of Tolkien's imagination when he came to write the march of the Ents upon Isengard. Back in Narnia, Lewis emphasizes the combination of Susan's yearning for the past and the way it brings her to the brink of tears. Her recollection of the past delights of Cair Paravel is accompanied not by a self-congratulating feeling of how important she was and how she enjoyed ruling, but by a profound sense of loss for a vanished Golden Age. Her recollections of past joys in the great hall also find parallels in the Anglo-Saxon elegiac poetry. One, known as 'The Wanderer', contains this outcry from its protagonist:

> Se þonne þisne wealsteal wise geþohte
> *He who thought wisely on this created world,*
> ond þis deorce lif deope geondþenceð,
> *and thought over deeply this dark life,*
> frod in ferðe, feor oft gemon
> *wise in spirit, remembered often in far times*
> wælsleahta worn, ond þas word acwið:
> *many slaughters, and spoke these words:*
> Hwær cwom mearg? Hwær cwom mago? Hwær cwom
>   maþþumgyfa?

> *Where is the horse gone? Where the rider? Where the giver of treasure?*
> Hwær cwom symbla gesetu? Hwær sindon seledreamas?
> *Where are the seats at the feast? Where are the revels in the hall?*
> Eala beorht bune! Eala byrnwiga!
> *Alas for the bright cup! Alas for the armoured warrior!*
> Eala þeodnes þrym! Hu seo þrag gewat,
> *Alas for the glory of the prince! How that time has passed away,*
> genap under nihthelm, swa heo no wære.
> *dark under the cover of night, as if it had never been.*

Susan's musings on the vanished splendours of the past are less concerned with the stern triumphs of armoured warriors and the martial society of the post-Roman Iron Age. Nonetheless, her lament engages strikingly with the tropes of Anglo-Saxon elegy. She stammers that the sight of the chess-piece 'brought back – oh, such lovely times' and the memory of 'my beautiful horse'. Her last wistful item is the first which bursts from the lips of the Wanderer, with his demand, 'Hwaer cwom mearg? Hwaer cwom mago?' ('Where is the horse? And where the rider?') Susan sobs that she 'remembered playing chess with fauns and good giants, and the mer-people singing in the sea' as well as her horse, depicting a world of communal enjoyment and fellowship rather like that depicted in the lament of the Wanderer. It is even noticeable, in passing, that Susan's nostalgia brings back memories of giants and Classical fauns. This is especially apt, given the tendency for Anglo-Saxon poets to muse upon Classical ruins and ascribe them to the giants they called 'ents'. Of all the Narnian creatures she could have lamented when sitting amidst the ruins of an ancient hall, it seems striking that giants spring to mind. Susan is increasingly taking the role of both horse-sick schoolgirl and world-sick Anglo-Saxon poet.

Earlier in the same chapter, the other Pevensies have already offered a less emotionally effusive version of the Wanderer's lament. Susan's tears over the chess-knight and her lost horse, which parallel 'Where is the horse gone? Where is the rider?', are only the most obvious connection between this elegy and the schoolchildren in Narnia. As they first explore the ruins, the siblings have the following conversation:

> 'I wonder, was it really the hall?' said Susan.
>
> 'What is that terrace kind of thing?'
>
> 'Why, you silly,' said Peter (who had become strangely excited), 'don't you see? That was the dais where the High Table was, where the King and the great lords sat. Anyone would think you had forgotten that we ourselves were once Kings and Queens and sat on a dais just like that, in our great hall.'
>
> 'In our castle of Cair Paravel,' continued Susan in a dreamy and rather sing-song voice, 'at the mouth of the great river of Narnia. How could I forget?'
>
> 'How it all comes back!' said Lucy. 'We could pretend we were in Cair Paravel now. This hall must have been very like the great hall we feasted in.'
>
> 'But unfortunately without the feast,' said Edmund. 'It's getting late, you know. Look how long the shadows are. And have you noticed that it isn't so hot?'
>
> 'We shall need a camp-fire if we've got to spend the night here,' said Peter. 'I've got matches. Let's go and see if we can collect some dry wood.'[7]

Many of the tropes of loss enumerated by the Anglo-Saxon poet appear in this prose passage, even occurring in roughly the same order. 'Where [is] the giver of treasure?' demands the Wanderer, using a poetic phrase for the king or chief of a people. As if in answer, Peter declares 'that was the dais ... where the King and the great lords sat'. 'Where are the seats at the feast?' and 'Where are the revels in the hall?' insists the elegy, whilst Peter comments that they 'sat on a dais just like that, in our great hall' and Lucy remarks that the place 'must have been very like the great hall we feasted in'. Edmund sardonically adds that they are 'unfortunately without the feast', and continues that it is 'getting late ... Look how long the shadows are'. Peter's agreement that they will need to build a fire 'if we've got to spend the night here' completes Edmund's version of the last image of mourning from the Wanderer: 'How that time has passed away, dark under the cover of night, as if it had never been'.

Unlike the anonymous Wanderer, however, the Pevensies are about to answer the questions in the poem. In the lament of an Anglo-Saxon poet, these are purely rhetorical declamations: 'Where is the horse?' is not an actual enquiry, merely an expressive way to depict his desolation. For the schoolchildren returning to Narnia, though, there are in fact answers to these questions. They are themselves the answers. Peter insists that 'it's about time we four started using our brains', and they deduce that the place they are sitting is not merely similar to Cair Paravel. It actually is the royal seat of the kings and queens of Narnia. The ensuing discussion of how the orchard could have grown wild and encroached on the ruins, and of how the peninsula could have become cut off from the mainland, allows them to understand how this could be the case. They are thinking their way back into the world they used to know, and accounting for the passage of years which has apparently cut them off from the ruins surrounding them. They even submit this theory to an experiment, by deducing that there should be a wooden door in the wall they are sitting against, and then tapping on the wall and clearing away the ivy to reveal exactly that door.

MOURNING AND DELVING

They then begin a descent into the treasure-chamber of Cair Paravel. I will discuss in a later chapter the origin of some of the details of this place, such as the locked boxes and the ivory. Here I am most interested in the way the Pevensies' exploration of the underground chamber brings back their memories — not only of the Narnian past, but of their role in it. To begin with the atmosphere is hushed and melancholy:

> the treasures were so covered with dust that unless they had realized where they were and remembered most of the things, they would hardly have known they were treasures. There was something sad and a little frightening about the place, because it all seemed so forsaken and long ago. That was why nobody said anything for at least a minute.[8]

This is the second time that Cair Paravel has been described in doleful language; when the children first find the arch and the clearing (which they eventually recognise as the hall) it is called 'a wide open place with walls all round it. In here there were no trees, only level grass and daisies, and ivy, and grey walls. It was a bright, secret, quiet place, and rather sad'.[9] The weight of the past is felt in these scenes, emphasizing one of the major themes I am exploring in *Prince Caspian*. The past is a problem; it can be a burden. The passing of time, and the traces of its passing, estrange the characters from the world they knew. This is the characteristic mood of poems like 'The Ruin', 'The Wanderer' and 'The Seafarer'. However, having inhabited this mood, the novel continues on through it. The tone of the scene in the treasure-chamber soon shifts:

> Then, of course, they began walking about and picking things up to look at. It was like meeting very old friends. If you had been there you would have heard them saying things like, 'Oh,

look! Our coronation rings – do you remember first wearing this? – Why, this is the little brooch we all thought was lost – I say, isn't that the armour you wore in the great tournament in the Lone Islands? – Do you remember the Dwarf making that for me? – Do you remember drinking out of that horn? – Do you remember, do you remember?"[10]

Then these memories become more focused, as they decide to take the gifts that Father Christmas gave them in *The Lion, the Witch and the Wardrobe*. They choose to take the objects which are most personal to them, and which define their roles in the previous story (including Edmund, who is reminded of his past by the fact that he was not with his siblings when they met Father Christmas). The Pevensies explore the traces of the Narnian past, are surrounded by memories of it, and then find themselves in that past. The sound of Susan plucking the string of her bow acts almost as a spell to restore the lost time:

> In a moment she had bent the bow and then she gave one little pluck to the string. It twanged: a chirruping twang that vibrated through the whole room. And that one small noise brought back the old days to the children's minds more than anything that had happened yet. All the battles and hunts and feasts came rushing into their heads together.[11]

I sometimes wonder if this passage was the inspiration for the harp music which accompanies the audiobook version of the *Chronicles of Narnia* recorded in the last decades of the previous century. The reappearance of a particular musical motif on the harp acts exactly in my memory (and perhaps in the memory of some others of my age) in the way described here: a lyrical, vibrating tone which brings Narnia rushing back. In any case, Susan's gift is a great step in the process

MOURNING AND DELVING

of meeting the past which the Pevensies embark upon down in the subterranean chamber. It contributes to the feeling that Susan takes the role of an Anglo-Saxon poet in these passages; their verses were recited to the accompaniment of a harp. As can be seen in some lines of *Beowulf* which I will quote later, the image of the harpist in the hall is one of the tropes of a joyous feast amongst Anglo-Saxon warriors. Susan plucks a string, and its sound brings hunts, battles and feasts rushing into the mind of her listeners. Peter then completes their journey into the past which Susan has called up:

> Next, Peter took down his gift – the shield with the great red lion on it, and the royal sword. He blew, and rapped them on the floor, to get off the dust. He fitted the shield on his arm and slung the sword by his side. He was afraid at first that it might be rusty and stick to the sheath. But it was not so. With one swift motion he drew it and held it up, shining in the torchlight.
> 'It is my sword Rhindon,' he said; 'with it I killed the Wolf.' There was a new tone in his voice, and the others all felt that he was really Peter the High King again.[12]

Peter's use of the present tense 'it is my sword' is mirrored by the reactions of the other Pevensies. They are not overwhelmed with memories of their brother as king. They recognise him as king at that very moment. I would like to explore the resonances of this scene further, both in the context of the novel and British culture of the time.

THE ARCHAEOLOGICAL IMAGINATION

The descent into the treasure chamber is paralleled by another scene where young adventurers descend into the Narnian past. When Trumpkin and the two Pevensie boys go to find Caspian at Aslan's How, they make a similar journey into the darkness and history. The How, which was built over the Stone Table, is described in this way when it first appears in the novel:

> Before sunrise they arrived at Aslan's How. It was certainly an awesome place, a round green hill on top of another hill, long since grown over with trees, and one little, low doorway leading into it. The tunnels inside were a perfect maze till you got to know them, and they were lined and roofed with smooth stones, and on the stones, peering in the twilight, Caspian saw strange characters and snaky patterns, and pictures in which the form of a Lion was repeated again and again. It all seemed to belong to an even older Narnia than the Narnia of which his nurse had told him.[13]

When the dwarf and the Pevensie boys enter the How, described as musty and dark, they also notice the carvings.

> 'I say, Peter,' whispered Edmund. 'Look at those carvings on the walls. Don't they look old? And yet we're older than that. When we were last here, they hadn't been made.'
> 'Yes,' said Peter. 'That makes one think.'[14]

Indeed, when they were challenged by the badger sentries at the entrance to the How, Trumpkin declared that he was '[b]ringing the High King Peter out of the far past'.[15] This all gives a slightly vertiginous effect, as the deep past and the present seem to mingle and swap over. The boy who stood on a railway station platform that morning is now being heralded as arriving 'out of the far past', and the ancient carvings on the stone walls are younger than he is. This picks up a theme from *The Lion, the Witch and the Wardrobe*, which was also expressed around the Stone Table. Aslan's resurrection was due to an incantation which the White Witch did not know about, because her

MOURNING AND DELVING

knowledge only stretched back to the beginning of time. The Deeper Magic from before time itself gave the lion's death its power, and led to his rising again. The modern schoolboy Peter is from the 'far past' because he is part of the story of Aslan. The How, with its mysterious barrow-like shape and its ancient carvings, is nonetheless younger than the Stone Table and the magic which surrounded it. There is perhaps an analogy here to our world, where relics of paganism, such as standing stones and carvings, are often seen as measurelessly ancient. They are sometimes referred to as 'pre-Christian remains', and much discussion of religion in Lewis's time framed them in that way. To a Christian, however, they are much younger, since the Christian story goes back before the creation of the world. According to that story the presence felt when coming to the altar or when searching the Scriptures is a presence older than the world itself. These dizzying swoops of time in the novel are part of its theological vision. They also tap into an interest, even an excitement, which was especially alive in British culture during the mid-twentieth century. They kindle what I would like to call the 'archaeological imagination'.

Probably the most famous archaeological dig of all time in Britain took place at Sutton Hoo in Suffolk. In the late 1930s, just before the Second World War broke out, a collection of mounds were excavated at Sutton Hoo. They revealed what appears to be the ship-burial of an Anglo-Saxon king, with an extraordinary collection of treasure and other artefacts. The discovery was reported with great excitement in the press; this article from the *Hull Daily Mail* provides a good example:

BURIAL SHIP YIELDS UP ITS SECRETS
Undisturbed for some 14 centuries, an 82 feet long Anglo-Saxon burial ship – the first ever found in this country – has now yielded up its secrets.

GOLD ON THE HORIZON

The discovery has just been made at Sutton Hoo, near Woodbridge, Suffolk, by Mrs. E. M. Pretty, whose enthusiasm and generosity have opened what may be a new chapter in Anglo-Saxon history.

Mrs. Pretty initiated investigations last year. Experts have placed the approximate date of the ship at A.D. 600.

SWORD AT HIS SIDE

Even on the continent such finds are rare. Interest is added to the Sutton Hoo discovery because of the remarkable collection of jewellery and personal articles revealed.

They were all found together in the centre of the ship, and their quality suggests that they could have belonged only to a king whose warriors had given him ceremonial burial, surrounded by his favourite treasures.

Among them are a handsome gold buckle, clasps and fasteners of kingly vestments, gold studs from a belt and small plaques of gold bearing figures of human beings and animals.

The king's sword has been placed by his side; little of it remains but the richly-ornamented gold and jewelled pommel. His soldiers had provided him with money, too, and remains of the purse were found beside some coins.

SPEARHEADS FOUND

Iron pots and spearheads have also been found. Another article had the appearance of a sceptre, with faces carved at each end.

The site, too, is worthy of a king. It is above the River Deben, which possibly his galleys once commanded. Up the steep face of the hill his warriors must have hauled the ship, which has a beam of almost 16ft.

There, on one of the highest points in Suffolk, they had laid him to rest – his kingdom at his feet. Over his ship they built a huge tumulus.[16]

MOURNING AND DELVING

The dramatic terms in which this newspaper reported the first Sutton Hoo finds reflects the excitement with which the excavations were greeted. The language of the burial yielding up its secrets and the richly-ornamented sword, on a site worthy of a king, goes beyond journalistic enthusiasm into the register of a historical novel. Certainly the last lines tip over into a heroic atmosphere, and one which highlights the role Sutton Hoo played in the imagination of the twentieth century. The famous helmet found there, with its intricately carved face-mask which mimics the features of a warrior wearing it, has become a symbol of the Anglo-Saxon world. The form of the object tantalizes us with the feeling that we have come face to face with the king who was buried beneath the Suffolk countryside. (Anyone who puts this book down for a moment, and searches online for 'Sutton Hoo helmet', may well find they recognise the image even if they do not know the name of Sutton Hoo.) One of the reasons why Sutton Hoo fired the imaginations of people in Britain was the resemblance between the burial site and the greatest work of poetry left by the Anglo-Saxons. *Beowulf* tells of the exploits of a great hero, who rids a kingdom of monsters and eventually dies after a battle with a dragon. In one episode, the poem relates the burial of an unknown king, in a barrow near the sea, in which treasures and weapons were placed. This passage ends with a similar lament to the elegies we saw above:

> næs hearpan wyn[17]
> *there is not harp's joy*
> gomen gleobeames ne god hafoc
> *delight of song-wood, nor good hawk*
> geond sæl swingeð ne se swifta mearh
> *soaring through the hall, nor swift horse*
> burhstede beateð bealocwealm hafað

GOLD ON THE HORIZON

stamping in the courtyard; baleful death has
fela feorhcynna forð onsended.
sent forth many of the human race.

When *Beowulf* comes to relate the death of its hero, his burial is rather similar. These are the last lines of the poem:

Geworhton ða Wedra leode
then wrought the Wederas' people
hlæw on hoe se wæs heah ond brad
a barrow on the hill, it was high and broad,
wegliðendum wide gesyne
to be seen far and wide by wave-travellers,
ond betimbredon on tyn dagum
and they constructed in ten days
beadurofes becn·
the war-chief's beacon

[…]

hi on beorg dydon beg ond siglu
they placed in the barrow rings and brooches,
eall swylce hyrsta swylce on horde aer
all such trappings, as before from the hoard
niðhedige men genumen hæfdon·
hostile men had taken;
forleton eorla gestreon eorðan healdan
they let the earth hold the heroes' treasure
gold on greote þaer hit nu gen lifað
gold in the gritty soil, where it now still lives,
eldum swa unnyt swa hyt aerer wæs.
as useless to men as it was before.

[…]

MOURNING AND DELVING

cwaedon þæt he waere wyruldcyninga
they said that he was, of all kings of the world,
manna mildust ond monðwaerust
the most generous of men, and the most gracious,
leodum liðost ond lofgeornost.
the most protective of his people, and keenest for glory.

Thus the poem ends with another king buried in a barrow overlooking the sea, with a hoard of treasure by his side, and his people lamenting. Perhaps some of the excitement which surrounded the Sutton Hoo discoveries can be attributed to a sense that people in 1939 had suddenly taken up the story at the very moment when *Beowulf* ends. We might compare it to a British Tutankhamun's tomb, if there had been a famous piece of Egyptian poetry from that time which detailed the entombment of the king and then tailed off. Of course *Beowulf* is not about whichever king was buried at Sutton Hoo (most probably Rædwald), but it provided a powerful sense that the Anglo-Saxon world had opened in front of the diggers.

If that newspaper report of the excavation suggested a blending of historical fact and imagination, the same combination can be seen in the novels of the decades either side of the Sutton Hoo excavation. What I am calling the 'archaeological imagination' was a powerful force in writing, especially in fantasy and children's literature. I have already mentioned that the heroes in *Prince Caspian* descend into the earth to find deep truths, in the treasure chamber and in Aslan's How. Caspian makes another similar descent when fleeing from Miraz's castle after Doctor Cornelius informs him that his life is in danger. The young prince is riding headlong through a wood at night, is knocked off his horse by a tree branch, and on waking up finds himself in a subterranean home. This is the first moment when he meets the Old Narnians in their own world, and the narrative has placed him beneath the earth. We might read this as a literalisation of the metaphor that there is an 'underground' group of Old Narnians, and a literalisation of the desire to find the ancient secrets which the earth holds. We might also see it as a neat inversion of another famous scene in which a lost woodland wanderer is rescued by a badger, in the Wild Wood episode of *The Wind in the Willows*. When Mole sets out, ill-advisedly, to explore the wood, he becomes lost and surrounded by the malevolent creatures of the wilderness. When Ratty finds him, the two creatures are despairing of finding their way out of the Wild Wood, when they trip over a door-scraper. This marks the entrance to Mr Badger's house, and the grumpy old brock takes them in. This passage is included in most adaptations of *The Wind in the Willows*, across TV, radio and film. Often left out, however, is a detail about the tunnels and chambers which adjoin Badger's own living quarters:

> Crossing the hall, they passed down one of the principal tunnels, and the wavering light of the lantern gave glimpses on either side of rooms both large and small, some mere cupboards, others nearly as broad and imposing as Toad's dining hall. A narrow passage at right angles led them into another corridor, and here the same thing was repeated. The Mole was staggered at the size, the extent, the ramifications of it all; at the length of the dim passages, the solid vaultings of the crammed store chambers, the masonry everywhere, the pillars, the arches, the pavements.
>
> 'How on earth, Badger,' he said at last, 'did you ever find time and strength to do all this? It's astonishing!'
>
> 'It would be astonishing indeed,' said the Badger simply, 'if I had done it. But as a matter of fact I did none of it—only cleaned out the passages and chambers, as far as I had need

MOURNING AND DELVING

of them. There's lots more of it, all round about. I see you don't understand, and I must explain it to you. Well, very long ago, on the spot where the Wild Wood waves now, before ever it had planted itself and grown up to what it now is, there was a city—a city of people, you know. Here, where we are standing, they lived, and walked, and talked, and slept, and carried on their business. Here they stabled their horses and feasted, from here they rode out to fight or drove out to trade. They were a powerful people, and rich, and great builders. They built to last, for they thought their city would last forever.'[18]

Badger goes on to explain that the city was gradually ruined and levelled by the weather (and possibly undermined by animals), and that the wood grew up amongst the remnants. He remarks that 'People come—they stay for a while, they flourish, they build—and they go. It is their way. But we remain. There were badgers here, I've been told, long before that same city ever came to be'.[19] Like Mr Badger, Trufflehunter takes the hero into his home, protects him from more dangerous inhabitants of Old Narnia, and later declares that his kind are tenacious physically and morally: 'I'm a beast and we don't change. I'm a badger, what's more, and we hold on.'[20] The episode is inverted, since in the Wild Wood some talking animals have discovered a subterranean city made by humans, and in Narnia a human wakes up in an underground lair of talking animals, but the same spark of the archaeological imagination animates both. Other fantastical and historical fiction displays the same impulse in the mid-century. *The Box of Delights* by John Masefield involves a scene in which the young hero visits an Iron Age hill-fort (known locally as 'King Arthur's Camp') at night, and finds it alive with people from the past. Rosemary Sutcliff's *Warrior Scarlet* depicts a young boy living in the Bronze Age, and the first chapter includes an episode of him eavesdropping on people talking about him. The passage involves Drem, the boy in question, wriggling down from higher ground into the rafters of the roundhouse where his family live, and lying there whilst he looks down on them. Sutcliff includes a great deal of detail for her young readers about what Drem sees, thus informing them of how a Bronze Age household lived and what objects would have been in a roundhouse. In sketching this scene, she puts Drem and the reader in the position of a modern archaeologist excavating a Bronze Age site. They are looking down from above at the past, noting the arrangement of the stones and the items within the roundhouse. There are good plot reasons provided for these delvings into the earth: Mr Badger and Trufflehunter naturally inhabit subterranean burrows, and Drem can remain out of sight by creeping down into the rafters. Nonetheless, I would argue that all these scenes testify to a powerful desire to recover the mysteries of the past by descending beneath the surface of the ground. The popular image of an archaeological dig seems to be reworked as a magical discovery of worlds beneath the ground, whether in delightful or terrifying modes. (Caspian's experience with the hag and werewolf chimes with the emotional tone of the scene in *The Fellowship of the Ring*, when Tolkien's hobbits become lost in the foggy downs and wake up in a barrow with a wight about to kill them.) In *Prince Caspian* there are no fewer than three episodes when this archaeological imagination sends the characters underground, and rewards them with wonderful discoveries.

MOURNING AND DELVING

The opening chapters of *Prince Caspian* show the characters imagining, scrutinising and exploring the past. As I have suggested, Susan's lament over her lost horse gives her the

MOURNING AND DELVING

double role of horse-sick schoolgirl and Anglo-Saxon poet mourning the lost glories of the past. The Pevensies become archaeologists who deduce the lives which were lived in the ruins, then descend into the earth and realize that those lives were their own. This scene also begins the sequence of descents below the surface of the ground, which yield similar truths later in the novel. These themes are a major part of the plot and imagery of *Prince Caspian*; they are also part of its religious vision. Archaeology thrilled the imagination of novelists and poets in the twentieth century. It also contributed to the spiritual imagination of the period. The archaeological remains of ancient societies, both in Britain and elsewhere, were used by some writers to argue that prehistoric peoples had worshipped a single mother Goddess, who had been displaced by later cults and religions (including the three Abrahamic monotheisms). The archaeologist and folklorist Margaret Murray argued, in a series of books including *God of the Witches* and *The Witch-Cult in Western Europe*, that not only had there been a prehistoric Goddess religion, but that it had survived through the centuries as witchcraft. In 1939, A. L. Armstrong apparently proved that this deity had been worshipped in Britain when he found a prehistoric carved chalk image of her during the dig at Grime's Graves in Norfolk (though later scholars are generally convinced this was a fraud).[21] This view of the prehistoric world was adopted by various strands of British paganism, and was built into the form of witchcraft known as Wicca when it emerged to public view in the 1950s. There might be no logically necessary connection between pagan witchcraft as a contemporary spiritual practice on one hand, and a belief that prehistoric sites in Britain testified to an ancient worship of the Goddess on the other, but the two were closely bound up in the mid-century. Later archaeologists, and indeed later practitioners of witchcraft, have often come to see this claim to prehistoric origins as more of an enabling myth or a symbolic image than a historical theory. For people at the time the association between the two sets of ideas was very potent, and it was part of the emotional drive of modern witchcraft. Its practitioners saw themselves as connecting with the ancient mysteries of the landscape, as liberating themselves from the centuries of Christian imposition, and as recovering the power of a past which had not yet been troubled by ideas of sin.

The archaeological imagination which courses through *Prince Caspian* makes an implicit counter-claim about what will be found by adventurers who delve deeply enough. Beneath the How is the broken stone table from which Aslan rose. Beneath the ruins of the castle are the treasures which mark the Pevensies as royalty crowned by the Lion himself. Beneath the woodland soil is a badger who remembers the old ways and still believes the King of the Wood will come to them and wake the trees. No one asserts it out loud, but the imagery of the novel presents a world in which the ancient past sits on something more ancient still. In *The Lion, the Witch and the Wardrobe*, the White Witch failed because her knowledge stretched back as far as time did; she did not know the Deeper Magic because only Aslan and the Emperor existed before time itself. That plot hinged on the opening line of Genesis, 'In the beginning, God created the heaven and the earth', and the opening line of John's Gospel, 'In the beginning was the Word, and the Word was with God, and the Word was God'.[22] The scenes I have been discussing show Susan finding that lament for the lost past can turn into recovering its splendours when she re-clothes herself as a Narnian queen, and they show that the power sleeping below the land is Aslan himself.

CHAPTER TWO
THE PRINCE UPON THE BATTLEMENTS

Once the Pevensies have realized where they are, and who they are, they are suddenly thrown into the immediate and current history of Narnia. They rescue a dwarf from soldiers intent on drowning him, and are told a brief biography of Prince Caspian himself. This contains some of the novel's most memorable images: the astronomy lessons on the high tower, the half-dwarf tutor in his hooded robe, the night-time flight through the castle and into the wood. From the melancholy of the ruins of Cair Paravel, the characters and reader are moved into a Narnia full of people whom they do not know. It prompts a question which this chapter will attempt to answer in rather oblique fashion: where do the Telmarines come from? Doctor Cornelius's history lesson to the young prince only mentions that they came into the land of Narnia from elsewhere. It is left to Aslan, near the end of the novel, to describe how they originated as a group of pirates who settled on an island and accidentally found their way into another world. (We might note, as Rowan Williams pointed out, that 'Narnia' can apparently mean two things in these books: an entire other world, and a specific country within that world.) The pirates found their way into the world of Narnia, then when they had become Telmarines they invaded the country of Narnia. We might read this as sloppy world-building by a novelist who was more interested in exploring moments of wonder and awe than in producing a coherent Tolkienesque secondary world. Alternatively, we might notice that what the reader understands 'Narnia' to be is opening up in this novel. In *The Lion, the Witch and the Wardrobe*, we only saw the Pevensies in the land from Lantern

GOLD ON THE HORIZON

Waste to Cair Paravel. With the arrival of the Telmarines in the story, it becomes clearer that there are other lands within this world. This will continue to develop in subsequent books, as *The Voyage of the Dawn Treader* actually takes the characters to the edge of the Narnian territory and beyond it into other islands (introducing the people of Calormen in passing), before touching the edge of the known world. *The Silver Chair* will show us Underland, a realm which apparently exists below parts of Narnia, with even a glimpse of Bism, a place which exists below that. *The Horse and His Boy* begins in neither the country of Narnia nor England, introducing us to Calormen, another civilization within the world of Narnia. We are shown this place from the inside, before the novel eventually brings its characters to the edge of the country of Narnia. *The Magician's Nephew* will take us a couple of generations into the past of England, and show us that there are other alternative worlds beside Narnia. There is even a 'wood between the worlds' which people can use to travel between them, if they can manage to do so without losing themselves. The end of *The Magician's Nephew* continues this cosmological scope, as we are present at the creation of the Narnian world itself. Then in *The Last Battle* we start in an odd corner of the Narnian world, and end up in an apocalypse where the borders between the distinct worlds seem to dissolve, and the deeper, truer, underlying reality of Aslan's country is glimpsed.

Whatever the significance of the unfolding of Narnian geography (and cosmology), the question remains: where did the Telmarines come from? In one sense, this is an unimportant question, since whatever their origins they are in Narnia and their king is threatening the life of the story's hero. In another sense, this question is a clue to a major strand of the novel's literary entanglements. The name 'Telmarines', and the land of 'Telmar', offer various possibilities for a reader

THE PRINCE UPON THE BATTLEMENTS

who is baffled by them and yet convinced there must be a secret here. To an English reader (or at least to this one), the syllables have a distinctly French ring to them. If 'Telmarine' is French, especially Norman French, then it appears to mean something like 'Someone of the sea' or 'To do with the sea'. (This assumes that 'Tel' has its general but indefinite meaning in modern French, and 'mar-' is a word which is in the process of deriving from the Latin 'mare' into the modern French 'mer'.) This makes paradoxical sense since, as we later discover, the Telmarines' hatred of the sea is connected with their vague memory that they are descended from pirates and a fear that someone will come from the sea and sweep them away. Alternatively, Telmar might be a neat swapping around, as in a crossword, of the syllables of the name 'Martel'. Charles Martel, the seventh-century Frankish prince and military commander, was the founder of the line of Carolingian kings, and the grandfather of the more famous Charlemagne. Like his grandson, 'Charles Le Magne' or Charles the Great, this Charles is known by his nickname, 'Charles Martel' or Charles the Hammer. This possibility taps into the same narratives and associations as 'Tel-Mar', making the Telmarines into a nation named after the founder of a conquering dynasty, and similarly placing them in the region covered by modern France.

This would fit with the narrative apparently being set up of a military aristocracy who arrived in a country, deposed its native hierarchy and took over the countryside. The Norman invasion of 1066, during which William the Conqueror defeated Harold at the Battle of Hastings and imported a French ruling class, was often cited in the twentieth century as the last successful invasion of Britain. (The Glorious Revolution of the 1680s is often offered as an alternative, but this is less picturesque as it did not involve the arrival of armies and a pitched battle with the British monarchy's forces.) The Norman invasion might well have

GOLD ON THE HORIZON

been on the mind of a novelist writing in the early 1950s, less than a decade after Britain had been threatened with another invasion by Continental forces launched from the shores of France. The Second World War had sharpened Britain's sense of itself as an island nation potentially menaced from the seas. Even before the war, there was a popular notion of the 'Norman yoke' as the imposition of French customs and laws on a freedom-loving English yeomanry. Rudyard Kipling, whose *Puck of Pook's Hill* was so influential on the previous Narnia novel, wrote a poem entitled 'Norman and Saxon' which is set forty years after the conquest and begins thus:

> 'My son,' said the Norman Baron, 'I am dying, and you will be heir
> To all the broad acres in England that William gave me for share
> When he conquered the Saxon at Hastings, and a nice little handful it is.
> But before you go over to rule it I want you to understand this:–
> 'The Saxon is not like us Normans. His manners are not so polite.
> But he never means anything serious till he talks about justice and right.
> When he stands like an ox in the furrow – with his sullen set eyes on your own,
> And grumbles, 'This isn't fair dealing,' my son, leave the Saxon alone.

This image of the Saxons as rough-mannered but good-hearted people, without polish or graces but with a powerful sense of fair play, is developed in a later stanza by reference to their lawless but steadfast character:

THE PRINCE UPON THE BATTLEMENTS

> They'll drink every hour of the daylight and poach every hour of the dark.
> It's the sport not the rabbits they're after (we've plenty of game in the park).
> Don't hang them or cut off their fingers. That's wasteful as well as unkind,
> For a hard-bitten, South-country poacher makes the best man-at-arms you can find.

The self-image produced, which of course Kipling meant to associate with the British people in implied contrast to some of their over-civilized and under-justified rulers, might be compared to the idea of the 'Scots Irish' tradition in the United States.[23] The point of mentioning Kipling and the Battle of Hastings is to underline the associations which many British readers of the 1950s might have had when faced with a story about a French-sounding military aristocracy who had imposed their own laws after conquest and driven the inhabitants to the fringes. When Doctor Cornelius explains that 'Caspian the First is called Caspian the Conqueror', it would sound a great deal like William I, who is also known as William the Conqueror.

If these puzzlings over the name of the Telmarines seem to locate them firmly in France, and in the part of the British cultural imagination which harped upon 1066 and William the Conqueror, there is another possibility in the name. Examining the English provincial newspapers in the decades before *Prince Caspian* was published throws up a couple of mentions of people with similar-sounding names. For example, in the early 1920s, the *Gloucester Citizen* newspaper received a letter to the editor, lamenting the attention lavished on one writer at the expense of another:

GOLD ON THE HORIZON

Sir,

Most cities of ancient lineage possess, I believe, societies or fellowships for the reading, recitation and worship of Charles Dickens. Gloucester is no exception to this honoured custom. But it has been a source of much mystery to me that, while men and women can make a cult concerning our greatest prose-writer, they should studiously ignore our greatest poet.

Will no one start a Shakespeare Society, Mr. Editor? We have three or four elocutionists of standing in the city who would do much to make readings hold interest and demand attention.

Besides, our children are taught Shakespeare in the schools. Just think of the prestige and dignity we lose when questions are propounded by them upon this subject which we are utterly unable to answer!

Yours truly,

TELMAH.[24]

This mysterious correspondent (whether a literary devotee or an elocution teacher hoping to drum up a little business) shared a name with a fortune-teller who appeared at church fetes in the same county a decade later. The papers record that in 1934 and 1935, the festivities held to benefit the parishes of Woolstone, Oxeton and Gotherington boasted a range of attractions, some more and some less familiar to the modern reader. These included a bring-and-buy stall, shove ha'penny, bowling for a pig, music from a gramophone, lavender bags, coin in the bath, cork stabbing, a play by 'the dramatic section of the Winchcome W.I.' (Women's Institute), quoits, bagatelle, cushion draw, and fortunes told by Madame Telmah 'the mystic of Winchcombe'.[25]

The explanation for these names, as readers have probably guessed by this point, is revealed by the fact that the master of ceremonies at the evening entertainment at Woolstone is

THE PRINCE UPON THE BATTLEMENTS

recorded as 'Mr. Hamlet'. Writing letters to the papers and telling fortunes at a fete both require a convenient pseudonym, and 'Hamlet' spelled backwards supplied 'Telmah' in both cases.

The case for 'Telmah' as the origin for the 'Telmarines' is strengthened by the appearance of the word in various novels. Lewis's Telmarines were not the last appearance of this reversed name in prose fiction. In the late 1990s, the Australian science-fiction writer Damien Broderick published *The White Abacus*. The protagonist, Telmah Lord Cima arrives on earth and befriends a character called Ratio. Both their names evoke Shakespeare's play, and the friendship between Hamlet and Horatio. J. N. Flint's romantic novel *Telmah* appeared in the 2010s, recounting the story of a 30-year-old singleton in Utah. Telmah's great-grandmother appears to her in a dream and instructs her to 'marry him!', leading to some soul-searching and partner-hunting by the young woman. As this synopsis suggests, *Telmah* translates elements of *Hamlet*'s revenge plot into a romance novel, pivoting the plot around the situation of a central character who is spurred to action to their family obligations but hindered by their uncertainty about committing themselves to the truth of that action. In the case of *Prince Caspian*, these echoes of Shakespeare's tragedy are most distinctly audible in the two scenes at the top of the Great Tower. They are present in earlier chapters (and will continue into later ones), but the connection is most obvious at this point.

Caspian finds himself on the top of the castle, rather like the characters at the beginning of *Hamlet* who are standing on the battlements of Elsinore. The prince, whose uncle is ruling as king, is told a story about the state of the land:

> 'Listen,' said the Doctor. 'All you have heard about Old Narnia is true. It is not the land of Men. It is the country of Aslan, the country of the Waking Trees and Visible Naiads, of Fauns and Satyrs, of Dwarfs and Giants, of the gods and the Centaurs, of Talking Beasts. It was against these that the first Caspian fought.

It is you Telmarines who silenced the beasts and the trees and the fountains, and who killed and drove away the Dwarfs and Fauns, and are now trying to cover up even the memory of them. The King does not allow them to be spoken of.'[26]

Narnia is a country which has gone fundamentally wrong in its government. There is, to adapt a line of *Hamlet* so famous as to have become also a proverb in its own right, 'something rotten in the state of Narnia'. This information, incidentally, comes from a character who turns out to be not entirely human. Doctor Cornelius reveals himself to be half-dwarf, putting him in a preternatural category which we might compare to the ghost who appears in *Hamlet*: part human, but nonetheless other-worldly. When Caspian and the Doctor make another visit to the top of the tower in the next chapter, the parallels with *Hamlet* grow stronger:

'What does it all mean? I don't understand,' said Caspian.

'I wonder you have never asked me before,' said the Doctor, 'why, being the son of King Caspian, you are not King Caspian yourself. Everyone except your Majesty knows that Miraz is a usurper. When he first began to rule he did not even pretend to be the King: he called himself Lord Protector. But then your royal mother died, the good Queen and the only Telmarine who was ever kind to me. And then, one by one, all the great lords, who had known your father, died or disappeared. Not by accident, either. Miraz weeded them out.

[…]

'Don't see!' exclaimed the Doctor. 'Have all my lessons in History and Politics taught you no more than that? Listen. As long as he had no children of his own, he was willing enough that you should be King after he died. He may not have cared much about you, but he would rather you should have the throne than a stranger. Now that he has a son of his own he

THE PRINCE UPON THE BATTLEMENTS

will want his own son to be the next King. You are in the way. He'll clear you out of the way.'

'Is he really as bad as that?' said Caspian. 'Would he really murder me?'

'He murdered your Father,' said Doctor Cornelius.

Caspian felt very queer and said nothing.

'I can tell you the whole story,' said the Doctor. 'But not now. There is no time. You must fly at once.'[27]

The rottenness in Narnia is connected both to the usurping king, and that king's murder of his own brother in order to seize the crown. In both cases the story is told to the dead king's son, and though *Hamlet* tells the story at more length than 'he murdered your Father', both versions involve the teller commenting on the lack of time to explain fully:

But soft! methinks I scent the morning air.
Brief let me be. Sleeping within my orchard,
My custom always of the afternoon,
Upon my secure hour thy uncle stole,
With juice of cursed hebona in a vial,
And in the porches of my ears did pour
The leperous distilment; whose effect
Holds such an enmity with blood of man
That swift as quicksilver it courses through
The natural gates and alleys of the body,
And with a sudden vigour it doth posset
And curd, like eager droppings into milk,
The thin and wholesome blood. So did it mine;
And a most instant tetter bark'd about,
Most lazar-like, with vile and loathsome crust
All my smooth body.
Thus was I, sleeping, by a brother's hand
Of life, of crown, of queen, at once dispatch'd;[28]

GOLD ON THE HORIZON

There are a couple of major differences which may strike the reader: that Cornelius is not asking Caspian to kill Miraz, and that Cornelius is a half-dwarf rather than a ghost. The question of revenge is diffused throughout the novel. In order to make it suitable for younger readers (and to alter the tone of the story), Lewis makes the imminent murder that of Caspian by Miraz rather than vice versa. In doing so, he glances at another Shakespearean archetype: a wicked uncle is making plans to have a nephew murdered, whilst that nephew is wandering round a tower. There is a strong air of *Richard III* and the Princes in the Tower about this reversal of the plot. Revenge is also transposed out of the personal key in which it appears in *Hamlet*, and into a broader and less morally suspect key of restoring the rightful rulers to Narnia. If, as Francis Bacon's famous essay *On Revenge* begins, 'Revenge is a kind of wild justice', then it is tamed in Caspian's case into a desire for proper monarchy (even if the revenge itself comes from the 'wild' lands of Old Narnia.)

The ghost is likewise displaced from the battlements of the great tower into the whole rest of the novel. *Prince Caspian* is a haunted novel in many senses, not least in the way people mention ghosts so regularly. The first appearance of the word (if not the theme) comes when the Pevensies rescue Trumpkin from the Telmarine soldiers:

> 'Anyway,' he continued, 'ghosts or not, you've saved my life and I'm extremely obliged to you.'
>
> 'But why should we be ghosts?' asked Lucy.
>
> 'I've been told all my life,' said the Dwarf, 'that these woods along the shore were as full of ghosts as they were of trees. That's what the story is. And that's why, when they want to get rid of anyone, they usually bring him down here (like they were doing with me) and say they'll leave him to the ghosts. But I always wondered if they didn't really drown 'em

THE PRINCE UPON THE BATTLEMENTS

> or cut their throats. I never quite believed in the ghosts. But those two cowards you've just shot believed all right. They were more frightened of taking me to my death than I was of going!'[29]

This seems an incidental detail at the time, but looking back from the Great Tower scenes it distinctly recalls *Hamlet*. Trumpkin has, unbeknownst to him, met the great kings and queens of Narnia, come out of the past to help a prince defeat his murderously usurping uncle. On seeing these kings and queens, he immediately assumes they are ghosts. Or that they might be ghosts, if ghosts exist, which he doubts. Later on, Caspian expresses a fear of ghosts in the woods around the ruins of Cair Paravel, but Doctor Cornelius assures him that the ghosts are a Telmarine superstition. True to form, when the Telmarines are defeated and offered the chance to stay in Narnia, some of them worry that this will mean living alongside talking animals and ghosts. The topic of ghosts returns for Trumpkin in a metaphorical sense when his principle of doubting and scoffing at everything he hasn't experienced personally comes up against the presence of Aslan:

> 'And now!' said Aslan in a much louder voice with just a hint of roar in it, while his tail lashed his flanks. 'And now, where is this little Dwarf, this famous swordsman and archer, who doesn't believe in lions? Come here, Son of Earth, come HERE!' – and the last word was no longer the hint of a roar but almost the real thing.
>
> 'Wraiths and wreckage!' gasped Trumpkin in the ghost of a voice.[30]

Trumpkin's characteristic habit of producing oaths suitable for any occasion throws up a phrase which might stand as epigraph for much of *Prince Caspian*. It is largely a novel about 'wraiths and wreckage'. The dwarf who met kings and queens on the beach and joked about them being ghosts has now met the King himself, Son of the Emperor-beyond-the-Sea. Susan once came close to asking Aslan if he was a ghost in *The Lion, the Witch and the Wardrobe*, and Trumpkin's 'ghost of a voice' brings the spectral theme into confrontation with Aslan. The angst and doubt which surround the ghost's appearances in *Hamlet* are dispelled by the reality of the lion's kingly presence.

WHEREON THE STARS IN SECRET INFLUENCE COMMENT

The useful prominence of Caspian and Cornelius's scenes on the Great Tower allow us to notice the ghosts flitting about the novel, and it also gives a useful perspective on the sky above them. The Doctor takes Caspian up to the tower with the promise of a practical lesson in astronomy. A first reading may suggest that this is merely a pretext for getting him alone on a quiet night to explain about the continuing existence of Old Narnia. However, their watching of the skies is described in dramatic detail:

> It was long and steep, but when they came out on the roof of the tower and Caspian had got his breath, he felt that it had been well worth it. Away on his right he could see, rather indistinctly, the Western Mountains. On his left was the gleam of the Great River, and everything was so quiet that he could hear the sound of the waterfall at Beaversdam, a mile away. There was no difficulty in picking out the two stars they had come to see. They hung rather low in the southern sky, almost as bright as two little moons and very close together.
>
> 'Are they going to have a collision?' he asked in an awestruck voice.
>
> 'Nay, dear Prince,' said the Doctor (and he too spoke in a whisper). 'The great lords of the upper sky know the steps

THE PRINCE UPON THE BATTLEMENTS

of their dance too well for that. Look well upon them. Their meeting is fortunate and means some great good for the sad realm of Narnia. Tarva, the Lord of Victory, salutes Alambil, the Lady of Peace. They are just coming to their nearest.'[31]

There is another allusion worth pausing on here, on the way back to *Hamlet*. For readers fond of the Psalms, there is surely a resonance with the hope and assurance expressed in the latter part of Psalm 85:

> For his salvation is nigh them that fear him; * that glory
>   may dwell in our land.
> Mercy and truth are met together: * righteousness and
>   peace have kissed each other.
> Truth shall flourish out of the earth, * and righteousness
> hath looked down from heaven.
> Yea, the LORD shall show loving-kindness; * and our land
>   shall give her increase.
> Righteousness shall go before him, * and shall direct his
>   going in the way.

The memorable image of righteousness and peace kissing is closer to Tarva saluting Alambil than might be obvious to a modern reader. We tend to associate 'salute' with the military gesture, which seems appropriate to a star known as the Lord of Victory. In earlier centuries, however, a 'salute' is simply a greeting, without the specialised overtones of army discipline. In the era when Shakespeare was writing *Hamlet*, salute had an additional particular meaning: a kiss given as a greeting. Cornelius' comment that the two planets are 'saluting' one implies that they are so close in the sky that they appear to have kissed. Victory and Peace, the titles of the stars in question, have done the same as Righteousness and Peace in the Psalm. The succeeding lines mention righteousness

GOLD ON THE HORIZON

looking down from the heavens and the land thriving. Lewis has loosely adapted the psalm verse, but made it happen in a more literal sense in Narnia. The two qualities are not simply associated but assigned to planets which then appear to 'kiss' in the heavens above. Just as Lewis literalises titles and metaphors from the Christian tradition elsewhere in Narnia – with the Lion of Judah saving those in captivity, or the Tables of Stone being present in the story – the two Narnians can look up and see the kissing of virtues in the heavens.

This stargazing is not only confined to the Bible, though. Caspian and Cornelius's attention to the sky binds them into an image system which runs throughout Shakespeare's play. We do not necessarily think of *Hamlet* as a play about stars and constellations; many of us probably mentally associate it with black cloaks, ghosts, skulls, battlements and drowned girls. Stars are nonetheless present all the way through the story. In the first scene of the play, when one of the guards on the battlements is telling the story of how the ghost appeared previously, he begins by reference to the constellations:

> Bernardo: Last night of all,
> When yond same star that's westward from the pole
> Had made his course t' illume that part of heaven
> Where now it burns, Marcellus and myself,
> The bell then beating one–
>
> Enter Ghost.
>
> Marcellus: Peace! break thee off! Look where it comes again![32]

In the same scene, Horatio worries that awful omens, including signs in the stars, have been warning them that the state of Denmark is corrupt and doomed:

THE PRINCE UPON THE BATTLEMENTS

> A mote it is to trouble the mind's eye.
> In the most high and palmy state of Rome,
> A little ere the mightiest Julius fell,
> The graves stood tenantless, and the sheeted dead
> Did squeak and gibber in the Roman streets;
> As stars with trains of fire, and dews of blood,
> Disasters in the sun; and the moist star
> Upon whose influence Neptune's empire stands
> Was sick almost to doomsday with eclipse.
> And even the like precurse of fierce events,
> As harbingers preceding still the fates
> And prologue to the omen coming on,
> Have heaven and earth together demonstrated
> Unto our climature and countrymen.[33]

The characters huddled on the top of Elsinore to await the ghost are clearly also concerned with what is happening in the stars above them. In this they parallel the Doctor and his royal pupil, as well as other Narnians. When Caspian ends up in Old Narnia he meets the centaur Glenstorm, who assumes the war against Miraz has started because he saw portents in the stars. He declares to Trufflehunter that

> I watch the skies, Badger, for it is mine to watch, as it is yours to remember. Tarva and Alambil have met in the halls of high heaven, and on earth a Son of Adam has once more arisen to rule and name the creatures.[34]

There are other instances in *Hamlet* where people invoke the stars, in that typically Renaissance blend of metaphor and occult implication. Hamlet swears in a poem to Ophelia that she might doubt that the stars are fire, but she should never doubt his love, whilst her father Polonius warns her that Hamlet is unsuitable because he is royal and thus 'out of thy star'.[35] Claudius describes Gertrude as so essential to him that she is like the sphere within which a star moves, and Hamlet advises Laertes that his own ignorance will make Laertes' skill flame like a star against a black night. In fact, there are as many stars in the play's imagery as ghosts, though none of them appear onstage. The stargazing which takes place on the top of the Great Tower borrows imagery from *Hamlet* and Psalm 85 to give a portentous significance to Caspian discovering the truth about Narnia.

Before considering how these Shakespearean echoes shape *Prince Caspian* as a novel, there are a handful of more faint traces. These are moments or details which probably would not be noticeable unless a reader had previously connected Narnia with *Hamlet*. They might be read as the kind of textual connections which only take place accidentally, when a writer has another work in mind as they write. One is a plot detail: the importance of education in *Prince Caspian*. The call which the Pevensies receive into Narnia both throws them into the story of Caspian and Miraz and rescues them from the prospect of going to school. Then Trumpkin's narrative about the prince stresses his process of education, both in the official curriculum and the secret learning about Old Narnia. The early scenes of *Hamlet* contain a certain amount of discussion of Laertes and the prince travelling away for their education. The next connection occurs when the Pevensies realize that the apple trees are the sprawling growth of the orchard which they had planted in their own time. They remember Lilygloves, the mole head gardener, and his team of other moles, putting in the trees. It is logical, given their skill in digging, that the moles should be the royal gardeners, though it might also remind a *Hamlet*-obsessed reader of one of the names which the prince calls the ghost. As Hamlet is enjoining Horatio to swear an oath not to reveal

THE PRINCE UPON THE BATTLEMENTS

what they have seen, they hear the ghost beneath them. It seems to be moving around under the ground, and Hamlet cries out an ironic commendation:

> Ghost [Beneath]: Swear.
> Hamlet: Well said, old mole! canst work i' the earth so fast? A worthy pioneer! Once more remove, good friends.

The children have cause to be glad that they, too, knew an old mole who was able to work in the earth so fast. Finally, the very first page of the novel has a slightly odd use of one verb, which recalls Hamlet's verbal quibbling. In briefly mentioning the events of *The Lion, the Witch and the Wardrobe*, the narrator states that

> While they were in Narnia they seemed to reign for years and years; but when they came back through the door and found themselves in England again, it all seemed to have taken no time at all. At any rate, no one noticed that they had ever been away, and they never told anyone except one very wise grown-up.[36]

That 'seemed' makes sense in giving an account of an apparently impossible happening, even though the characters (and the reader) know that 'seem' is not quite the right word. They did in fact reign for decades, and it had only taken up a minute or so of our world's time. The early scenes of *Hamlet* also call attention to this word, when Gertrude and the prince are discussing the grief at his father's death. She comments that it seems to be very bitter for him, and Hamlet picks up her choice of word:

> Queen Gertrude: If it be,
> Why seems it so particular with thee?

GOLD ON THE HORIZON

> Hamlet: Seems, madam! nay it is; I know not 'seems.'
> 'Tis not alone my inky cloak, good mother,
> Nor customary suits of solemn black,
> Nor windy suspiration of forced breath,
> No, nor the fruitful river in the eye,
> Nor the dejected 'havior of the visage,
> Together with all forms, moods, shapes of grief,
> That can denote me truly: these indeed seem,
> For they are actions that a man might play:
> But I have that within which passeth show;
> These but the trappings and the suits of woe.

Hamlet's famous denunciation of appearances and deceit in Elsinore has become a famous quotation. It may be Lewis's creative imagination almost accidentally borrowing a word from the play which he intended to weave into his novel later on, or it may be a personal textual joke, or it may be the near-paranoia of a literary critic seeing literary allusions in every line. Nonetheless, I now find it difficult to read the narrator's 'they seemed to reign for years and years' without immediately imagining Lucy Pevensie entering page left, dressed in black breeches and cloak, with a moustache of burnt cork smeared on her upper lip, and throwing out her arm to declaim, 'Seems, good sir? Nay, it is. I know not "seems".'

THE MEANING OF THE PRINCE

Having seen how closely *Hamlet* is interlaced with crucial elements of *Prince Caspian*, it is worth thinking about what effect this has on the novel. From one point of view, the presence of *Hamlet* needs no explanation or even consideration. The play was one of the most famous pieces of European literature in the nineteenth and twentieth centuries. It was regarded by many as the supreme achievement of the greatest literary artist who had ever lived. (During the twentieth century this

THE PRINCE UPON THE BATTLEMENTS

judgement tended to shift from *Hamlet* to *King Lear*, but Lewis was still living in the *Hamlet* supremacy.) Not only England regarded the play as presenting something crucial about the world: the German poet Freiligrath had declared in the 1840s that 'Deutschland ist Hamlet!' ('Germany is Hamlet!'), and a couple of decades after *Prince Caspian*, the playwright Heiner Müller would create the postmodern Marxist play *Die Hamletmaschine* ('Hamletmachine') which drew parallels between the drama at Elsinore and a totalitarian surveillance state. The use of *Hamlet* to explore the state of the nation, or the condition of a symbolic person, was a long and continuing tradition. The play was also well known enough for allusions to appear in detective novels, advertising slogans, and jokes. However, this major significance which *Hamlet* had in European culture prompts us to consider what it is doing in a children's fantasy novel. Amongst all the incidental detail and the creativity with which Lewis weaves the Shakespearean play into his novel, some major themes stand out.

Firstly, that *Hamlet* is a play about a young man faced with a usurping king on the throne, and his own rights displaced. Alan Jacobs has described the common thread of all the Narnia novels as the need to restore the rightful monarch to the throne. He writes that

> If we then try to consider the seven Narnia stories as a single story, what is that story about? I contend that the best answer is disputed sovereignty. More than any other single thing, the story of Narnia concerns an unacknowledged but true King and the efforts of his loyalists to reclaim or protect his throne from would-be usurpers.[37]

This theme links the apparently disparate narratives of novels from *The Lion, the Witch and the Wardrobe*, through *Prince Caspian*, to *The Silver Chair* and *The Last Battle*. It was also

GOLD ON THE HORIZON

one of Lewis's ways of characterising the situation in which Christians found themselves in the world, not because of any changed attitude towards Christianity but because of the state of sin. In *Mere Christianity*, which is based on talks he gave during the Second World War, he presents this idea with a blend of contemporary military imagery and kingly symbolism:

> Christianity agrees with Dualism that this universe is at war. But it does not think this is a war between independent powers. It thinks it is a civil war, a rebellion, and that we are living in a part of the universe occupied by the rebel.
>
> Enemy-occupied territory—that is what this world is. Christianity is the story of how the rightful king has landed, you might say landed in disguise, and is calling us all to take part in a great campaign of sabotage. When you go to church you are really listening-in to the secret wireless from our friends: that is why the enemy is so anxious to prevent us from going. He does it by playing on our conceit and laziness and intellectual snobbery. I know someone will ask me, 'Do you really mean, at this time of day, to re-introduce our old friend the devil—hoofs and horns and all?' Well, what the time of day has to do with it I do not know. And I am not particular about the hoofs and horns. But in other respects my answer is 'Yes, I do.'[38]

Hamlet provides an example of this usurpation narrative, and one which is already fleshed out with characters, narrative, plot-line and imagery. It is no doubt misleading to suggest that Lewis had this abstract notion of what Christianity involved, and then looked around until he found a suitable existing story which he could adapt to express his idea in a children's novel. It is much more likely that the *Hamlet* material suggested itself to him as he composed *Prince Caspian*, adding depth and symbols to this tale of a young man faced with

THE PRINCE UPON THE BATTLEMENTS

usurpation. It is striking that *Hamlet* had become associated with the problems of modernity: the play had been read in terms of political ennui, of philosophical angst, of existentialist crisis and Marxist analysis. *Prince Caspian* shows Lewis also borrowing materials from Shakespeare's play, but using them to put forward a very different vision of the modern world.

This highlights another parallel in the two princes' situations. The young prince of Narnia is not oppressed by philosophical indecision or by modern angst. He is, however, challenged by a supernatural revelation. Just as Hamlet is visited by a ghost from another realm, Caspian meets a half-dwarf (a kind of creature he has been taught does not exist) who tells him about the existence of a secret world within the country he knows. In the narrative itself, Caspian does not have much time to ponder what to do about this, because the novel moves on to another scene on the Great Tower and the necessity for him fleeing immediately. In both stories, however, the young protagonist is given the news of the usurpation via means which give him a glimpse into a wider reality. Both receive, in different senses, a supernatural message. This puts into narrative form a similar idea to the passage I quoted above from *Mere Christianity*: it shows the hero as the subject of 'messages' from the world of the usurped king. This further dramatizes one of the main themes of *Prince Caspian*: the question of how we are to deal with the past, and with supernatural revelations (a question which will be dealt with in more detail when Lucy has her night-time meeting with Aslan.) All the way through the book, characters are faced with the problem of whether and how to believe in the past. Caspian wants to believe in Old Narnia, but is told it is all childish rubbish. (He eventually does meet people with horns and hooves, at Dancing Lawn, though they are much more pleasant than the horns and hooves described above.) Some Old Narnians believe that Aslan exists, that he did what it says he did in the stories about the past, and that he may come again to save them. Some disbelieve in the four kings and queens. The Pevensies have to decide what to do when Lucy claims to have seen Aslan on their travels. Even though they have themselves met Aslan, even though they are the actual people in the stories about which other people are sceptical, they find it difficult to bring that belief to bear on what they are doing in this later Narnia. *Hamlet*, woven through the story of the young prince and the return of the Pevensies, provides images which are central to the novel's most lively concerns. In the process, Lewis quietly recasts *Hamlet* as a story which can represent the dilemma of modern life, but which resolves that dilemma by reasserting the spiritual world which would have seemed obvious to most people when Shakespeare's play was written.

CHAPTER THREE
LUCY THE PROPHET

Hearing the story of Caspian and the Old Narnians presents the Pevensies with the next stage of their quest, but it does not allow them to skip through the arduous matter of walking across Narnia. They are once again headed for the Stone Table (or the hill where they remember it being), retracing the triumphal journey which they made from the Table to Cair Paravel during the latter chapters of *The Lion, the Witch and the Wardrobe*. This time, however, they are hurrying to meet up with Caspian, assure him that they are real, and aid him in his rebellion. Uncertainties, difficult terrain and enemies hinder them, though Lucy is aware of another presence on the journey. In this chapter I would like to explore one of the central scenes of *Prince Caspian*: Lucy's night-time walk in the wood. In some ways it is the emotional heart of the novel, the point at which Lucy is rewarded for her perseverance through uncertainty by a meeting with Aslan. After being doubted, and doubting herself, after struggling with her family, the landscape and danger on the path, she is validated and reassured. Except that I think that would be slightly too simple a reading of this episode. I am going to suggest that Lucy receives a calling in this episode. She is given a vision into the heart of reality, and returns from it as an anointed prophet of Aslan.

To begin with, it is worth quoting the opening at length:

> Lucy woke out of the deepest sleep you can imagine, with the feeling that the voice she liked best in the world had been calling her name. She thought at first it was her father's voice, but that did not seem quite right. Then she thought

it was Peter's voice, but that did not seem to fit either. She did not want to get up; not because she was still tired – on the contrary she was wonderfully rested and all the aches had gone from her bones – but because she felt so extremely happy and comfortable. She was looking straight up at the Narnian moon, which is larger than ours, and at the starry sky, for the place where they had bivouacked was comparatively open.

'Lucy,' came the call again, neither her father's voice nor Peter's. She sat up, trembling with excitement but not with fear. The moon was so bright that the whole forest landscape around her was almost as clear as day, though it looked wilder.[39]

The image of Lucy hearing 'the voice she liked best in the world calling her name' suggests the theme of this episode. Though not everything in Narnia could or should be reduced to a 'real-world' equivalent, there are times when particular scenes seem to gesture towards an experience in our reality. The clue, perhaps, is in the word 'calling', which is still used in modern English in a technical sense. It is the term for a particular profession or way of life: one's 'calling' can be that of a musician, or a plumber or a lawyer. It can also be used in a more specialized sense still, to refer to the call to religious ministry. In this case many people use the Latin equivalent, 'vocation', from the verb 'vocare', to call. Lucy is experiencing a form of vocation in this episode. The fact that she does not initially realize whose voice is speaking her name suggests an allusion to a particular biblical story of calling. The prophet Samuel was sent to live in the temple as a child, and experienced a similar calling of his name:

> And the child Samuel ministered unto the Lord before Eli. And the word of the Lord was precious in those days; there was no open vision. And it came to pass at that time, when Eli was

LUCY THE PROPHET

> laid down in his place, and his eyes began to wax dim, that he could not see; And ere the lamp of God went out in the temple of the Lord, where the ark of God was, and Samuel was laid down to sleep;
>
> That the Lord called Samuel: and he answered, Here am I. And he ran unto Eli, and said, Here am I; for thou calledst me. And he said, I called not; lie down again. And he went and lay down.
>
> And the Lord called yet again, Samuel. And Samuel arose and went to Eli, and said, Here am I; for thou didst call me. And he answered, I called not, my son; lie down again.
>
> Now Samuel did not yet know the Lord, neither was the word of the Lord yet revealed unto him. And the Lord called Samuel again the third time. And he arose and went to Eli, and said, Here am I; for thou didst call me. And Eli perceived that the Lord had called the child.
>
> Therefore Eli said unto Samuel, Go, lie down: and it shall be, if he call thee, that thou shalt say, Speak, Lord; for thy servant heareth. So Samuel went and lay down in his place. And the Lord came, and stood, and called as at other times, Samuel, Samuel. Then Samuel answered, Speak; for thy servant heareth. And the Lord said to Samuel, Behold, I will do a thing in Israel, at which both the ears of every one that heareth it shall tingle.

As with so many of Lewis's biblical parallels, some of the elements have been moved around. As soon as Samuel is called by the Lord, he gets up and goes to see Eli, who tells him to go back to sleep. This happens to Lucy, but at the other end of her vision, when she wakes Susan and her sister says 'in her most annoying grown-up voice, "You've been dreaming, Lucy. Go to sleep again."'[40] Lucy does still make the same mistake as Samuel: where the young boy assumes that his master Eli has been calling him, Lucy initially thinks the voice might be her father, and then perhaps Peter. There is even a mild pun here based on the fact that Eli addresses Samuel as 'my son', though the boy is not related to him, as a term of affectionate authority. In Narnia this phrase is literalised, as Lucy actually (if momentarily) thinks her father is calling her. As she follows the voice, Lucy sees the trees apparently coming to life around her. She has already walked in the woods and felt that they might be about to quicken, but this time it actually happens. Lucy is experiencing several marks of a biblical prophet; so far she has heard a calling and now she is undergoing a vision. It has something of the quality of Isaiah's vision in the temple when he was called, and the cherubim began flying around and calling out. The form that this takes for Lucy is distinctively Narnian.

A VERY, VERY COUNTRY DANCE

At one point Lucy mingles with the dancing trees, on her way to following the voice:

> She went fearlessly in among them, dancing herself as she leapt this way and that to avoid being run into by these huge partners. But she was only half interested in them. She wanted to get beyond them to something else; it was from beyond them that the dear voice had called.
>
> She soon got through them (half wondering whether she had been using her arms to push branches aside, or to take hands in a Great Chain with big dancers who stooped to reach her) for they were really a ring of trees round a central open place. She stepped out from among their shifting confusion of lovely lights and shadows.[41]

The emphasis laid on the trees' dance, Lucy's brief participation in it, and the intriguing term 'Great Chain', brings together two systems of images from literature and culture in the mid-

LUCY THE PROPHET

twentieth century: folk-dancing and Elizabethan cosmology. The novel has already described the girl's wish to dance, and her sense that the trees are following a particular pattern:

> Yet it was not exactly an ordinary tree-noise either. Lucy felt there was a tune in it, but she could not catch the tune any more than she had been able to catch the words when the trees had so nearly talked to her the night before. But there was, at least, a lilt; she felt her own feet wanting to dance as she got nearer. And now there was no doubt that the trees were really moving – moving in and out through one another as if in a complicated country dance. ('And I suppose,' thought Lucy, 'when trees dance, it must be a very, very country dance indeed.')[42]

The remark about the trees performing 'a very, very country dance indeed' is based on the distinction in English dancing tradition between the more formal dances at a ball, and the more robust and rural dances which were customary in the country. In practice, many people of Jane Austen's time, for example, would dance the more courtly dances at the beginning of a party, and then finish the evening with a series of country dances. If the 'country dances' are called that because they are rural and earthy, Lucy seems to be joking to herself, then actual trees wading their roots through the soil must be the most 'country' dance of all.

Of course, Lucy does not live in Jane Austen's time, and almost certainly has not attended balls at a local Assembly Rooms. However, as a mid-twentieth-century schoolgirl, she is one of the people in her society most likely to have some knowledge of country dances. There was a great revival of interest in folk music and folk dancing in the late-nineteenth and early-twentieth centuries in Britain. It had an effect on the classical art music of the time: there is a strong folk-song influence audible in the work of composers like Ralph Vaughan Williams, Peter Warlock and Frederick Delius. It also expressed itself in clubs and societies which attempted to revitalise the traditions, such as the Folk Song Society and the English Folk Dance Society. The latter was founded by Cecil Sharp, whose writings make clear how he hoped a folk revival would invigorate British culture. *The Country Dance Book* commends the form to readers:

> The Country Dance, on the other hand ... has played altogether another part in the social life of the village [unlike Morris dancing]. No ceremony or formality has ever been associated with its performance. It was, and so far as it is practised it still is, the ordinary, everyday dance of the country-folk, performed not merely on festal days, but whenever the opportunity offered and the spirit of merrymaking was abroad. So far from being a man's dance, it is performed in couples, or partners of opposite sexes. No special dress is needed, not even holiday clothes. The steps and figures are simple and easily learned, so that anyone of ordinary intelligence and of average physique can without difficulty qualify as a competent performer.
>
> Nor has the Country Dance ever been regarded as a spectacle or pageant, like the Morris. It has always been danced purely for its own sake, for the pleasure it afforded the performers and the social intercourse that it provided.[43]

Sharp goes on to specifically commend the increasing enthusiasm to teach country dancing in schools:

> The movement has, no doubt, for its chief objective the quickening of the national spirit, and this will most certainly be one of its immediate and most beneficent effects. But there are other motives as well. Educationalists, for instance,

LUCY THE PROPHET

> advocate folk-dancing in schools for the sake of physical exercise that it promotes under the guise of recreation, seeing in it a corrective to the 'hockey walk', the 'rowing slouch' and the wooden stiffness of bearing induced by military drill.
>
> [People] attracted by the simple, rhythmic beauty of their movements, and of the tunes to which they are allied, think that these ancient national dances are on their own merits far too good to be lost, and advocate wholeheartedly their revival and practice, particularly in the schools and by young people.
>
> Among those who take this latter view must be reckoned the Educational Authorities, who, in their new Syllabus of Physical Exercises, propose that the Morris and Country Dances shall forthwith be placed in the curriculum of the elementary school.[44]

He continues to outline the grace of movement, physical health and artistic feeling which country dancing can help young people develop. The idea of schoolchildren frolicking through country dances did not stay in the writings of folk revivalists and educational theorists; it also appears in the school stories of the mid-century. Contemporary readers, especially of fiction for young people, would probably have been used to the idea of folk dancing as an enjoyable pastime for characters not occupied at the time with dormitory feasts, clifftop rescues, treasure-hunting or standing up to bullies. The hugely popular *Chalet School* series by Elinor Brent-Dyer features a great deal of folk dancing, as does the *Abbey Girls* series by Elsie Oxenham. The novel *Two Joans at the Abbey*, published in 1945, ends with a scene of country dancing:

> The first party in the tithe-barn was long remembered as one of the jolliest the Hamlet Club had known. Invited and rung in by Cecilia, the dancers came from every quarter and crowded

on the floor, eagerly making long lines or rounds, or squares, as the choice of dance demanded. Violinists were there who gave music that was perfect in lilt and rhythm, for they had played for the Club for years.

[…]

Jen, in her blue dancing-frock, claimed one after another of her friends as a partner, and then took up her little pipe, mounted the ladder to the musicians' gallery, and whistled a gay 'Newcastle' for the family set, while the crowd drew back to the walls to look on. Janice and Littlejean and the twins were closely watched by the other four and came through without mishap, though a grin went round the barn as Margaret was firmly seized and pulled into her line by Rosamund, when if left to herself she would have dashed across and made five on one side and three on the other.[45]

As this scene suggests, the dancing scenes in Oxenham's novels are not merely an impressionistic account of whirling music and bright dresses. The enjoyment, and sometimes suspense, for the girls, is largely vested in the technical elements of the dances. (I chose the barn dance scene from a very large selection because it has rather more lyricism than most: many are simply lists of tunes and dance figures.) So Lucy, falling in with the dance pattern the waking trees tread around the edge of the clearing, is not as unusual a figure as she might first appear. Anthropomorphic foliage aside, a schoolgirl joining a country dance in an English novel was a familiar trope. Indeed, in this scene in Narnia, some of the aspirations vested in folk dancing are realized in a more dramatic way. The 'quickening of the national spirit', or enlivening of the cultural traditions of the country, which Cecil Sharp hoped for, takes place to a remarkable extent. The young Pevensie ends up dancing with the trees themselves, with partners who are wading through the earth of Narnia. The country dance is apparently a sign that

LUCY THE PROPHET

Old Narnia is stirring on an even more fundamental level than Caspian has yet experienced, that the spirits of the land are gradually awakening at Aslan's call. Like so many other things in this novel, folk dancing can be seen as a way of meeting the past. It involves exploring old traditions (which still just about survived in rural areas, but were in danger of finally disappearing, according to the enthusiasts) and bringing them back to life by inhabiting them physically. The country dance which Lucy sees, and in which she briefly participates, looks rather like the archaeology that happens at Cair Paravel; the youngsters meet the past, and find their truest selves there. It is a much slighter example, but the theme of the past is being played out here, too.

There is even a suggestion that Lucy, like the girls of the Abbey and the Chalet, can reel off the names of dances when required. The narrator comments that she worked her way through the dancing trees, and when she arrived in the clearing she was 'half wondering whether she had been using her arms to push branches aside, or to take hands in a Great Chain with big dancers who stooped to reach her'.[46] The capitalisation of the name indicates that this is not simply Lucy's name for it, but the proper title of a dance. A 'chain' is a figure, or pattern, in dancing in which dancers thread their way through each other by moving in opposite directions and passing each other on the way. There are various kinds of 'chain' in country dancing, such as the 'Ladies' Chain' and the 'Grand Chain'. Hugh Stewart's book *The Elements of English Country Dance*, explains the figure thus:

Grand Chain
You face your partner and pass your partner giving right hands. As you let go of your partner's hand you take the left hand of the person coming towards you, and pass them by the left. Keep on passing right and left alternately until told to stop.

> This will typically be when you meet your partner half way round a square set.
>
> Conventionally this results in the men going anti-clockwise round the set and ladies clockwise. Square dancers talk about a 'wrong way grand [chain]' if you go in the other direction.
>
> As described it is a mistake if you meet someone of your sex, but some English dances have chains in them where this is supposed to happen.[47]

I have not, however, been able to find any reference to a 'Great Chain' in works on country dancing from the mid-century (or by subsequent writers). It is possible to regard this as a simple mistake: either Lucy or Lewis has got the names of country dancing figures muddled, and she mentally compared the weaving in and out of the trees with a 'Great Chain' when she meant a 'Grand Chain'. However, I would suggest a more interesting possibility: that there is no dance called the Great Chain, but that Lewis wrote the term deliberately.

THE CHAIN STRETCHED FROM THE FOOT OF GOD'S THRONE

The 'Great Chain of Being' is the name generally used for a particular way of looking at the world which is evident in medieval and Renaissance literature and philosophy. In the late 1930s it was discussed as part of the history of philosophical ideas by Arthur Loveday in *The Great Chain of Being* and from a literary point of view by E. M. W. Tillyard, in a book called *The Elizabethan World Picture*. Lewis would certainly have been aware of these books, both because they were part of the general knowledge of scholars of Renaissance literature in the mid-century, and because he had a distinct personal interest in the topic. He gave lectures on the worldview of medieval and Renaissance literature, which were eventually published as *The Discarded Image*. Indeed, we know that Lewis engaged

LUCY THE PROPHET

energetically with the literary ideas of E. M. W. Tillyard; in the mid-1930s they disagreed about the connection between literature and the author's personality via some articles published in the journal *Essays and Studies*. These were collected and published, with some additional articles in which the two scholars continued their disagreement, as a volume called *The Personal Heresy*. Lewis and Tillyard also held a public debate on the subject at Magdalen College in Oxford. Thus Tillyard's work had definitely occupied Lewis's mind at various times, both on points with which he agreed and disagreed with the other scholar.

Tillyard's *The Elizabethan World Picture* describes the great chain as one of the typical metaphors used to consider the world:

> The metaphor served to express the unimaginable plenitude of God's creation, its unfaltering order and its ultimate unity. The chain stretched from the foot of God's throne to the meanest of inanimate objects. Every speck of creation was a link in the chain, and every link except those at the two extremities was simultaneously bigger and smaller than another: there could be no gap. The precise magnitude of the chain raised metaphysical difficulties; but the safest option made it short of infinity though a finitude quite outside man's imagination.[48]

He cites various works of the time, and summarizes the vision of the world put forward under the idea of the great chain:

> First there is mere existence, the inanimate class: the elements, liquids, and metals. But in spite of this common lack of life there is vast difference of virtue; water is nobler than earth, the ruby than the topaz, gold than brass: the links in the chain are there. Next there is existence and life, the vegetative class, where again the oak is nobler than the bramble. Next there

> is existence life and feeling, the sensitive class. In it there are three grades. First the creatures having touch but not hearing memory or movement. Such are shellfish and parasites on the base of trees. Then there are animals having touch memory and movement but not hearing, for instance ants. And finally there are the higher animals, horses and dogs etc., that have all these faculties. The three classes lead up to man, who has not only existence, life and feeling, but understanding: he sums up in himself the total faculties of earthly phenomena. (For this reason he was called the little world or microcosm.)[49]

It might appear that humanity was the end of the chain, from this account, since it is both the highest point mentioned, and can act as a summary of what has been elaborated. However, seen from another point of view, humanity was only the hinge or midpoint:

> But as there had been an inanimate class, so to balance it there must be a purely rational or spiritual. These are the angels, linked to man by community of the understanding, but freed from simultaneous attachment to the lower faculties. There are vast numbers of angels and they are as precisely ordered along the chain of being as the elements of the metals. Now, although the creatures are assigned their precise place in the chain of being, there is at the same time the possibility of a change. The chain is also a ladder. The elements are alimental. There is a progression in the way the elements nourish plants, the fruits of plants beasts, and the flesh of beasts men. And this is all one with the tendency of man upwards towards God. The chain of being is educative both in the marvels of its static self and in its implications of ascent.[50]

Lucy's experience of dancing with the waking trees involves something of this finely-graded overlapping of faculties and links in the chain. The narrator comments that the first tree

LUCY THE PROPHET

she saw 'seemed at first glance to be not a tree at all but a huge man with a shaggy beard and great bushes of hair ... But when she looked again he was only a tree, though he was still moving'.[51] As she watches the trees, they sometimes seem to be giant humans, and sometimes seem to be trees again, '[b]ut when they looked like trees, it was like strangely human trees, and when they looked like people, it was like strangely branchy and leafy people'.[52] As the youngest Pevensie moves amongst them, it is rather as if she is taking part in a pageant of the Great Chain: the trees have their roots in earth (though they wade as if it were water), they possess the faculty of movement, and use that movement in ways which suggest they are teetering on the edge of other faculties, such as the memory which brings personality to a creature, or even the 'understanding', the reason or consciousness, which would put them on a par with humans. The story stresses, however, that they do not have that conscious quality: '"They are almost awake, not quite," said Lucy. She knew she herself was wide awake, wider than anyone usually is'.[53] That wakefulness was caused by someone calling her name, and Lucy's sense of vocation takes her through the dancing trees and to the presence of Aslan. As she embraces him, '[h]is warm breath came all around her'.[54] That breath, the same breath which revived the Narnians who had been turned to stone (in *The Lion, the Witch and the Wardrobe*) implies that Lucy has reached the empyrean, the realm of spirit. She has ascended through the elements and realms, the faculties and ranks, until she is (literally) face to face with Aslan. In Tillyard's term she has made her way up the chain to 'the throne of God' where it ends. In doing so, she has arrived at the same point as various Biblical prophets. The breath of Aslan also echoes the spirit which prophets receive.

The fact that she has reached Aslan by moving through a dance called the 'Great Chain' is made doubly apt by the way medieval and renaissance writers imagined the universe as a dance as well as a chain. To quote from Tillyard again:

> There was the further notion that the created universe was itself in a state of music, that it was one perpetual dance ... The idea of creation as a dance implies 'degree' but degree in motion. The static battalions of the earthly, celestial and divine hierarchies are sped on a varied but controlled peregrination to the accompaniment of music.[55]

The scholar quotes from the Elizabethan poet Sir John Davies, to the effect that the sea itself dances:

> And lo the sea, that fleets about the land
> And like a girdle clips her solid waist,
> Music and measure both doth understand;
> For his great chrystal eye is always cast
> Up to the moon and on her fixed fast.
> And as she danceth in her pallid sphere
> So danceth he about his centre here[56]

The same poem mentions plants and trees dancing, in a way which strongly recalls the Narnian trees:

> See how those flowers that have sweet beauty too
> (The only jewels that the earth doth wear,
> When the young sun in bravery her doth woo),
> And oft as they the whistling wind do hear,
> Do wave their tender bodies here and there;
> And though their dance no perfect measure is,
> Yet oftentimes their music makes them kiss.
>
> What makes the vine about the elm to dance
> With turnings windings and embracements round?

LUCY THE PROPHET

> What makes the loadstone to the north dance
> His subtile point, as if from thence he found
> His chief attractive virtue to redound?
> Kind nature first doth cause all things to love;
> Love makes them dance and in just order move.[57]

In these verses there are the incidental details of the wind whistling through the trees, and producing a tune to which they dance, but also the more profound sense that this is all set in motion by the influence of 'love'. In an Elizabethan poet this is not merely the fondness of one person for another, but the moving power of God, what the last line of Dante's *Divine Comedy* calls *'l'amor che move il sole e l'altre stelle'*, the love that moves the sun and the other stars. (Those stars including Tarva and Alambil, in this world.) Lucy moves through the dance of the trees to meet the radiant origin of that love.

When she has enjoyed the presence of Aslan for a little while, her vocation comes into focus again. The prophetic echoes which were visible (or rather, audible) when she was woken by the mysterious voice become more pronounced. In admitting her failure the previous day, Lucy begins to excuse herself by blaming the others, only to be brought back to truth by 'the faintest suggestion of a growl'.[58] When she accepts that her calling is to go and wake the others up, and alert them to the need to follow Aslan immediately, she takes on a prophetic office, awaking others as she had been woken. She has seen Aslan face to face, the evasions and self-deceptions of her speech have been purged by looking into his eyes, and she recognizes her duty to tell the others. This does not, however, mean she is unaware of the problems her office will involve. When she asks, 'Will the others see you too?' and Aslan answers 'Certainly not at first ... Later, it depends', the reader might be reminded of the opening lines of Samuel's calling, 'And the word of the Lord was precious in those days;

there was no open vision'.[59] The following pages bear out her worry, as the others do not have her clear vision when it comes to seeing Aslan amongst the trees.

By the end of this extraordinary episode, Lucy has passed through several of the distinctive experiences of a prophet like Samuel or Isaiah. She has been woken from sleep by a mysterious calling, seen a vision of unusual creatures that show that the world is alive with the power of the Lord, come face to face with Aslan, received an infusion of his breath, had her speech purged by his presence, and been sent back to her people with an imperative message which they will not want to hear. These scenes are redolent with the prophetic imagery of the Hebrew Bible, and filled with the medieval world's images of chains and dances. Through it all, Lucy remains herself. She is a prophet and a schoolgirl; an English youngster who trips some country dance steps and a seer who passes through the great chain of being. What she sees there gives her a personal job to do, and foreshadows the fate of the land of Narnia.

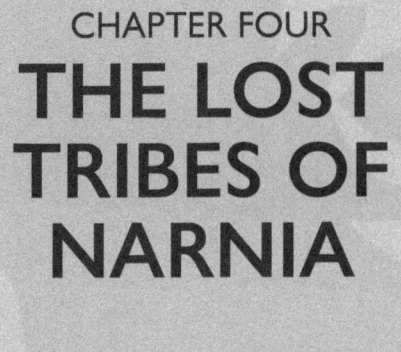

CHAPTER FOUR
THE LOST TRIBES OF NARNIA

Lucy persuades the others to follow her, and as they travel in the right direction they begin to see the lion more clearly. Finally Aslan appears, and sends the Pevensie boys, along with Trumpkin, off to the Mound on the hill of the Stone Table. The girls join him, to begin a glorious romp across Narnia, which I will discuss in a later chapter. For the moment, I will concentrate on the three adventurers who disappear beneath the hill, meeting a hag and a werewolf, and the literary echoes they set up. To introduce the next novel which appears to be interlaced with *Prince Caspian*, I should really have started at the scenes in the treasure house at Cair Paravel. The key detail is the stacks of ivory, and the open caskets of jewels. Even given Narnia's medieval trappings, it might strike us as odd that the kings and queens of Cair Paravel kept the tusks of elephants in their treasury. We might feel certain that these were not talking elephants, but nonetheless it has an odd feel for monarchs whose courtiers are talking animals to keep trophies which are so clearly part of an animal. This is a clue which I will have to explore by going back to the 1880s and a novel about a wily old elephant-hunter.

King Solomon's Mines by H. Rider Haggard was published in 1885, and became one of the most influential adventure novels in English. Its theme of a 'lost world' being discovered by European explorers inspired works like Arthur Conan Doyle's *The Lost World* and Charlotte Perkins Gilman's *Herland*. I will be focusing on some specific scenes in my discussion of how it is connected to *Prince Caspian*, but I will summarize the novel at some length. This should help readers to appreciate how

GOLD ON THE HORIZON

many elements of the story echo in Narnia, and allow them to spot similarities for themselves. The novel tells the story of Allan Quatermain, a grizzled trader and hunter in southern Africa. He meets an English baronet called Sir Henry and an ex-naval captain called John Good, who are searching for Sir Henry's brother. They believe he was lost on a journey to find the fabled diamond mines of King Solomon. The three men, with a number of African servants, decide to look for the lost brother by going to search for the mines themselves. They have various clues from an old document copied from the account of a sixteenth-century Spaniard who also tried to find the mines. One of their servants is a Zulu named Umbopa, who asks to join their expedition without expecting any wages, and who clearly has some secret which he is not telling them. After travelling through scorching deserts and snowy mountains, the group find their way through a hidden pass into a country called Kukuanaland. They meet a group of the Kukuana people, and claim to be 'white men from the stars' as an explanation as to what they are doing in the country. When they are taken to meet Twala, the King of the Kukuanas, they discover that he is a cruel tyrant. He is not the legitimate king, having killed the true king, who was his brother, and sent his infant nephew into exile with the ex-queen. Twala maintains his rule by intimidation and violence: the explorers witness an example first-hand when a 'witch-hunt' is held and men are summarily executed for supposed witchcraft against the king. The victims are chosen by a band of 'witch-doctresses' under the command of Gagool, an ally of Twala who is herself a witch and prophetess. Quatermain, Good and Curtis are horrified by the king's tyranny, and discover that several noblemen are on the point of rebelling under the leadership of a general of the royal blood called Infadoos.

At this point Umbopa reveals himself to be the infant nephew whom Twala hoped had died, and the rightful king of the Kukuanas. Under his real name, Ignosi, he declares

THE LOST TRIBES OF NARNIA

he will lead the rebellion. Infadoos is unsure that enough regiments will join them in overthrowing the king, and the adventurers offer to provide a sign of their great magic and power. Having consulted an almanac, they realize that the next day should be an eclipse, and they state that they will blot out the moon as a proof. This apparent demonstration of their supernatural and celestial power convinces enough of the Kukuanas, though Gagool is not persuaded, since she claims to have seen this happen before, many years ago. A brief but dramatic campaign is fought between the armies of Ignosi and Twala, in which Sir Henry fights in the line of battle, outfitted as a Kukuana warrior. Ignosi's rebellion succeeds, and he is crowned king. He orders Gagool, under threat of death, to lead the adventurers into the secret passages under the nearby mountain, where King Solomon's mines are said to be located. Gagool grudgingly agrees, and leads them through a series of strange chambers. One appears to have carvings made by ancient Hebrew or Phoenician engineers. One contains enormous numbers of stalactites and stalagmites. One contains the bodies of generations of dead Kukuana kings, which have been petrified by the slow dripping of the water until they are turned into the equivalent of human stalagmites. Gagool opens a hidden door in the rock, and leads them into a chamber full of treasures which include chests of diamonds. However, she then creeps out again, intending to trap them there and leave them to die, but is caught and killed by the secret mechanism of the rock door. The adventurers are trapped underground but, after resigning themselves to death by starvation, realize that the air has not run out and thus there must be some gap in the rock somewhere. After blundering around in the dark, and trying to save their remaining matches, they find an ancient stone ring and pull up a slab. They escape through a series of underground tunnels and come out on the slopes of the mountain. They then leave Kukuanaland, with Ignosi swearing brotherhood to them, but also taking an oath that no white men will ever be allowed to set foot in his kingdom again.

TREASURE CHAMBERS LOST AND FOUND

The detail about ivory in the treasure chamber of Cair Paravel, which I mentioned as sounding a little inappropriate for Narnian monarchs, draws attention to the parallels between the scenes in both novels during which adventurers descend into the earth and find treasure. The two passages are worth quoting at length, and putting side-by-side. Firstly, the Pevensies descend into the earth through the door they have discovered. Even before they get to the chamber, they make a point of asking the first person to count the steps as they go, to see if it is the same number as the treasure house they remember:

> They tried to use long sticks as torches but this was not a success. If you held them with the lighted end up they went out, and if you held them the other way they scorched your hand and the smoke got in your eyes. In the end they had to use Edmund's electric torch; luckily it had been a birthday present less than a week ago and the battery was almost new. He went first, with the light. Then came Lucy, then Susan, and Peter brought up the rear.
> 'I've come to the top of the steps,' said Edmund. 'Count them,' said Peter. 'One – two – three,' said Edmund, as he went cautiously down, and so up to sixteen. 'And this is the bottom,' he shouted back.
> 'Then it really must be Cair Paravel,' said Lucy. 'There were sixteen.'[60]

Much of this circumstantial detail, which seems so particular to the Pevensies' situation as children in the unusual situation of exploring a stone staircase which may have led to their treasury when they were monarchs of a fantastical land, can be seen in the equivalent scene of *King Solomon's Mines*. When the adventurers have been trapped in the treasure chamber, and eventually find a way out, they are also confronted with steps to count and burned fingers:

> 'Come on, Quatermain,' repeated Sir Henry, who was already standing on the first step of the stone stair.
>
> 'Steady, I will go first.'
>
> 'Mind where you put your feet, there may be some awful hole underneath,' I answered.
>
> 'Much more likely to be another room,' said Sir Henry, while he descended slowly, counting the steps as he went. When he got to 'fifteen' he stopped. 'Here's the bottom,' he said. 'Thank goodness! I think it's a passage. Follow me down.'
>
> Good went next, and I came last, carrying the basket, and on reaching the bottom lit one of the two remaining matches. By its light we could just see that we were standing in a narrow tunnel, which ran right and left at right angles to the staircase we had descended. Before we could make out any more, the match burnt my fingers and went out.[61]

Many of the details have changed in their significance: for the Pevensies the counting of the steps is not to avoid falling into an unseen abyss, but to check if it is the same place they remember, and the burned fingers are not the end of the explorers' light, but a cause of them using a better light source. It is even noticeable that one of each party has to be hurried along into tackling the steps: Quatermain because he is busy filling his pockets with diamonds from the caskets, and Susan because she is ostensibly sceptical about it being Cair Paravel, and possibly scared of a descent into the dark. Both sequences begin with characters rapping on a stone wall until it rings hollow, and Quatermain and his friends are desperately 'groping about on our hands and knees, feeling for the slightest indication of a draught' to show where the air gets into the stone chamber, whilst Susan comments that she doesn't want an open door at her back which 'anything might come out of, besides the draught and damp'.[62] Those details are still nonetheless present, and the extent to which they have changed their meaning underlines how precise the textual connections are. The escape from the treasure chamber in Kukuanaland has been transformed into the discovery of the treasure chamber in Narnia. Those chambers also involve remarkably similar details. In Narnia it looks like this:

> For now all knew that it was indeed the ancient treasure chamber of Cair Paravel where they had once reigned as Kings and Queens of Narnia. There was a kind of path up the middle (as it might be in a greenhouse), and along each side at intervals stood rich suits of armour, like knights guarding the treasures. In between the suits of armour, and on each side of the path, were shelves covered with precious things – necklaces and arm rings and finger rings and golden bowls and dishes and long tusks of ivory, brooches and coronets and chains of gold, and heaps of unset stones lying piled anyhow as if they were marbles or potatoes – diamonds, rubies, carbuncles, emeralds, topazes, and amethysts. Under the shelves stood great chests of oak strengthened with iron bars and heavily padlocked. And it was bitterly cold, and so still that they could hear themselves breathing, and the treasures were so covered with dust that unless they had realized where they were and remembered most of the things, they would hardly have known they were treasures. There was something sad and a little frightening about the place, because it all seemed so forsaken and long ago. That was why nobody said anything for at least a minute.[63]

THE LOST TRIBES OF NARNIA

Beneath the mountains of Kukuanaland, Quatermain and his companions' discovery is described thus:

> At first, all that the somewhat faint light given by the lamp revealed was a room hewn out of the living rock, and apparently not more than ten feet square. Next there came into sight, stored one on the other to the arch of the roof, a splendid collection of elephant-tusks. How many of them there were we did not know, for of course we could not see to what depth they went back, but there could not have been less than the ends of four or five hundred tusks of the first quality visible to our eyes. There, alone, was enough ivory to make a man wealthy for life. Perhaps, I thought, it was from this very store that Solomon drew the raw material for his 'great throne of ivory,' of which 'there was not the like made in any kingdom.'
>
> On the opposite side of the chamber were about a score of wooden boxes, something like Martini-Henry ammunition boxes, only rather larger, and painted red. 'There are the diamonds,' cried I; 'bring the light.' Sir Henry did so, holding it close to the top box, of which the lid, rendered rotten by time even in that dry place, appeared to have been smashed in, probably by Da Silvestra himself. Pushing my hand through the hole in the lid I drew it out full, not of diamonds, but of gold pieces, of a shape that none of us had seen before, and with what looked like Hebrew characters stamped upon them.[64]

The diamonds themselves are found in 'three stone chests' found 'in a nook' or 'recess', and when they look into one it is 'three-parts full of uncut diamonds'.[65] Much of the two treasure houses could be simply the description of any fantastically wealthy monarch's stores, but some details stand out. The 'uncut' diamonds in *King Solomon's Mines* are paralleled by the 'unset' precious stones in *Prince Caspian*. Quatermain remarks

GOLD ON THE HORIZON

on the wooden cases 'like Martini-Henry ammunition boxes', and might have expected a reader to recognise the name of the Martini-Henry arms company, which made a rifle used generally in the late nineteenth-century wars. The boxes in question were made of hardwoods like teak and mahogany, and reinforced with metal bands. When we turn to Cair Paravel, there are also heavy wooden chests reinforced with metal, though they are never opened. Then there is the ivory. I remarked at the beginning of this dive into *King Solomon's Mines* on the oddness of finding ivory in the Pevensies' treasury. Certainly an earlier generation would be less squeamish than me about ivory as a decorative and expensive material, since they were not raised on stories in which conservationists, rather than hunters, were the heroes. Quatermain especially notes the ivory because he is himself a professional hunter, and part of his fee for undertaking the trip was the rights to any ivory they found. He also mentions Solomon, however, and this is the detail which ties the two treasure chambers to an even earlier text.

When Quatermain refers to Solomon's throne, he is citing the passage in the book of Kings in which the Queen of Sheba's visit to Solomon is recounted, and in which Solomon's magnificence is expounded.

> Moreover the king made a great throne of ivory, and overlaid it with the best gold.
>
> The throne had six steps, and the top of the throne was round behind: and there were stays on either side on the place of the seat, and two lions stood beside the stays.
>
> And twelve lions stood there on the one side and on the other upon the six steps: there was not the like made in any kingdom.
>
> And all king Solomon's drinking vessels were of gold, and all the vessels of the house of the forest of Lebanon were of

> pure gold; none were of silver: it was nothing accounted of in the days of Solomon.
>
> For the king had at sea a navy of Tharshish with the navy of Hiram: once in three years came the navy of Tharshish, bringing gold, and silver, ivory, and apes, and peacocks.
>
> So king Solomon exceeded all the kings of the earth for riches and for wisdom[66]

Here we see a possible source for the golden vessels and dishes in Cair Paravel: they are echoes of the golden crockery in Solomon's court, which no-one thought much about. The Narnian analogue to Solomon's throne is not in *Prince Caspian*, except for the mention of ivory in the chamber. It comes near the end of the previous novel of Narnia, *The Lion, the Witch and the Wardrobe*.

> But the next day was more solemn. For then, in the Great Hall of Cair Paravel – that wonderful hall with the ivory roof and the west wall hung with peacocks' feathers and the eastern door which looks towards the sea, in the presence of all their friends and to the sound of trumpets, Aslan solemnly crowned them and led them to the four thrones amid deafening shouts.[67]

The coronation of the Pevensies borrows from the description in 1 Kings of Solomon's glory. The items are, as usual, a little transformed but are still visible. The ivory has become the material for the roof rather than the throne, and the peacocks which arrive from Tharshish have given up their tail feathers to adorn the west wall. The statues of lions surrounding the throne have become a real lion, Aslan, who conducts the new kings and queens to their seats. The ivory in the treasure house beneath the ruins of Cair Paravel is a trace of the splendour of the Great Hall in the Narnian Golden Age, but it is also a trace of two other sources: the piles of

GOLD ON THE HORIZON

ivory that Hunter Quatermain finds in Kukuanaland, and the throne-room of Solomon which stands behind both stories. The search for the origins of the ivory has illuminated a whole series of connections between the Pevensies' adventures and those of Allan Quatermain, not least in the matter of burnt fingers and suspect draughts. The treasure-chambers are not, however, the only places where Kukuanaland has apparently influenced Narnia.

THE AGES OF THE WITCH

The scene beneath Aslan's How, where Caspian meets a hag and a werewolf, and ends up fighting with them, is thick with details which recall *King Solomon's Mines*. The suggestion that they call up the White Witch, now that the Pevensies have apparently not returned, is met by both moral and practical objections. Chief amongst the latter is Doctor Cornelius' point that Aslan killed the Witch. The hag is not convinced this is a problem:

> And then the shrill, whining voice began, 'Oh, bless his heart, his dear little Majesty needn't mind about the White Lady – that's what we call her – being dead. The Worshipful Master Doctor is only making game of a poor old woman like me when he says that. Sweet Master Doctor, learned Master Doctor, who ever heard of a witch that really died? You can always get them back.'[68]

The idea that witches may be so incredibly long-lived as to be basically immortal hovers around the weird figure of Gagool in Haggard's novel. She is described as unbelievably shrivelled and wrinkled, and almost unrecognisable as a human. No one in Kukuanaland can remember when she was young, as discussed by Ignosi after her death:

THE LOST TRIBES OF NARNIA

He listened with intense interest to our wonderful story; but when we told him of old Gagool's frightful end he grew thoughtful.

'Come hither,' he called, to a very old Induna or councillor, who was sitting with others in a circle round the king, but out of ear-shot. The ancient man rose, approached, saluted, and seated himself.

'Thou art aged,' said Ignosi.

'Ay, my lord the king! Thy father's father and I were born on the same day.'

'Tell me, when thou wast little, didst thou know Gagaoola the witch doctress?'

'Ay, my lord the king!'

'How was she then—young, like thee?'

'Not so, my lord the king! She was even as she is now and as she was in the days of my great grandfather before me; old and dried, very ugly, and full of wickedness.'

'She is no more; she is dead.'

'So, O king! then is an ancient curse taken from the land.'[69]

In fact, Gagool boasts of her own age in an earlier scene, when she begins to wail in a 'thin, piercing voice' rather like the hag's:

'I am old! I am old! I have seen much blood; ha, ha! but I shall see more ere I die, and be merry. How old am I, think ye? Your fathers knew me, and their fathers knew me, and their fathers' fathers' fathers. I have seen the white man and know his desires. I am old, but the mountains are older than I. Who made the great road, tell me? Who wrote the pictures on the rocks, tell me? Who reared up the three Silent Ones yonder, that gaze across the pit, tell me?' and she pointed towards the three precipitous mountains which we had noticed on the previous night.

> 'Ye know not, but I know. It was a white people who were before ye are, who shall be when ye are not, who shall eat you up and destroy you. Yea! yea! yea!
>
> 'And what came they for, the White Ones, the Terrible Ones, the skilled in magic and all learning, the strong, the unswerving? What is that bright stone upon thy forehead, O king? Whose hands made the iron garments upon thy breast, O king? Ye know not, but I know. I the Old One, I the Wise One, I the Isanusi, the witch doctress!'[70]

This speech brings together three ideas which recur in the scenes inside Aslan's How. Gagool insists on the ability of witches (or isanusis) to live an unfathomably long time so that they meet generation after generation of people. She taunts her listeners with the knowledge that she has gained by this longevity, but also defers to others who are even more 'skilled in magic and all learning', just as the hag verbally grovels to the 'learned Master Doctor'. She points out that no one present except her knows who carved pictures on the walls of the caverns. When Caspian is first taken into Aslan's How, he notices pictures on the rocks which indicate great antiquity:

> The tunnels inside were a perfect maze till you got to know them, and they were lined and roofed with smooth stones, and on the stones, peering in the twilight, Caspian saw strange characters and snaky patterns, and pictures in which the form of a Lion was repeated again and again. It all seemed to belong to an even older Narnia than the Narnia of which his nurse had told him.[71]

These pictures are also noticed by the two Pevensie boys in one of the moments of chronological vertigo which are strewn throughout *Prince Caspian*:

THE LOST TRIBES OF NARNIA

> 'I say, Peter,' whispered Edmund. 'Look at those carvings on the walls. Don't they look old? And yet we're older than that. When we were last here, they hadn't been made.'
>
> 'Yes,' said Peter. 'That makes one think.'[72]

There is even another detail in Gagool's speech which reappears in the How, but assigned to another speaker. She raves about blood and a coming war: 'Blood! blood! blood! rivers of blood; blood everywhere. I see it, I smell it, I taste it—it is salt! it runs red upon the ground, it rains down from the skies'.[73] The phrase 'rivers of blood' is picked up by the werewolf as she describes his supernatural powers to the assembled company: 'I can fast a hundred years and not die. I can lie a hundred nights on the ice and not freeze. I can drink a river of blood and not burst.'[74] The hag and the werewolf are almost completely incidental characters in the narrative of *Prince Caspian*. From a plot point of view, they are merely present to show that not all Old Narnians are loyal to Aslan, and that the rebels are growing desperate in the face of the apparent failure of summoning the kings and queens. (In symbolic terms it also provides Caspian with a chance to kill a wolf-creature and thus demonstrate his likeness to King Peter Wolf's-Bane and his suitability to fill the same throne.) On rereading the book I am often struck by how vividly I remembered these two characters, and the disproportionate shiver they produce in the memory when compared to their significance in the novel. It may be that Lewis freighted this scene with this uncanny quality because he was channelling the much more adult gruesomeness of Gagool. Almost all the unsettling and sinister elements of the earlier novel are altered or avoided in *Prince Caspian*, except in this scene. Here they glisten briefly in the darkness of Aslan's How, before they are resolved by the arrival of Peter and Edmund.

GOLD ON THE HORIZON

THE ECLIPSE OF THE USURPER

As I mentioned in the synopsis earlier in this chapter, the movement of celestial bodies provides a hinge in the plot of *King Solomon's Mines*, just as it does in *Prince Caspian*. I suggested in the exploration of *Hamlet* that the scenes of stargazing on the top of the Great Tower of Miraz's castle both provide a parallel to the moments when the ghost visits Hamlet on the battlements, and ties the narrative of *Prince Caspian* into the star imagery which is scattered throughout Shakespeare's play. Rider Haggard's novel supplies other overtones which are present in the scene. The stars are themselves a running topic in *King Solomon's Mines*. When they are first discovered in Kukuanaland, the adventurers are asked to explain their presence since no strangers are allowed in the country, on pain of death. Quatermain improvises, and declares to the Kukuanas that 'Nay, ye shall know the truth. We come from another world, though we are men such as ye; we come ... from the biggest star that shines at night'[75]

When Ignosi reveals in secret that he is the true king of the Kukuanas, and the adventurers decide to join with him to depose Twala, a number of the chiefs refuse to rebel unless they are sent a sign. The lunar eclipse provides an opportunity for the 'men from the stars' to show their celestial mastery:

> 'Now tell me, can any mortal man put out that moon before her hour of setting, and bring the curtain of black night down upon the land?'
>
> The chief laughed a little at the question. 'No, my lord, that no man can do. The moon is stronger than man who looks on her, nor can she vary in her courses.'
>
> 'Ye say so. Yet I tell you that to-morrow night, about two hours before midnight, we will cause the moon to be eaten up for a space of an hour and half an hour. Yes, deep darkness shall cover the earth, and it shall be for a sign that Ignosi is

indeed king of the Kukuanas. If we do this thing, will ye be satisfied?'

'Yea, my lords,' answered the old chief with a smile, which was reflected on the faces of his companions; 'if ye do this thing, we will be satisfied indeed.'[76]

When the time comes, there is a double suspense, since the English travellers have interrupted Twala's intentions to offer the most beautiful girl at the dance as a human sacrifice. In the moment, they declare that the eclipse is to show their power and stop the girl's death, though they have also claimed it as a sign to the chiefs of the various regiments. The eclipse is described in a combination of dramatic and comic tones:

I glanced up at the moon despairingly, and now to my intense joy and relief saw that we—or rather the almanack—had made no mistake. On the edge of the great orb lay a faint rim of shadow, while a smoky hue grew and gathered upon its bright surface.[77]

As the eclipse builds, Quatermain hurriedly makes gestures to imply that he is causing it:

Then I lifted my hand solemnly towards the sky, an example which Sir Henry and Good followed, and quoted a line or two from the 'Ingoldsby Legends' at it in the most impressive tones that I could command. Sir Henry followed suit with a verse out of the Old Testament, and something about Balbus building a wall, in Latin, whilst Good addressed the Queen of Night in a volume of the most classical bad language which he could think of.[78]

Quatermain demands of Twala and Gagool, and of the surrounding Kukuanas 'see if the white men from the Stars keep their word, or if they be but empty liars'. In his

GOLD ON THE HORIZON

elevated language he nearly gives away a crucial detail of their intentions to Twala, given that the rebellion has not been yet begun:

> The moon grows black before your eyes; soon there will be darkness—ay, darkness in the hour of the full moon. Ye have asked for a sign; it is given to you. Grow dark, O Moon! withdraw thy light, thou pure and holy One; bring the proud heart of usurping murderers to the dust, and eat up the world with shadows.[79]

This rather pointed reference to people who occupy thrones which do not belong to them passes unremarked, and Gagool claims it is all a trick and she has seen something similar before. Quatermain and his friends succeed in overbearing her claims by a dramatic performance of their mystical rites as wizards from the moon, drawing on whatever incantations they can bring to mind:

> 'O Moon! Moon! Moon! wherefore art thou so cold and fickle?' This appropriate quotation was from the pages of a popular romance that I chanced to have read recently, though now I come to think of it, it was ungrateful of me to abuse the Lady of the Heavens, who was showing herself to be the truest of friends to us, however she may have behaved to the impassioned lover in the novel. Then I added: 'Keep it up, Good, I can't remember any more poetry. Curse away, there's a good fellow.'
>
> Good responded nobly to this tax upon his inventive faculties. Never before had I the faintest conception of the breadth and depth and height of a naval officer's objurgatory powers. For ten minutes he went on in several languages without stopping, and he scarcely ever repeated himself.[80]

THE LOST TRIBES OF NARNIA

Admittedly neither Doctor Cornelius nor Prince Caspian swear at the heavens whose movements they observe, but there are notable parallels here in the plot. We could see connections here with the scene of Cornelius and Caspian observing the conjunction of Tarva and Alambil from the castle battlements, and the careful scrutiny of the stars by which Glenstorm discerns that there is to be war in Narnia. It is a rare and dramatic coming together of celestial bodies, which acts as an omen that there will be an upheaval in the land. It persuades some of the watchers that the time has come for a usurper to be overthrown, and for his nephew to take the throne as rightful king. Both astronomical observations act as catalysts for the same kind of plot, though their tone is rather different.

ECHOES BENEATH THE MOUNTAINS

Rider Haggard's novel is a significant presence in *Prince Caspian*. There are several major elements or themes which appear to have been incorporated into the later work from the story of Allan Quatermain. We cannot, of course, say that Lewis deliberately chose these portions and decided to incorporate them into Narnia. We cannot even be sure he knew that he had drawn so much from the adventures in Kukuanaland, though the weight of connections makes it probable that he was at least aware of an influence. We do also know that Lewis praised Rider Haggard as a writer whose imagination produced not only exciting stories, but 'myths', large symbols which struck a chord beyond the immediate story. Comparing him to John Buchan (the writer of thrillers such as *The Thirty-Nine Steps*), Lewis wrote:

> The myth-loving boy, if he is also literary, will soon discover that Buchan is by far the better writer; but he will still be aware of reaching through Haggard something which is quite incommensurable with mere excitement. Reading Buchan, he

asks 'Will the hero escape?' Reading Haggard, he feels 'I shall never escape this. This will never escape me. These images have struck roots far below the surface of my mind.'

As with the other texts we explore, it is worth asking what impact this has on Lewis's novel. Firstly, *King Solomon's Mines* is an adventure story with a background of biblical references and images. This may not be immediately obvious from the passages I have quoted above, but the whole premise of the book is bound up with biblical narrative. Quatermain and his friends are setting out to find the legendary Solomon diamond mines, part of the source of King Solomon's wealth. When the hunter sticks his hand in the wooden box in the treasure chamber, he pulls out gold pieces marked with Hebrew characters, and he speculates that the ivory is part of the store used to make Solomon's throne. Much of the incidental narrative, with its big game hunting, diplomacy, treasure-seeking and civil war, may have little to do with the Bible. However, the overall story concerns people who (in a sense) stumble back into the past, and what they find is the traces of the Israelite kingdom. This is the first 'lost world' novel, and other novelists took the form in different directions. Charlotte Perkins Gilman depicted a lost nation of women who live without the need for men. Arthur Conan Doyle imagined a volcanic plateau in South America which had cut off a portion of the country from the rest of the world, so his adventurers arrived to find that dinosaurs still lived there. In more recent fiction, the *Black Panther* graphic novels and film depend on a similar notion: that there is a 'lost' or hidden civilization which exists in parallel to the world we know. In Rider Haggard's original version, the Kukuanas are a 'lost' African nation, but the land they inhabit preserves the traces of biblical characters. There are echoes of biblical texts in some of the dialogue as well. When Quatermain tells the chiefs that 'deep darkness shall cover the earth, and it shall be for a sign that Ignosi is indeed king of the Kukuanas', he is slipping into the language of Genesis. Perhaps aptly, since he is discussing a lunar eclipse, his words are redolent of the creation of the sun and moon: 'And God said, Let there be lights in the firmament of the heaven to divide the day from the night; and let them be for signs, and for seasons, and for days, and years' (Gen 1:14). His reference to not having understood 'the breadth and depth and height' of a naval officer's ability to swear uninterruptedly has an echo of the Epistle to the Ephesians' discussion of comprehending those same parameters, and being in the love of Christ. Elsewhere in the novel, Gagool calls upon the Kukuanas to listen as she sees a vision of blood and death, which begins:

> 'Listen, O king! Listen, O warriors! Listen, O mountains and plains and rivers, home of the Kukuana race! Listen, O skies and sun, O rain and storm and mist! Listen, O men and women, O youths and maidens, and O ye babes unborn! Listen, all things that live and must die! Listen, all dead things that shall live again—again to die! Listen, the spirit of life is in me and I prophesy. I prophesy! I prophesy!'[81]

This has decided echoes of the various prophecies of the Hebrew Scriptures, with the 'spirit of life' substituting for the 'Spirit of the LORD' which comes upon the prophets. The invocation of the various categories of people, places and things also recalls the liturgical prayer known as the 'Benedicite' in the Book of Common Prayer, which itself draws on Psalm 148. At another point, the story of Ignosi's mother fleeing with him is compared to that of Hagar. *King Solomon's Mines* does not feature biblical characters or retell a biblical narrative, but it offers a model of an adventure story taking place amongst the remains of the Bible. Both setting and occasional verbal echoes summon up the Bible behind the story being related. *Prince Caspian* takes on the same genre in many places. Unlike *The Lion, the Witch and the Wardrobe*, there is no major set of biblical narratives being reworked in this novel. The accounts of Jesus' arrest, death and resurrection structure the plot of the last part of *The Lion, the Witch and the Wardrobe*, and are repeatedly invoked by the narrative. This later story does not have an equivalent source; instead it tells a tale of adventure which evokes more scattered parts of the Bible here and there. This mode of adventure fiction may well have been borrowed from, or influenced by, *King Solomon's Mines*.

Secondly, the Pevensies are called into Narnia for a second time to establish someone else as king. This is a much less complex element of the novel, but it is essential to both *Prince Caspian* and *King Solomon's Mines*. In both books, the adventurers from the reader's own 'world' become embroiled in the struggle to displace a murderous usurper and crown his nephew as the rightful king. As Peter emphasizes, the kings and queens from the Golden Age have not come to reclaim their old titles: '"Your Majesty is very welcome," said Caspian. "And so is your Majesty," said Peter. "I haven't come to take your place, you know, but to put you into it".'[82] Unlike *Hamlet*, for example, the overall narrative is not framed from the prince's point of view. Given how closely Lewis's novel engages with Rider Haggard's, we might see this as another element that *King Solomon's Mines* provided, which was then used to rather different effect in the Narnian story. Thirdly, there is a strong, but generally unstated, theme which runs through the adventures of Quatermain and his friends which can be summed up as an adventurer finding his double in the lost world. When the three men first meet on a ship, Sir Henry's appearance is described in striking terms:

THE LOST TRIBES OF NARNIA

> Among these passengers who came on board were two who excited my curiosity. One, a gentleman of about thirty, was perhaps the biggest-chested and longest-armed man I ever saw. He had yellow hair, a thick yellow beard, clear-cut features, and large grey eyes set deep in his head. I never saw a finer-looking man, and somehow he reminded me of an ancient Dane. Not that I know much of ancient Danes, though I knew a modern Dane who did me out of ten pounds; but I remember once seeing a picture of some of those gentry, who, I take it, were a kind of white Zulus. They were drinking out of big horns, and their long hair hung down their backs. As I looked at my friend standing there by the companion-ladder, I thought that if he only let his grow a little, put one of those chain shirts on to his great shoulders, and took hold of a battle-axe and a horn mug, he might have sat as a model for that picture. And by the way it is a curious thing, and just shows how the blood will out, I discovered afterwards that Sir Henry Curtis, for that was the big man's name, is of Danish blood. He also reminded me strongly of somebody else, but at the time I could not remember who it was.[83]

There is a touch of humour in the deftly-reversed perspective of a white hunter whose only frame of reference for describing Vikings is 'a kind of white Zulu'. Less to modern taste is the racial and cultural politics suggested by the idea that 'blood will out', and the assertion that Sir Henry looked like an ancient Dane in modern clothing. It gestures towards contemporary anxieties that European nations had become 'decadent' somehow, and presents this character as an atavistic proof that there is still vitality in their bloodlines. When Ignosi, calling himself Umbopa, asks to join their expedition without accepting wages, Sir Henry is compared to another figure:

GOLD ON THE HORIZON

Sir Henry told me to ask him to stand up. Umbopa did so, at the same time slipping off the long military great coat which he wore, and revealing himself naked except for the moocha round his centre and a necklace of lions' claws. Certainly he was a magnificent-looking man; I never saw a finer native. Standing about six foot three high he was broad in proportion, and very shapely. In that light, too, his skin looked scarcely more than dark, except here and there where deep black scars marked old assegai wounds. Sir Henry walked up to him and looked into his proud, handsome face.

'They make a good pair, don't they?' said Good; 'one as big as the other.'

'I like your looks, Mr. Umbopa, and I will take you as my servant,' said Sir Henry in English. Umbopa evidently understood him, for he answered in Zulu,

'It is well'; and then added, with a glance at the white man's great stature and breadth, 'We are men, thou and I.'[84]

Again the racial politics of this passage are unpleasant to a modern reader, with the suggestion that Ignosi looks handsome because his skin accidentally appears lighter. The theme I am tracing comes out strongly nonetheless: that Sir Henry and Ignosi recognise each other as the same kind of man, even though they come from widely different backgrounds and cultures. Later in the novel, when Sir Henry and the others join the rebellion against Twala, Quatermain relates how they prepared for battle:

We rose and dressed ourselves for the fray, each putting on his chain armour shirt, for which garments at the present juncture we felt exceedingly thankful. Sir Henry went the whole length about the matter, and dressed himself like a native warrior. 'When you are in Kukuanaland, do as the Kukuanas do,' he remarked, as he drew the shining steel over his broad breast,

> which it fitted like a glove. Nor did he stop there. At his request Infadoos had provided him with a complete set of native war uniform. Round his throat he fastened the leopard-skin cloak of a commanding officer, on his brows he bound the plume of black ostrich feathers worn only by generals of high rank, and about his middle a magnificent moocha of white ox-tails. A pair of sandals, a leglet of goat's hair, a heavy battle-axe with a rhinoceros-horn handle, a round iron shield covered with white ox-hide, and the regulation number of tollas, or throwing-knives, made up his equipment, to which, however, he added his revolver. The dress was, no doubt, a savage one, but I am bound to say that I seldom saw a finer sight than Sir Henry Curtis presented in this guise. It showed off his magnificent physique to the greatest advantage, and when Ignosi arrived presently, arrayed in a similar costume, I thought to myself that I had never before seen two such splendid men.[85]

Dressed in Kukuana war-gear, Sir Henry looks even more like a 'kind of white Zulu', in Quatermain's earlier terms. The Viking strain which the hunter suspected within the English aristocrat has been drawn out by their adventures in Africa, and Sir Henry dives into the battle the way his ancestors might have.

In *Prince Caspian* there is no such speculation on bloodlines and atavistic elements flowering in modern men, but there is an extended theme of the Pevensies recovering who they were in their 'past life' as Narnians. They arrive as schoolchildren, but gradually begin to regain their previous selves. When Peter finds his sister failing to rise to the challenge on the island, he remarks 'Cheer up, Su. It's no good behaving like kids now that we are back in Narnia. You're a Queen here'.[86] As they descend to the treasure chamber, Lucy, Susan and Peter each become a little more royal as they take up the

GOLD ON THE HORIZON

gifts which Father Christmas bestowed on them. When Susan plucks the string of her bow, the atmosphere changes, in a passage which I discussed above:

> But whether by some magic in the air of the treasure chamber or not, the bow was still in working order. Archery and swimming were the things Susan was good at. In a moment she had bent the bow and then she gave one little pluck to the string. It twanged: a chirruping twang that vibrated through the whole room. And that one small noise brought back the old days to the children's minds more than anything that had happened yet. All the battles and hunts and feasts came rushing into their heads together. [87]

When it comes to Peter, a parallel with Sir Henry suggests itself. The English schoolboy puts on the armour and weaponry of this land, and everyone suddenly sees him as a warrior king from the past:

> Next, Peter took down his gift – the shield with the great red lion on it, and the royal sword. He blew, and rapped them on the floor, to get off the dust. He fitted the shield on his arm and slung the sword by his side. He was afraid at first that it might be rusty and stick to the sheath. But it was not so. With one swift motion he drew it and held it up, shining in the torchlight.
>
> 'It is my sword Rhindon,' he said; 'with it I killed the Wolf.' There was a new tone in his voice, and the others all felt that he was really Peter the High King again.[88]

The Pevensies soon have to prove to Trumpkin that they are not only who they say they are, but that they still have the abilities they possessed as Narnian monarchs. The narrator comments that Edmund would not have been able to fight

THE LOST TRIBES OF NARNIA

the dwarf twenty-four hours earlier 'But the air of Narnia had been working upon him ever since they arrived on the island, and all his old battles came back to him, and his arms and fingers remembered their old skill'.[89] This strand of *Prince Caspian* is partly a necessity of the plot, to describe how the Pevensies are waiting to go to school in one chapter, and ready to be part of an armed resistance a few chapters later. It is also a major theme of the novel, and part of its concern for how we relate to the past. The children know they have been kings and queens in Narnia, but have to recover their old selves in order to be part of this story. They have to do so despite the fact that, in Narnia, those old selves are apparently hundreds of years distant. The theme of Sir Henry venturing into Africa and embodying his own warrior ancestors is reworked to show the Pevensies (especially Peter) embodying their own royal selves from the past. The adaptation of this theme in *Prince Caspian* encapsulates one of the excitements and challenges which many of the chronicles pose: how to be your Narnian self.

CHAPTER FIVE
THE WISDOM OF THE DOCTOR

The events beneath Aslan's How have clarified matters, if in a slightly horrific way. The Old Narnians are now committed to the leadership of Caspian, and he has acknowledged the Pevensies as royalty from the far past. Their rebellion is being held in Aslan's name. In order to clarify things even further, Peter issues a challenge to Miraz, and two of the Telmarine king's nobles manipulate him into accepting it. The single combat between the High King and the usurper ends in false claims of treachery, followed by real treachery as Miraz is stabbed by one of his own men. Then, in a scene reminiscent of *Macbeth*, the usurping army is routed by the trees themselves coming to life. (Both Lewis and Tolkien seem to have rewritten the end of that Shakespeare play, scorning the trick of an army carrying branches and showing actual vengeful trees rising against evil in the land.)

Whilst Peter and Miraz battle each other, with the ground held by marshals from each army, I would like to pause and suggest a literary connection. *Tom Brown's School Days* is a novel from the middle of the nineteenth century, written by Thomas Hughes. As the title suggests, it is a school story, relating the scrapes and triumphs of characters at Rugby School in the 1830s. It has been enormously influential on the genre since. The titular character is a good-hearted, hot-tempered, fair-play-loving youngster whose physical courage is tempered through the novel by the acquisition of moral courage. The other characters include his chum East, the headmaster Doctor Arnold, the introverted but brilliant Arthur, and the bully Flashman. As the existence of that latter figure implies, *Tom Brown's School Days* does not paint a particularly rosy picture of life at a British public school. The place is full of violence, injustice and bullying, as well as friendship, games and food. Some of the most memorable, and famous, passages in the novel concern the campaign of bullying which Flashman and his cronies wage against the younger boys. This is handled with some social and psychological insight by the author: a number of the older boys dislike Flashman and are repulsed by his pleasure in brutality, but they still think the youngsters need putting in their place when they rebel and are unwilling to lose their status in the upper school. When Tom and East do stand out against the bullies, and eventually triumph over Flashman at some cost to themselves, they find it difficult to settle back into obeying the legitimate authorities and become semi-permanent rebels and outcasts. Amidst these plot-lines there is plenty of sport, including cross-country running, rugby and cricket, and an outbreak of dangerous fever in the school.

Prince Caspian and *Tom Brown's School Days* come closest to each other in a lengthy episode which does not appear to have much to do with school: the fight sequences. In Narnia, Peter fights Miraz on behalf of Caspian, in order to save bloodshed and determine their rival claims to the throne. There is a significant fight sequence in Hughes' novel, which takes place when Tom fights 'Slogger' Wilson on behalf of his friend Arthur. Wilson has been bullying Arthur, who is nominally head of the form but rather younger and weaker than most of the other boys, and Tom steps in to challenge Wilson to a fight. The rumour spreads through the school that the two boys will fight, and the customary (though against school rules) meeting happens. Both sides have their 'seconds', with Tom's friend East acting as his cornerman.

The account of the beginning of the single combat in *Prince Caspian* uses some strikingly similar terms to the Victorian school story. Both stories stress that the hero is lighter and younger, but more skilful, than the antagonist:

THE WISDOM OF THE DOCTOR

> 'Well done, Peter, oh, well done!' shouted Edmund as he saw Miraz reel back a whole pace and a half. 'Follow it up, quick!' And Peter did, and for a few seconds it looked as if the fight might be won. But then Miraz pulled himself together – began to make real use of his height and weight. 'Miraz! Miraz! The King! The King!' came the roar of the Telmarines. Caspian and Edmund grew white with sickening anxiety.[90]

A similar early flurry at Rugby School is followed by the fight turning against the hero and shouts from the other side:

> Hard all is the word; the two stand to one another like men; rally follows rally in quick succession, each fighting as if he thought to finish the whole thing out of hand. 'Can't last at this rate,' say the knowing ones, while the partisans of each make the air ring with their shouts and counter-shouts of encouragement, approval, and defiance.
>
> ...
>
> A very severe round follows, in which Tom gets out and out the worst of it, and is at last hit clean off his legs, and deposited on the grass by a right-hander from the Slogger. Loud shouts rise from the boys of Slogger's house, and the School-house are silent and vicious, ready to pick quarrels anywhere.[91]

In between rounds, East tries to persuade Tom not to stand and trade punches with Slogger, but to fight more skilfully, using his opponent's weight and heft against him. Tom sees the logic of this, and changes his tactics:

> 'Tom, old boy,' whispers he, 'this may be fun for you, but it's death to me. He'll hit all the fight out of you in another five minutes, and then I shall go and drown myself in the island ditch. Feint him; use your legs; draw him about. He'll lose his

> wind then in no time, and you can go into him. Hit at his body too; we'll take care of his frontispiece by-and-by.'
>
> Tom felt the wisdom of the counsel, and saw already that he couldn't go in and finish the Slogger off at mere hammer and tongs, so changed his tactics completely in the third round. He now fights cautiously, getting away from and parrying the Slogger's lunging hits, instead of trying to counter, and leading his enemy a dance all round the ring after him. 'He's funking; go in, Williams,' 'Catch him up,' 'Finish him off,' scream the small boys of the Slogger party.[92]

In the single combat between Peter and Miraz, the initial flurry in which the hero gets the worst of it is similarly followed by a shift to a more scientific style. As well as this narrative similarity, Lewis echoes the idea that the younger and lighter combatant is booed by his opponent's supporters as a result, and that the fight has become a 'dance':

> But the new bout went well. Peter now seemed to be able to make some use of his shield, and he certainly made good use of his feet. He was almost playing Tig with Miraz now, keeping out of range, shifting his ground, making the enemy work. 'Coward!' booed the Telmarines. 'Why don't you stand up to him? Don't you like it, eh? Thought you'd come to fight, not dance. Yah!'
>
> 'Oh, I do hope he won't listen to them,' said Caspian.
>
> 'Not he,' said Edmund. 'You don't know him.'[93]

The repetition of 'dance' is not the only distinct verbal parallel between the two fights. Tom's realization that he will not be able to beat Slogger at 'mere hammer and tongs' finds a resonance in Narnia:

THE WISDOM OF THE DOCTOR

> They were certainly at it hammer and tongs now: such a flurry of blows that it seemed impossible for either not to be killed. As the excitement grew, the shouting almost died away. The spectators were holding their breath. It was most horrible and most magnificent.[94]

A third verbal echo has East crying out 'Now then, Tom!' whilst 'dancing with delight' as his friend starts to get the better of the match.[95] As Peter recovers from a fall by grabbing Miraz's arm, Trumpkin calls 'The High King! The High King!' as he is 'dancing with delight'.[96] The narrative describes high deeds and single combat between two claimants to the throne of Narnia, but much of the incidental detail might remind the reader of a fist-fight behind the gym in a school story. The echoes of *Tom Brown's School Days* are oddly precise, and suggest that Lewis's may have had the older novel in mind when constructing his scene. This produces the kind of double-vision in the text which we have seen in previous chapters. Peter is both a schoolboy from England, and the rightful king of Narnia. Susan is both a bereft schoolgirl weeping because she has been separated from her horse, and an Anglo-Saxon poet lamenting the transience of worldly glory. Lucy is both a youngster who went for a walk on a wakeful night, prancing a few steps of a country dance, and a prophet who is granted a vision of the interwoven fabric of creation. This is one of the characteristic techniques of the Narnia novels, and it feels especially present in *Prince Caspian*. It can have a powerful effect on readers, even if they are unaware of the literary echoes in the text, or never notice the way the royal single combat is curiously like a bare-knuckle bout at an English public school. The way the Pevensies carry out their roles, and the way they tackle their adventures, presents them to the audience as both schoolchildren and chivalric heroes.

GOLD ON THE HORIZON

This may be part of the reason why the Narnia novels have exerted such a force upon so many readers: they offer a form of a fiction where characters feel as if they inhabit two worlds, making it easier for the audience to see how they could do likewise.

The apparent connections between the two texts are most visible, and most verbally precise, in the fight sequence. Once they are noticed, however, more subtle similarities appear. One of the most striking parallels between *Prince Caspian* and *Tom Brown's School Days* is the presence of a wise older man, almost a father-figure at times, who is called 'the Doctor'. In Caspian's case this is Doctor Cornelius, who is almost always called by his full title and name, or simply called 'the Doctor'. (For those fond of the kind of statistics which electronic texts can provide, I believe he is called 'Cornelius' only five times, 'Doctor Cornelius' forty-six times, and 'the Doctor' forty-nine times.) This name makes sense, since he is Caspian's tutor, and the word 'doctor' derives from the Latin *docere*, to teach. This is why a number of great theologians are known as the 'doctors of the Church', not because they are imagined as healing spiritual sickness, but because they provided significant teaching in the faith. Therefore it is not incongruous that Caspian should have a teacher who is frequently referred to as 'the Doctor'. It does, however, become significant when the novel is compared with *Tom Brown's School Days*. The headmaster at Rugby School is Dr Thomas Arnold, an educational reformer who was the actual head of the school in the mid-nineteenth century. He is called 'Arnold' a handful of times in the text, but he is overwhelmingly called by the same name as Cornelius: 'the Doctor'. (Again, for enthusiasts of numbers: about four to one hundred and eighty-ish.)

This juggling with nomenclature is not to argue any numerological significance, but rather to suggest that there

THE WISDOM OF THE DOCTOR

is a strong parallel between two characters which might easily pass unnoticed if a reader is not thinking of *Tom Brown's School Days* in the background of the guerilla war against Miraz. For the generations reading the Narnia novels in the early-twenty-first century, 'the Doctor' is more likely to summon up the time-travelling science fiction TV show. Before the 1960s and 1970s, though, I would suggest that 'the Doctor' was more likely to summon up Arnold of Rugby to an audience's mind. In *Tom Brown's School Days* the Doctor plays a rather similar role to Cornelius, early on in the text. When Tom has only been a few days at Rugby, he attends the school chapel:

> And then came that great event in his, as in every Rugby boy's life of that day—the first sermon from the Doctor. More worthy pens than mine have described that scene—the oak pulpit standing out by itself above the School seats; the tall, gallant form, the kindling eye, the voice, now soft as the low notes of a flute, now clear and stirring as the call of the light-infantry bugle, of him who stood there Sunday after Sunday, witnessing and pleading for his Lord, the King of righteousness and love and glory, with whose Spirit he was filled, and in whose power he spoke; the long lines of young faces, rising tier above tier down the whole length of the chapel, from the little boy's who had just left his mother to the young man's who was going out next week into the great world, rejoicing in his strength. It was a great and solemn sight, and never more so than at this time of year, when the only lights in the chapel were in the pulpit and at the seats of the prepostors of the week, and the soft twilight stole over the rest of the chapel, deepening into darkness in the high gallery behind the organ.[97]

This dramatic description of the headmaster preaching alerts the reader to the importance of this scene in the narrative.

GOLD ON THE HORIZON

Hughes goes on to describe the impact which that sermon (and others like it) had upon the boys, and what marked out the Doctor's preaching:

> It was not the cold, clear voice of one giving advice and warning from serene heights to those who were struggling and sinning below, but the warm, living voice of one who was fighting for us and by our sides, and calling on us to help him and ourselves and one another. And so, wearily and little by little, but surely and steadily on the whole, was brought home to the young boy, for the first time, the meaning of his life—that it was no fool's or sluggard's paradise into which he had wandered by chance, but a battlefield ordained from of old, where there are no spectators, but the youngest must take his side, and the stakes are life and death. And he who roused this consciousness in them showed them at the same time, by every word he spoke in the pulpit, and by his whole daily life, how that battle was to be fought, and stood there before them their fellow-soldier and the captain of their band.[98]

Caspian's own 'Doctor' plays a similar role on the top of the tower, when he reveals to the young prince what is really going on in Narnia. The metaphors which Hughes employs, that life is a battlefield in which everyone must choose sides and carry on the war, are going to become literally true for Caspian. I suspect that Hughes' imagery may have been influenced by the works of the great allegorist John Bunyan, whose *Pilgrim's Progress* and *The Holy War* strongly informed the Christian imagination in the nineteenth century. If so, then Hughes is drawing on a source which Lewis also appears to have been influenced by in his more fantastical writings. Either way, the two 'Doctors' influence young men by telling them about the state of the world, and calling them to take their part in a war (whether literal or metaphorical). Cornelius is regarded with less awe by the narrator and main characters than the great Doctor Arnold, but he has a similar effect on the narrative. He reveals – like the Doctor of Rugby – that the young hero's education is not simply a training in certain subjects in order to become proficient at them for their own sake, but is a preparation for existential struggles.

LET US PRAISE NOW TALKING BEASTS

The parallels between these two novels might cause a reader some surprise. Lewis is not an obvious writer to start channelling the British school story tradition. His own experience at school had been miserably unhappy, and the depiction of school life at the beginning of *The Silver Chair* shows a tyrannical and unpleasant institution. Not only schools themselves, but school stories seem suspect to him, for example in this comment in *An Experiment in Criticism*:

> No one can deceive you unless he makes you think he is telling the truth. The unblushingly romantic has far less power to deceive than the apparently realistic. Admitted fantasy is precisely the kind of literature which never deceives at all. Children are not deceived by fairy-tales; they are often and gravely deceived by school-stories. Adults are not deceived by science-fiction; they can be deceived by the stories in the women's magazines. None of us are deceived by the Odyssey, the Kalevala, Beowulf, or Malory. The real danger lurks in sober-faced novels where all appears to be very probable but all is in fact contrived to put across some social or ethical or religious or anti-religious 'comment on life'.[99]

This passage comes – as readers may have deduced – from a defence of fantastical writing as a legitimate literary form. With typically Lewisian irony, and an insistence on turning opponents' arguments round on them, he declares that realistic fiction is much more deceptive than admitted fantasy. (I have heard a similar argument deployed more recently by enthusiasts of 'paranormal romance' and 'dark romance' novels; asserting that these forms of the genre are much less likely to instil harmful attitudes to relationships in their readers than the more realistic and thus insidious contemporary romances.) Schools fare badly elsewhere in Narnia. In *The Lion, the Witch and the Wardrobe*, there is a strong suggestion that Edmund's moral character has been damaged by his time at school. When he first meets the White Witch, and she asks what he is, Edmund identifies himself as 'at school' rather than as a boy or a Son of Adam. When the Pevensies become monarchs of Narnia, they stop people sending the young satyrs to school, and when Aslan and his retinue romp through the land in the later chapters of *Prince Caspian* they liberate various Narnians from schools.

Despite this apparent distaste for both school and novels about them, Lewis does seem to have borrowed from *Tom Brown's School Days*. Noticing this brings into focus just how much *Prince Caspian* is concerned with education. This theme may not be the one which produces the most memorable scenes in the book. Most people, including me, if asked to recall the striking moments in *Prince Caspian* would probably mention images like the underground treasure chamber, Lucy's vision, the darkness inside Aslan's How and the door in the air. Less noticeably, learning and education are threaded through the story. When they are called into Narnia, the children are sitting on a railway station platform, about to move definitively from holidays to term:

> The first part of the journey, when they were all together, always seemed to be part of the holidays; but now when they would be saying goodbye and going different ways so soon, everyone felt that the holidays were really over and everyone

THE WISDOM OF THE DOCTOR

felt their term-time feelings beginning again, and they were all rather gloomy and no one could think of anything to say. Lucy was going to boarding school for the first time.[100]

When they meet Trumpkin and he settles down to tell them why he was under order of execution by the Telmarines, he begins with an account of Prince Caspian's education. The move from the stories of his Nurse to the lessons with his tutor marks the beginning of Caspian's coming-of-age. It is the time we join his story, the point at which he both begins to learn more about the land of Narnia and potentially become more of a threat to his uncle. The subjects which Cornelius teaches him are apparently very dry and tedious (I suspect the author of his grammar book, 'Pulverulentus Siccus' is a joke meaning something like 'Crushingly Dry'), but they do keep leading him towards the truth about Narnia. This may be because Doctor Cornelius is priming him to learn about the people who are living in hiding, but it may also be Lewis's gesture towards the fact that truth is indivisible. You cannot teach the facts of Narnian history, for example, such as the regnal name and number of Caspian the Conqueror, without sometimes prompting the question of who was in Narnia before the Telmarines. We might also notice that the apparently tedious lessons in grammar are teaching Caspian a skill which will allow him to notice something crucial about his tutor:

> 'But, Doctor,' said Caspian, 'why do you say my race? After all, I suppose you're a Telmarine too.'
> 'Am I?' said the Doctor.
> 'Well, you're a Man anyway,' said Caspian.
> 'Am I?' repeated the Doctor in a deeper voice.[101]

Education is an ambiguous matter in these early chapters: it can be an unappealing prospect, and a means of directing young minds away from important matters, but it can also train them to notice and enquire. This may well be the distinction needed to appreciate the borrowings from *Tom Brown's School Days*: Lewis is less interested in schools than in education more broadly. The fight between Tom and Slogger, and the figure of the Doctor, are elements which come from a school story, but are not necessarily defined by the school setting. Lewis's borrowings do not include the cricket match, or the speech by Tom's head of house, which are more obviously episodes from a school story. Indeed, there are some striking elements which the two novels have in common which do not involve a school at all.

The opening chapters of *Tom Brown's School Days* are nothing to do with Rugby School, and instead detail Tom's childhood in the English countryside. Hughes is both rhapsodic and didactic about the glories of the rural counties, apostrophizing the reader thus:

> O young England! young England! you who are born into these racing railroad times, when there's a Great Exhibition, or some monster sight, every year, and you can get over a couple of thousand miles of ground for three pound ten in a five-weeks' holiday, why don't you know more of your own birthplaces?[102]

He decries the tendency amongst modern youth to either disappear off to Ireland, or Switzerland, or France, or sit at home reading books. The kind of sophistication this gives, according to Hughes, cannot compete with a knowledge of the countryside:

> All I say is, you don't know your own lanes and woods and fields. Though you may be choke-full of science, not one in twenty of you knows where to find the wood-sorrel, or bee-orchis, which grow in the next wood, or on the down three miles off, or what the bog-bean and wood-sage are good for.

THE WISDOM OF THE DOCTOR

> And as for the country legends, the stories of the old gable-ended farmhouses, the place where the last skirmish was fought in the civil wars, where the parish butts stood, where the last highwayman turned to bay, where the last ghost was laid by the parson, they're gone out of date altogether.[103]

As a means of remedying this defect amongst his readership, Hughes conducts them on an imaginary tour of the region of Berkshire where Tom Brown grew up, known as the Vale of the White Horse. Whilst pointing out features of interest, he gestures at the history and the legends of the land:

> And then what a hill is the White Horse Hill! There it stands right up above all the rest, nine hundred feet above the sea, and the boldest, bravest shape for a chalk hill that you ever saw. Let us go up to the top of him, and see what is to be found there. Ay, you may well wonder and think it odd you never heard of this before; but wonder or not, as you please, there are hundreds of such things lying about England, which wiser folk than you know nothing of, and care nothing for. Yes, it's a magnificent Roman camp, and no mistake, with gates and ditch and mounds, all as complete as it was twenty years after the strong old rogues left it.
>
> [...]
>
> And now we leave the camp, and descend towards the west, and are on the Ashdown. We are treading on heroes. It is sacred ground for Englishmen—more sacred than all but one or two fields where their bones lie whitening. For this is the actual place where our Alfred won his great battle, the battle of Ashdown ('Aescendum' in the chroniclers), which broke the Danish power, and made England a Christian land.[104]

He continues on, relating the legend that Dragon's Hill is so-called because some hero such as St George killed a dragon there, and then directs the reader's attention to the barrows on the downs:

> There are the barrows still, solemn and silent, like ships in the calm sea, the sepulchres of some sons of men. But of whom? It is three miles from the White Horse—too far for the slain of Ashdown to be buried there. Who shall say what heroes are waiting there?[105]

The English youngsters walking (if only in imagination) over the traces of the glorious past, the heroes waiting in barrows beneath the earth, find echoes in *Prince Caspian*. I discussed the 'archaeological imagination' of the novel in an earlier chapter, and suggested that both Caspian and the Pevensies end up disappearing under the ground to seek their true selves. The thrill and depth of the past are strongly present in these early passages of *Tom Brown's School Days*. It would only take a little alteration to make them sound like Kipling's *Puck of Pook's Hill*, the children's stories in which people appear from England's past. A visit to a local pub on Hughes' imaginary tour yields another (and even more literal) echo resounding between the two books. The narrator asks the landlord a question, and amongst copious 'yokelry' dialect and heavy humour, it is answered:

> 'What is the name of your hill, landlord?'
>> 'Blawing STWUN Hill, sir, to be sure.'
>> [READER. 'Stuym?'
>> AUTHOR: 'Stone, stupid—the Blowing Stone.']
>> 'And of your house? I can't make out the sign.'
>> 'Blawing Stwun, sir,' says the landlord, pouring out his old ale from a Toby Philpot jug, with a melodious crash, into the long-necked glass.
>> 'What queer names!' say we, sighing at the end of our draught, and holding out the glass to be replenished.

THE WISDOM OF THE DOCTOR

> 'Bean't queer at all, as I can see, sir,' says mine host, handing back our glass, 'seeing as this here is the Blawing Stwun, his self,' putting his hand on a square lump of stone, some three feet and a half high, perforated with two or three queer holes, like petrified antediluvian rat-holes, which lies there close under the oak, under our very nose. [106]

The landlord offers to show them why the stone is called that, with the following results:

> We are ready for anything; and he, without waiting for a reply, applies his mouth to one of the ratholes. Something must come of it, if he doesn't burst. Good heavens! I hope he has no apoplectic tendencies. Yes, here it comes, sure enough, a gruesome sound between a moan and a roar, and spreads itself away over the valley, and up the hillside, and into the woods at the back of the house, a ghost-like, awful voice. [107]

The landlord says that the sound can be heard for miles around, and the narrator wonders whether 'the blowing of the stone [could] have been a summons', like a beacon sent around the landscape 'in the old times? What old times? Who knows? We pay for our beer and are thankful'.[108]

A ghostly noise, which reverberates across the land when someone blows an ancient relic, is one of the central plot points of *Prince Caspian*. I do not claim that this echo proves that Lewis was deliberately reworking the earlier novel, but it is remarkable how similar the imaginative landscapes of the two books appear on close inspection. These other elements of *Tom Brown's School Days*, such as the mysterious barrows and the Blowing Stone, suggest a further development of the way *Prince Caspian* engages with the Victorian novel. Lewis has produced a novel which is profoundly concerned with education, in various senses, but which is somewhat sceptical of schools themselves. Examining the passages which find a parallel in Hughes' book emphasizes how *Caspian* both engages with and differs from the mainstream British school story. It borrows from a book which was formative in that genre, but which also contained a lot of material which never became part of the classic school story. Indeed, much of what Lewis appears to have borrowed (or shared) with *Tom Brown's School Days* is material which the twentieth-century school story found irrelevant or indigestible. The two books resonate with each other most strongly when the characters' horizons open up beyond school life, in the fight (which is itself against school rules), or the Doctor's sermons, or the sound of the stone echoing across the hill. This connection sums up the role of education in *Prince Caspian*, and can be seen most clearly via its echoes of *Tom Brown*: it is a story about education, but about an education which includes grammar and history alongside legends, folk-tales, standing up against injustice, and sensing the secrets of the land. It is about how education must lead us far beyond itself if it is to do any good.

CHAPTER SIX
LEWIS AMONG THE CLERKS

After the single combat between Peter and Miraz, as the Telmarines are terrified by the landscape itself waking up and turning against them, the story loops back on itself. Suitably for a novel so concerned with different time-schemes, the reader is now taken back to the moment when three of the adventurers set off for Aslan's How, and the others stayed with the lion. The romp which Aslan, the Pevensie girls and a number of Classical figure (led by Bacchus and Silenus) make across Narnia brings together a fascinating blend of images and symbols. Wild gods appear, people are healed, violence ceases, the natural world quickens. In this chapter I will be exploring the way these passages blend together Christian and Classical elements. In the process I would like to suggest that Lewis produces a Christianized recasting of episodes from the Roman poet Ovid, and that doing so put him in a long line of medieval clerks who also sought to reconcile the worlds of pagan myth and faith in Christ.

One of the most striking moments in this divine progress across the land involves the healing of an old lady, who turns out to be Caspian's nurse. Here Lewis brings together elements from a number of Gospel episodes. As told in *Prince Caspian*, it happens this way:

> Then Aslan went to go in at the door of the cottage, but it was too small for him. So, when he had got his head through, he pushed with his shoulders (Lucy and Susan fell off when he did this) and lifted the whole house up and it fell backwards and apart. And there, still in her bed, though the bed was now

in the open air, lay a little old woman who looked as if she had Dwarf blood in her. She was at death's door, but when she opened her eyes and saw the bright, hairy head of the lion staring into her face, she did not scream or faint. She said, 'Oh, Aslan! I knew it was true. I've been waiting for this all my life. Have you come to take me away?'

'Yes, Dearest,' said Aslan. 'But not the long journey yet.' And as he spoke, like the flush creeping along the underside of a cloud at sunrise, the colour came back to her white face and her eyes grew bright and she sat up and said, 'Why, I do declare I feel *that* better. I think I could take a little breakfast this morning.'

'Here you are, mother,' said Bacchus, dipping a pitcher in the cottage well and handing it to her. But what was in it now was not water but the richest wine, red as redcurrant jelly, smooth as oil, strong as beef, warming as tea, cool as dew.

'Eh, you've done something to our well,' said the old woman. 'That makes a nice change, that does.'[109]

The curious detail at the beginning, where Aslan knocks down the house in order to reach the ill woman, evokes the story of Jesus healing a palsied man. In this story, it is the man's friends who are unable to reach Jesus, so they resort to dismantling the roof above him:

And again he entered into Capernaum after some days; and it was noised that he was in the house. And straightway many were gathered together, insomuch that there was no room to receive them, no, not so much as about the door: and he preached the word unto them. And they come unto him, bringing one sick of the palsy, which was borne of four. And when they could not come nigh unto him for the press, they uncovered the roof where he was: and when they had broken it up, they let down the bed wherein the sick of the

> palsy lay. When Jesus saw their faith, he said unto the sick of
> the palsy, Son, thy sins be forgiven thee (Mark 2:1-5)

The parallel is not exact, but it there is a similar sense of the healing happening in a space which is suddenly open to the sky. Likewise, the restoration of the woman takes place simply by Aslan's words, and she changes before the eyes of the observers. The transformation of the water from the well supplies an echo of another miracle in the Gospels. The episode of the wedding at Cana does not involve any healing, but it does occur during a scene of merry-making, and testifies to the power of the Messianic figure.

> And the third day there was a marriage in Cana of Galilee; and the mother of Jesus was there: And both Jesus was called, and his disciples, to the marriage. And when they wanted wine, the mother of Jesus saith unto him, They have no wine.
>
> Jesus saith unto her, Woman, what have I to do with thee? mine hour is not yet come. His mother saith unto the servants, Whatsoever he saith unto you, do it. And there were set there six waterpots of stone, after the manner of the purifying of the Jews, containing two or three firkins apiece. Jesus saith unto them, Fill the waterpots with water. And they filled them up to the brim. And he saith unto them, Draw out now, and bear unto the governor of the feast. And they bare it.
>
> When the ruler of the feast had tasted the water that was made wine, and knew not whence it was: (but the servants which drew the water knew;) the governor of the feast called the bridegroom, And saith unto him, Every man at the beginning doth set forth good wine; and when men have well drunk, then that which is worse: but thou hast kept the good wine until now.
>
> This beginning of miracles did Jesus in Cana of Galilee, and manifested forth his glory; and his disciples believed on him
> (John 2:1-11)

Several details connect the healing of Caspian's nurse to the wedding scene here. There is the turning of the water into wine, most obviously. There is also the fact that neither Jesus or Aslan apparently do anything to the liquid; it is drawn from the source of water by someone else, and then found to be wine when it is drunk. There are even possible traces of Jesus' conversation with Mary in the brief dialogue here. Jesus is talking to his mother Mary, whilst Bacchus addresses the nurse with the phrase 'Here you are, Mother', and Jesus tells Mary that 'mine hour is not yet come', whilst Aslan tells the old lady that it is 'not the long journey yet'. The combination of the wedding at Cana with the healing miracles binds together the renewal and restoration which Jesus and Aslan both bring, with the images of celebration and feasting which also accompany them. There is no single Gospel episode in which someone is healed and then drinks wine drawn from a well, but in typically Narnian fashion this episode borrows images and elements from a range of passages and rearranges them together. The mention of a well, and the nurse's comment that the water is different, even brings in a suggestion of Jesus' dialogue with the Samaritan woman at the well:

> Jesus answered and said unto her, Whosoever drinketh of this water shall thirst again: But whosoever drinketh of the water that I shall give him shall never thirst; but the water that I shall give him shall be in him a well of water springing up into everlasting life. The woman saith unto him, Sir, give me this water, that I thirst not, neither come hither to draw. (John 4:13-15)

The healing of Caspian's nurse acts almost as an anthology of healing and restoration in the Gospels. Healing, new life, merrymaking and the presence of the divine are all combined in a rapid series of images. At the very end of the passage, the old woman makes a remark which might direct our attention to another text which Lewis is drawing upon. 'Eh, you've done something to our well ... That makes a nice change, that does.'

That comment about how it 'makes a nice change' points towards a Classical, rather than a biblical source, and brings in one of the most famous texts of the Classical tradition in English literature. The *Metamorphoses* is a poetic collection by the Roman author Publius Ovidius Naso, more commonly known as Ovid. It contains an array of mythological tales and acted as something of a handbook of Classical myth for many later writers. The connecting theme is a somewhat odd one, encapsulated in the work's title: they are stories about things that change into other things. Within this thematic framework Ovid weaves myths in and out of each other, with the text itself becoming a shifting and metamorphic surface. One story's turns provide the conditions for another to start, and the characters in that story tell each other another story, taking us deeper into a maze of myth and tale. The nurse's remark that whatever Aslan has done to the well 'makes a nice change' picks up the major theme of Ovid's book. We can use the *Metamorphoses* to read several of the stories of Aslan's triumphant progress, with Classical myth weaving in and out of Gospel texts just as the Ovidian narratives do to each other.

The episode with the pig-boys exemplifies this blending of the Gospels and the *Metamorphoses*. Like so many episodes in this chapter, it briefly narrates a transformation which sets one of the characters free:

> they came to another school, where a tired-looking girl was teaching arithmetic to a number of boys who looked very like pigs. She looked out of the window and saw the divine revellers singing up the street and a stab of joy went through her heart. Aslan stopped right under the window and looked up at her.

> 'Oh, don't, don't,' she said. 'I'd love to. But I mustn't. I must stick to my work. And the children would be frightened if they saw you.'
>
> 'Frightened?' said the most pig-like of the boys. 'Who's she talking to out of the window? Let's tell the inspector she talks to people out of the window when she ought to be teaching us.'
>
> 'Let's go and see who it is,' said another boy, and they all came crowding to the window. But as soon as their mean little faces looked out, Bacchus gave a great cry of Euan, euoi-oi-oi-oi and the boys all began howling with fright and trampling one another down to get out of the door and jumping out of the windows. And it was said afterwards (whether truly or not) that those particular little boys were never seen again, but that there were a lot of very fine little pigs in that part of the country which had never been there before.
>
> 'Now, Dear Heart,' said Aslan to the Mistress; and she jumped down and joined them.[110]

The mention of humans who seem pig-like, who stampede at the end of the story as they are banished, and who have possibly been turned into pigs, recalls the episode in the Gospels often known as 'the Gadarene swine'. It appears in all three of the Synoptic Gospels, but I will quote it from Luke:

> And they arrived at the country of the Gadarenes, which is over against Galilee. And when he went forth to land, there met him out of the city a certain man, which had devils long time, and ware no clothes, neither abode in any house, but in the tombs.
>
> When he saw Jesus, he cried out, and fell down before him, and with a loud voice said, What have I to do with thee, Jesus, thou Son of God most high? I beseech thee, torment me not.

> (For he had commanded the unclean spirit to come out of the man. For oftentimes it had caught him: and he was kept bound with chains and in fetters; and he brake the bands, and was driven of the devil into the wilderness.)
>
> And Jesus asked him, saying, What is thy name? And he said, Legion: because many devils were entered into him.
>
> And they besought him that he would not command them to go out into the deep.
>
> And there was there an herd of many swine feeding on the mountain: and they besought him that he would suffer them to enter into them. And he suffered them. Then went the devils out of the man, and entered into the swine: and the herd ran violently down a steep place into the lake, and were choked. When they that fed them saw what was done, they fled, and went and told it in the city and in the country.

Other versions differ in some details, but the central story remains, of a tormented man who was freed by unclean spirits being transferred from him into a herd of pigs. The echo found of this tale in Narnia is considerably less terrifying and lacks a number of the more violent details. There is no possession, no demons or devils and the pigs do not die at the end. The story is, however, suffused with a similar sense that someone is being constrained or hampered, and that the coming of the Messiah brings them liberation. As ever with Lewis, there are little narrative touches which have been retained, but slightly changed in their meaning. Thus when the possessed man meets Jesus, he cries out asking Jesus to leave him alone: 'What have I to do with thee, Jesus, thou Son of God most high? I beseech thee, torment me not.' It is not clear in the Bible if this is the evil spirits speaking through him, and recognising Jesus, or if the man himself is speaking. In Narnia this same detail is transposed into a quieter and more emotionally everyday form, as the teacher sees Aslan and similarly asks him to go away: 'Oh don't, don't...I'd love to. But I mustn't.' At the end of the episode from Luke's Gospel, the text notes that when the swineherds 'saw what was done, they fled, and went and told it in the city and in the country'. The Narnian version picks up on the idea of rumours circulating in the area, but uses it to suggest the boys' transformation was complete: 'it was said afterwards (whether truly or not) that those particular little boys were never seen again, but that there were a lot of very fine little pigs in that part of the country'.

That transformation is the basis for the blending of Gospels and Ovid that I mentioned, since the *Metamorphoses* also contains a story of humans becoming pigs. The episode itself has an earlier origin in Homer's *Odyssey*, but I think it makes most sense to see Ovid as Lewis's source. Odysseus (called Ulysses in Latin) and his men arrive at a series of islands on their long sea journey, one of which is inhabited by the divine sorceress named Circe. She gives the men wine which is mixed with a secret magical substance, which turns them all into pigs. There are numerous translations of the *Metamorphoses*, and Lewis would have read Ovid in the original Latin, but I will quote the passage from the 1950s translation by Mary Innes. One of Ulysses' companions gives his account of the transformation:

> When she saw us, and received our greeting, she bade us welcome, and her smiling face seemed to augur well for the success of our plans. Immediately she gave orders for a concoction of toasted barley, honey, strong wine, and cheese to be prepared, and to these ingredients she added juices whose taste would be concealed by the sweetness of the rest. We took from the goddess' hand the cups she gave us, and drained them greedily, for we were parched. As soon as we had done so, the dread goddess touched our hair lightly

> with her wand and that at that – ashamed though I am, I shall tell you – my body began to bristle with stiff hairs, and I was no longer able to speak, but uttered harsh grunts instead of words. My body bent forward and down, until my face looked straight at the ground, and I felt my mouth hardening into a turned-up snout, my neck swelling with muscles. My hands, which had lately held the goblet, now left prints, like feet, upon the ground.[111]

The Classical parallel here provides an element which was missing from the Gospels: the idea that the little boys have been physically turned into pigs. It also offers an image which is visible in the Narnian version, of a learned woman surrounded by grunting and hog-like males. The instinctive sympathies of the story may be somewhat reversed here, as Circe is a sorceress who needs to be defeated if Odysseus and his crew are to continue their long journey home, and the Narnian teacher is a careworn girl carrying out an irksome duty. Ovid nonetheless supplies a source for the episode which maps onto what we see in the schoolroom here. The connection emphasizes the transformative effect of Aslan's presence, and the way in which Classical and biblical imagery an inhabit the same narrative space within Narnia.

Another brief, but tellingly Ovidian, episode is glimpsed as the joyous convoy passes by. The narrator informs us of a sight they saw:

> At a well in a yard they met a man who was beating a boy. The stick burst into flower in the man's hand. He tried to drop it, but it stuck to his hand. His arm became a branch, his body the trunk of a tree, his feet took root. The boy, who had been crying a moment before, burst out laughing and joined them.[112]

GOLD ON THE HORIZON

Here again, the liberation and justice offered by Aslan's presence is effected via a form of transformation. We might see this as a microcosm of Telmarine rule: something from the natural world is being used to harm and dominate, rather than being part of harmony and flourishing. The scene shows that natural world rebelling against its misuse, and conquering via a sudden burst of Spring-like growth. The previous Narnian novel, *The Lion, the Witch and the Wardrobe*, has a remarkable chapter in which Edmund and the White Witch are travelling through a snowy landscape when the natural world begins to reawaken. Rapturous description of the flowers, birds, water and wind in that chapter suggest that the Spring is a sign of Aslan's return to the land. Here we see the same idea repeated in more compressed and supernatural form. The response of the natural world to Aslan is itself a means of stopping a violent injustice, as the stick flowers and encompasses the man. This transformation is itself a reworking of imagery from the *Metamorphoses*. Ovid's poetic collection contains more than one tale in which a person changing into a plant avoids violence. At one point the god Mercury tells (in slightly haphazard fashion) the story of how Pan chased the nymph Syrinx, and how she escaped from him:

> In the chill mountains of Arcadia there lived a nymph, the most famous of all the wood-nymphs of Nonacris. The other nymphs called her Syrinx. Many a time she had eluded the pursuit of satyrs and of other spirits who haunt the shady woodlands or the fertile fields...As she was returning from Mount Lycaus Pan caught sight of her...
>
> [...]
>
> she, scorning his prayers, ran off through the pathless forest until she came to the still water of sandy Ladon. When the rivers halted her flight, she prayed her sisters of the stream to transform her; and when Pan thought that he had at last caught

hold of Syrinx, he found that instead of the nymph's body he held a handful of marsh reeds. As he stood sighing the wind blew through the reeds, and produced a thin plaintive sound. The god was enchanted by this new device and by the sweetness of the music 'You and I shall always talk together so!' he cried; then he took the reeds of unequal length, and fastened them together with wax. These preserved the girl's name.[113]

Ovid's collection tells at greater length the story of how Apollo similarly chased the nymph Daphne, and I will quote just the end of that passage:

He gave the fleeing maiden no respite, but followed close on her heels, and his breath touched the locks that lay scattered on her neck, till Daphne's strength was spent, and she grew pale and weary with the effort of her swift flight. Then she saw the waters of the Peneus: 'O father', she cried, 'help me! If you rivers really have divine powers, work some transformation, and destroy this beauty which makes me please all too well!' Her prayer was scarcely ended when a deep languor took hold on her limbs, her soft breast was enclosed in thin bark, her hair grew into leaves, her arms into branches, and her feet that were lately so swift were held fast by sluggish roots, while her face became the treetop. Nothing of her was left, except her shining loveliness.

Even as a tree, Phoebus loved her. He placed his hand against her trunk, and felt her heart still beating under the new bark. Embracing the branches as if they were limbs he kissed the wood: but, even as a tree, she shrank from his kisses. [114]

This working of a similar theme has even closer parallels with the version which Aslan's retinue see before the boy joins them. Ovid details the way Daphne's skin became bark, her hair became leaves, her arms changed into boughs and her

GOLD ON THE HORIZON

feet rooted into the ground. Lewis's narrator tells us that the man was unable to drop the stick, and '[h]is arm became a branch, his body the trunk of a tree, his feet took root'. People changing into plants, and thus escaping violence, is a distinctly Ovidian theme. There is no obvious parallel in the Gospels, no healing which Jesus accomplishes by making a plant suddenly sprout, no reproving of evil-doers with a stick. However, Jesus' genealogies in the Gospels of Matthew and Luke contain his descent from Jesse, the father of King David. This is a crucial element of his Messianic identity and his status as the inheritor of the Davidic kingship. One of the great Messianic prophecies of the Hebrew Scriptures occurs in Isaiah:

> And there shall come forth a rod out of the stem of Jesse, and a Branch shall grow out of his roots: And the spirit of the Lord shall rest upon him, the spirit of wisdom and understanding, the spirit of counsel and might, the spirit of knowledge and of the fear of the Lord; And shall make him of quick understanding in the fear of the Lord: and he shall not judge after the sight of his eyes, neither reprove after the hearing of his ears:
>
> But with righteousness shall he judge the poor, and reprove with equity for the meek of the earth: and he shall smite the earth: with the rod of his mouth, and with the breath of his lips shall he slay the wicked. And righteousness shall be the girdle of his loins, and faithfulness the girdle of his reins.
>
> The wolf also shall dwell with the lamb, and the leopard shall lie down with the kid; and the calf and the young lion and the fatling together; and a little child shall lead them.
>
> (Isaiah 11:1-6)

Jesus may not himself cause a stick to flower, but his identity as the Christ is expressed in the image of a stem blossoming. In the prophecies of Isaiah, as applied to Jesus by Paul and other Christians, that image is in turn connected to the idea of justice being brought into an unjust world. Just as Aslan himself can be read as a figure who makes into literal reality the figurative title of the Messiah as 'lion of the tribe of Judah', this brief scene shows justice 'flowering' from the stem of Jesse. The establishment of righteousness and the punishment of wrongdoing is intertwined with the Messiah's identity as a new shoot from the stock. The process of transforming a person into a plant to avoid violence and the end the abuse of power is borrowed from Ovid to supply the fantastical means of connecting flowering sticks and the coming of justice in Narnia. The biblical and Ovidian sources map across each other, adding complementary material to the scene. The echoes of Isaiah underline one major difference here between the stories of Daphne and Syrinx, and the episode which Lucy and Susan witness. In both tales from the *Metamorphoses*, the transformation avoids physical violence but nearly obliterates the identity of the person being saved. At best they are consolatory episodes, in which the nymphs do not suffer the violence they fear, but they becomes something else in the process. More than that, both nymphs are symbolically 'possessed' by Pan and Apollo, by being physically handled and made into a symbol of the male deities. Lewis's version inverts this process, putting the transformation onto the person carrying out the violence, and enabling the victim to escape. This produces a shift in not only the emotional tone, but also the genre of the episodes. The Daphne and Syrinx tales are essentially aetiological myths; they are stories which explain the familiar state of affairs. It seems almost certain that readers of Ovid would not be learning for the first time that Pan carried the pan-pipes, or that the laurel was sacred to Apollo, by reading this poetry. On the contrary, like the 'origin stories' of modern superhero cinema, the poet assumes the audience knows that this is the case, and proceeds to tell a story explaining why. (Some of the purest forms of aetiological tale occur in Rudyard Kipling's *Just So Stories*, with titles such as 'How the Camel Got His Hump' and 'How the Leopard Got His Spots'.) In the Narnian version, infused with the prophetic material of Isaiah, the opposite is true. The existing state of affairs is not to be explained or justified, but to be overturned and abolished as righteousness is ushered in. Aetiological tales are used to construct a messianic scene, as the arrival of Aslan and his company transforms the state of things in Narnia.

OVID AND THE CLERKS

There is something more particular about combining material from Ovid with a specifically Christian narrative. In *Prince Caspian* this gives an intoxicating blend of pagan myth and Gospel themes, but it also places Lewis in a specific literary tradition. Ovid provided a mythological source-book for centuries upon centuries of later writers, most of whom lived in very different cultures to ancient Rome. His work was adapted and alluded to in a variety of works, providing both an opportunity and a challenge for those who wished to incorporate his tales into their view of the world. (I must thank Rebecca Menmuir heartily for her generosity in expounding the world of the medieval Ovids to me.) One of the most famous examples of this is an anonymous medieval French work known as the *Ovide Moralisé*, or 'moralized Ovid'. This text translates and retells the tales of the *Metamorphoses*, along with some other Classical myths, and provides an extensive commentary on each story. The commentary treats Ovid as a source for allegorical and symbolic interpretations which purport to reveal a Christian meaning within the pagan narrative. The tales which I identified above as woven into the story of Aslan's triumphant progress provide good examples of the way the *Ovide Moralisé* treats the text. In the case of Pan's pursuit of Syrinx, and her transformation into reeds, it has this to say:

{T}he tale can have another meaning: whoever might put effort into learning might well expect to profit from it. We can take Pan to mean the world: 'Pan' in Greek means 'everything' in French. Syrinx denotes the pretensions and the vain earthly delights that everyone has chosen as their goal. Syrinx means the same as 'attraction': everyone is attracted by these fickle and vain delights, which are false and deceiving, but they think they are worth a lot. Many people do not wish for another paradise, one can see this clearly, for there is no one, whether from the woods or the plains, city or rural village, knight, layperson, scholar, or priest who does not seek after these vain delights. Syrinx was 'a river's daughter' because these delights are more vain and changing than fleeting water, and every day they flee away without stopping. No one can hurry after them so much that they don't abandon them in a short time.

Syrinx was 'a virgin and a huntress,' for those who pursue worldly delights are deluded and their hunt is in vain, for no good fruit can come of it. Syrinx 'wished to behave in the fashion of Diana' for, just as the moon is now full, now horned, and now there is none, these worldly goods are unable to be in one place very long; thus there are many who foolishly put their heart and attention into them. Whoever trusts in them and ardently desires to wed them is very foolish. Whoever wishes to rest their heart there – when they have hunted for a long time and think to have acquired everything and conquered what they hoped of the worldly delights they sought – is left 'holding a fistful of reeds.' From night to morning they have completely lost these goods full of changeability, either through death or sickness, or some other circumstance of fortune. Those goods are more changeable than the moon or reeds that bend before the wind; they can all be lost in a single breath. No wise person places their hope in goods full of such deception, for many lose the eternal goods for such vain, fickle ones.[115]

GOLD ON THE HORIZON

The interpretation which this puts upon the Ovidian tale is likely to strike many modern readers as strained, fanciful and even wilfully perverse. Even for those who studied English Literature at school or university, and are used to paying close attention to details of a narrative in order to extrapolate larger themes, this is an unfamiliar method of reading. The *Ovide Moralisé* indulges in an allegorical method, in which characters are identified with abstract moral or philosophical ideas. The identification happens, in this case, by the association of their names. The recognition that the god Pan's name also meant 'all' in Greek was used by various Renaissance thinkers and poets to suggest a connection with Christ, but here 'all' is identified with 'everything' and thus 'the world'. Syrinx's name is similarly read as 'attraction', and thus the pursuit of a virgin huntress becomes the world's chasing after attractive things which do not breed any good. The goddess Diana, to whom Syrinx was a sworn follower, is also scrutinised. She was associated with the moon, and the moon is fickle because it waxes and wanes, thus worldly attractions are fickle and delusive. As I said, to most modern readers this is likely to seem a schematic and mechanical imposition of pre-determined meanings on the story. To many medieval readers, however, it would have felt satisfying and persuasive: the allegorical and symbolic habit of mind provided an aesthetic pleasure in this kind of 'discovery' of meanings. To a modern reader, the most convincing aspect might be the feeling at the end of the tale that Pan has been left holding a bunch of reeds which only produce a faint and fleeting music. This emotional tone suits the idea that Pan and Syrinx's story is 'really' about the vain pursuit of elusive worldly goods.

The *Ovide Moralisé* takes this symbolic reading a stage further when commenting upon the other tale of a human transforming into a plant which I mentioned. Daphne's pursuit by Apollo is initially discussed in terms which extrapolate moral themes from the text:

LEWIS AMONG THE CLERKS

> Daphne, who fled so quickly from carnal relations and was then transformed into a tree, signifies that anyone wanting to be a perfect virgin must guard the heart and the body and the mind entirely, without any carnal impulse, without any thought of defilement, and without any interruption. And then she will be made a tree that no wind can blow over, for just as the wind cannot dislodge a strong tree by shaking it, so no gifts, promise, or entreaty, which are all winds of vanity, should sway or move the virgin heart in any way to lose its virginity. Daphne was changed into a laurel tree, rather than into an oak or a mulberry tree, or any other tree one sees. For just as the laurel grows green and never at any time loses its greenery, either through heat or through cold – rather, it grows green in every season without bearing any fruit – thus it stands to reason that virginity must grow green and live without bearing fruit. For it has never happened, and never will, that a woman living her life as a virgin is capable of giving birth. That is, except for the one who, contrary to nature, gave birth to her Father and her Master, God, who resolved to be born of the Virgin. She wisely, out of charity, will keep her virginity and be able to preserve it until the end. God will give her, as a sign and in the name of victory, in his great delightful glory, the crown that virgins have who are crowned in heaven.[116]

This praise of chastity and virginity probably seems more reasonably derived, to a modern reader, from the tale as it is told. Daphne is a symbol of avoiding sexual involvement, since that is what she flees to escape during the story. The fact that she turns into a laurel tree is then used as the basis for an allegorical reading, with the laurel's evergreen leaves representing the continual state of virginity. However, unsurprisingly in a medieval Christian commentary, the topic of perpetual virginity leads to a mention of the Virgin

GOLD ON THE HORIZON

Mary. This leads to another, more abstruse reading of the tale, as the text declares that 'I can put forth another interpretation', in which Daphne is 'that glorious maiden, a pure, graceful, and beautiful virgin, whom God chose pre-eminently and clearly above all others'.[117] In this rereading, Apollo the god of healing and the sun, represents Christ since the latter is

> light of the world, the sun that illuminates every man, the master who has invented every discipline, every art, all wisdom, and all knowledge, the doctor who knows all cures and all the properties of herbs, who can heal and raise from death all the sick and all the dead.[118]

The pursuit of the nymph is expounded as a mystical symbol of Christ's Incarnation, which resulted in Mary being perpetually a virgin like Syrinx.[119] This interpretation does not so much develop from the previous moral reading, as use the theme of virginity as the link to an entirely different interpretation. The fact that the laurel leaves are Apollo's symbol, especially when made into a crown and worn around the head, is interpreted in terms of Christ's intimate connection with Mary, and the way her body contained his. The laurel crown also implicitly seems to symbolize a sign of victory, in Christ's role as triumphant over death, and Mary's status as queen of heaven.

I would hesitate to assume what every modern reader will feel about this kind of interpretation, but I suspect many people will find it jarring or forced. Perhaps the most radical shift in this second reading of the tale is that Apollo's pursuit of the nymph has gone from being a source of danger and moral taint, to an emblem of the incarnation, Christ's love for humanity, and Jesus' relationship with Mary. The emotional landscape and the instinctive sympathies of the reader are expected to shift rapidly between one interpretation and the next. It is worth noting that Lewis's own narrative engages in some of the same kinds of transformation as we see here, though in a way which feels less jarring to modern sensibilities. His figure of Aslan also involves identifying another character with aspects of Christ, making the lion into the 'Son of the Emperor-beyond-the-Sea', a kingly lion and a saviour figure who rose from the Stone Table just as the sun was coming up above the horizon. His apparent borrowings from the *Metamorphoses* sometimes alter the sympathies of the original text, or switch around the roles of characters. It is not simply that Lewis combined Christian and Ovidian material, but that in doing so he took part in a long tradition of reconciling these rich and strange texts with each other. A set of Classical echoes might suggest Lewis the enthusiast for Greek and Roman literature, but this specific kind of echo suggests Lewis taking the role of medieval clerk. The mode of theological fantasy which is produced in Narnia in these passages is not 'medieval' because it shows us armoured knights or cathedrals. Rather, it could be called 'medieval' because it inhabits the same intellectual and imaginative worlds as medieval authors, blending Ovidian myth with Christian doctrine.

The incorporation of Ovid (and other Classical sources of myth) into a Christian framework was not confined to fourteenth-century France. Allusions and adaptations appear across medieval and Renaissance literature in English, and Jonathan Bate's *Shakespeare and Ovid* has identified the playwright's close and imaginative engagement with the Roman poet. A striking example of Classical myth being allegorised for its moral value appears in Robert Henryson's *The Tale of Orpheus and Euridices His Quene*. This poem in Older Scots follows a similar technique to the *Ovide Moralisé*, in providing

GOLD ON THE HORIZON

allegorical notes at the end of the tale. The scene in which Orpheus succeeds in lulling Cerberus, the three-headed guard-dog of the Underworld, by playing his harp, receives this comment:

> ... the monster mervellus[120]
> *the fantastical monster*
> With thre heidis that we call Cerberus
> *With three heads, that we call Cerberus*
> Quhilk fenyeid is to haif so mony heidis
> *Is represented as having so many heads*
> For to betakin thre maner of deidis
> *In order to signify three kinds of death*
> The first is in the tendir yong bernage
> *The first is in young age and childhood*
> The second deid is in the middill age
> *The second death is in middle age*
> The hird is in greit eild quhen men ar taen.
> *The third is in great age when men are taken*
> Thus Cerberus to swelly sparis nane,
> *Thus Cerberus spares no-one from being swallowed.*
> Bot quhen our mynd is myngit with sapience
> *But when our mind is infused with prudence*
> And plais upoun the herp of eloquence,
> *And plays upon the harp of eloquence*
> That is to say, makis persuasioun
> *That is to say, makes an appeal*
> To draw our will and our affectioun
> *To draw our will and our desire*
> In every eild fra syn and fowl delyte,
> *At every age from sin and foul delights*
> The dog our sawll na power hes to byte
> *This dog has no power to bite our soul*

LEWIS AMONG THE CLERKS

This bringing together of Ovidian material and Christian principles was a widespread tendency in medieval literature. It is the sort of imaginative reconciling and creative synthesis which Lewis particularly admired in medieval culture. In *The Discarded Image*, he remarked that '[a]t his most characteristic, medieval man was not a dreamer nor a wanderer. He was an organiser, a codifier, a builder of systems', and that '[t]hough full of turbulent activities, he was equally full of the impulse to formalise them'.[121] The two greatest achievements of the period, for Lewis, were Dante's *Divine Comedy* and Aquinas' *Summa Theologica*. In them he saw a characteristically medieval impulse of 'tranquil, indefatigable, exultant energy' where 'passionately systematic minds br[ought] huge masses of heterogeneous material into unity'.[122] The third great work of the era, for him, was the medieval worldview itself, which synthesized so much apparently jarring or irrelevant material into a grand vision of the universe and its relationship to God. When we recognize the blending of biblical and Ovidian material in these passages, I think the joyful and liberating royal progress across Narnia exhibits the same impulse in fictional form. Images and themes from the two texts are interwoven, exchanged, recast and synthesized in dazzling ways. In one sense these scenes are an answer to the problem which *Prince Caspian* implicitly poses throughout its pages; the problem of the past. Both the Classical and the Christian past can be enjoyed, inhabited and witnessed within this triumphant meander through Narnia. There is a further aspect to this reconciling, since (as I mentioned) by combining the Gospels with the *Metamorphoses* Lewis is taking up the role of a medieval clerk. This sweeps another era of the past into the book, and asserts that a grand, imaginative, liberating synthesis is possible. It seems symbolic to the point of allegory that the old woman whose healing brings together echoes from a range of Gospel stories turns out to be the old nurse who first told Caspian the stories of Old Narnia. Similarly to the prince and the Pevensies, the reader lives in a later world. But Lewis, like a sound medieval clerk, shows them how their world is quickened with the life which fills the old stories.

THE VOYAGE OF THE DAWN TREADER

INTRODUCTION
ORIENTED FOR THE JOURNEY

'On the breeze which was blowing in their faces from the far-off sea'

The Lion, the Witch and the Wardrobe

The Voyage of the Dawn Treader is a novel about questing. That might seem absolutely obvious, since as soon as the Pevensies and their cousin are onboard the titular ship, their old friend Caspian explains his voyage.

> 'And where are we heading for?' asked Edmund.
> 'Well,' said Caspian, 'that's rather a long story. Perhaps you remember that when I was a child my usurping uncle Miraz got rid of seven friends of my father's (who might have taken my part) by sending them off to explore the unknown Eastern Seas beyond the Lone Islands.'
> 'Yes,' said Lucy, 'and none of them ever came back.'
> 'Right. Well, on my coronation day, with Aslan's approval, I swore an oath that, if once I established peace in Narnia, I would sail east myself for a year and a day to find my father's friends or to learn of their deaths and avenge them if I could.[123]

However, as soon as this quest is detailed, another one appears in the story. Not everyone on board the Dawn Treader is looking for the seven lost lords of Narnia, or is not merely looking for them:

> 'That is my main intention. But Reepicheep here has an even higher hope.' Everyone's eyes turned to the Mouse.
> 'As high as my spirit,' it said. 'Though perhaps as small as

my stature. Why should we not come to the very eastern end of the world? And what might we find there? I expect to find Aslan's own country. It is always from the east, across the sea, that the great Lion comes to us.'

'I say, that is an idea,' said Edmund in an awed voice.[124]

These two quests provide a structure for the narrative, since they can trace (or actually find and recruit) the lost lords, and a horizon, since they are always moving towards the east (and implicitly towards Aslan's country) during their voyage. Various places and people they encounter along the way provide them with inset tasks or quests, such as Lucy venturing upstairs in the wizard's house in order to find the spell for the Dufflepuds. There are even parodic quests, such as Eustace's encounter with the dragon. He first watches in horror as the monster dies by the side of a pool, then eventually comes to feel as if he has fought and killed it himself. When he plunders its hoard and sleeps on a pile of treasure, Eustace wakes to find that not only is he far from a dragon-slaying knight, he has actually become a dragon. The questing mode borrows from medieval romance, and from tales of sea voyages. The island-hopping provides a useful structure for individual moral tests or allegorical episodes, suggesting that Lewis also had John Bunyan's *Pilgrim's Progress* in the back of his mind. The fact that this quest involves a journey across the seas prompts me to notice some things about how Narnia is constructed.

In order to explore what the oceans, and voyaging across them, might mean in Narnia, I'd like to return for a moment to the end of *The Lion, the Witch and the Wardrobe*. The glorious coronation scene in Cair Paravel involves some particular details about the great hall, as well as the arrival of some new creatures:

> But the next day was more solemn. For then, in the Great Hall of Cair Paravel – that wonderful hall with the ivory roof and the west wall hung with peacock's feathers and the eastern door which looks towards the sea, in the presence of all their friends and to the sound of trumpets, Aslan solemnly crowned the in and led them to the four thrones amid deafening shouts of, 'Long Live King Peter! Long Live Queen Susan! Long Live King Edmund! Long Live Queen Lucy!'
>
> 'Once a kind or queen in Narnia, always a king or queen. Bear it well, Sons of Adam! Bear it well, Daughters of Eve!' said Aslan.
>
> And through the eastern door, which was wide open, came the voices of the mermen and the mermaids swimming close to the shore and singing in honour of their new Kings and Queens.
>
> [...]
>
> And that night there was a great feast in Cair Paravel, and revelry and dancing, and gold flashed and wine flowed, and answering to the music inside, but stranger, sweeter and more piercing, came the music of the sea people. [125]

Lewis is quite specific in mentioning that there is a door which looks to the sea in Cair Paravel, that it was open when the children were crowned, and that it was still open during the ceremonial feasting. Since the same page involves a catalogue of the fantastical characters to whom the Pevensies gave honours and gifts, such as the centaurs and the talking beavers, it is also notable that the merpeople suddenly enter the story. They take no part in the plot, but it is obviously significant in some way that they are present at the ceremony and the celebration. (They reappear, in greater and vertiginous detail, near the end of *The Voyage of the Dawn Treader*.) I would suggest that this is the first hint of Narnia's unusual cosmology: it is an almost completely horizontal world. In fact, much of Narnia (in the early novels at least) appears to resemble our world turned through ninety geometrical degrees. Rather than being a world where height is the most significant idea, the Narnia of *Dawn Treader* appears to be a world where distance is most important. Its axis is not vertical, but horizontal.

If this is the case, then the sea is roughly equivalent to the heavens, and the merpeople are the equivalent of angels. There are a few details in *The Lion, the Witch and the Wardrobe* which hint at this connection. When the children first hear about Aslan, it is from Mr Beaver:

> 'Aslan a man!' said Mr Beaver sternly. 'Certainly. I tell you he is the King of the wood and the son of the great Emperor-beyond-the-Sea. Don't you know who is the King of Beasts? Aslan is a lion – the Lion, the great Lion.'[126]

Amidst the insistence on Aslan's animal nature here, there is also the comment that he is the son of the Emperor-beyond-the-Sea. The association between Aslan and the sea continues, in subtle ways, through the novel. When the Pevensies arrive at the hill where they will meet him, the horizon shows them something:

> They were on a green open space from which you could look down on the forest spreading as far as one could see in every direction – except right ahead. There, far to the East, was something twinkling and moving. 'By gum!' whispered Peter to Susan, 'The sea!' In the very middle of this open hill-top was the Stone Table.[127]

Thus the children's first encounter with the site where Aslan's death and resurrection will take place is joined with a far-off glimpse of the sea. The description of it as something twinkling and moving in the far distance even sounds like a description of a star, strengthening the sense that the expanses of the ocean are somehow equivalent to the arches of the firmament above. (The stars also exist in Narnia, of course, and *Prince Caspian* has a significant scene of star-gazing. Nonetheless, in *Dawn Treader* they become mixed up a good deal with the sea.) In the same sequence, the moment before the Pevensies actually see Aslan, they look at a pavilion with his heraldry on it:

> A wonderful pavilion it was – and especially now when the light of the setting sun fell on it – with sides of what looked like yellow silk and cords of crimson and tent-pegs of ivory; and high above it on a pole a banner which bore a red rampant lion fluttering in the breeze which was blowing in their faces from the far-off sea.[128]

Both Aslan himself, and Aslan's role as saviour, is associated with the sea once again, when the hill-top becomes the site of his resurrection:

> They walked to the eastern edge of the hill and looked down. The one big star had almost disappeared. The country all looked dark grey, but beyond, at the very end of the world, the sea showed pale. The sky began to turn red. They walked to and fro more times than they could count between the dead Aslan and the eastern ridge, trying to keep warm; and oh, how tired their legs felt. Then at last, as they stood for a moment looking out towards the sea and Cair Paravel (which they could now just make out) the red turned to gold along the line where the sea and the sky met and very slowly up came the edge of the sun. At that moment they heard from behind them a loud noise[129]

The great east door of the hall of Cair Paravel, and the music of the merpeople which can be heard through it during the

GOLD ON THE HORIZON

feast, make rather more sense when we start noticing these references throughout the novel. Aslan is the son of the Emperor-beyond-the-Sea, the sun rises from the sea every dawn at the hill of the Stone Table, Cair Paravel is built at the shore where Narnia meets the sea, onto which its great eastern door opens. Taken together, these moments build up a symbolism in the novel where the sea is both the realm of mystery and the source of salvation. This imagery continues through *Prince Caspian*. The young prince first betrays that he knows some of the old Narnian stories when his uncle catches him referring to Aslan and asks who he means. Caspian replies that 'Aslan is the great Lion who comes from over the sea', causing Miraz to explode in fury.[130] When Doctor Cornelius teaches the prince more about Old Narnia, the sea reappears:

> Cair Paravel. No man alive has seen that blessed place and perhaps even the ruins of it have now vanished. But we believe it was far from here, down at the mouth of the Great River, on the very shore of the sea.[131]

Caspian's horror at the location of the castle, in the ghost-haunted woods, cause Cornelius to explain further:

> 'Your Highness speaks as you have been taught,' said the Doctor. 'But it is all lies. There are no ghosts there. That is a story invented by the Telmarines. Your Kings are in deadly fear of the sea because they can never quite forget that in all stories Aslan comes from over the sea. They don't want to go near it and they don't want anyone else to go near it. So they have let great woods grow up to cut their people off from the coast. But because they have quarrelled with the trees, they are afraid of the woods. And because they are afraid of the woods they imagine that they are full of ghosts. And the Kings and great men, hating both the sea and the wood, partly

believe these stories, and partly encourage them. They feel safer if no one in Narnia dares to go down to the coast and look out to sea – towards Aslan's land and the morning and the eastern end of the world.[132]

Aslan's identity as the lion from the sea becomes part of the landscape, and even the politics, of Narnia in this novel. The Pevensies, in their role as the kings and queens called out of the far past, become unknowingly part of this connection. They are summoned by the winding of Susan's horn in the hour of Narnia's need, and they appear on the shore by Cair Paravel, just as if they have landed from the sea.

It might sound like a quibble or a pun to say that Narnia is an 'oriented' world, since that word literally means 'aligned towards the east'. However, that is one of the most significant features about Narnia in this novel. The seas are the equivalent of the heavens, and they are the horizon across which the light comes from the Emperor-beyond-the-Sea. This implies that the Narnian world is oriented in another sense: space has meaning in Narnia. This is one of the corollaries of the quest form in *The Voyage of the Dawn Treader*: the universe contains meaning and there is something vital to be found in it. Whether or not the world as we know it becomes mysteriously different at the end of the quest, the quest has led us to that point. Every movement in the voyage has either been towards or away from Aslan.

The question of whether the world has inherent meaning in the modern age – and how that might affect human behaviour – was handled by various writers in the mid-century. Einstein's theory of relativity had made its way into the public presses, and for many seemed to suggest that everything which had apparently been objective and fixed was now relative. Dorothy L. Sayers' *The Documents in the Case* plays with the idea of modern physics and cosmology in a detective novel, a form which notoriously depends upon Newtonian rather than Einsteinian physics. In a world in which space and time did not behave as predictably and comprehensibly as everyone thought, it would become very difficult to sort out alibis, calculate times or rule out suspects. Though it resolves these issues without deconstructing the genre itself, *The Documents in the Case* does feature a lot of discussion of how science influences people's view of human life, such as this extract from a letter:

> but why Victorian, more than anything else? At any rate, they had the consolation of feeling that this earth and its affairs were extremely large and important—though why they should have thought so, when they were convinced they were only the mechanical outcome of a cast-iron law of evolution on a very three-by-four planet, whirling round a fifth-rate star in illimitable space, passes human comprehension. It would be more reasonable to think so to-day, if Eddington and those people are right in supposing that we are rather a freak sort of planet, with quite unusual facilities for being inhabited, and that space is a sort of cosy little thing which God could fold up and put in his pocket without our ever noticing the difference. Anyhow, if time and space and straightness and curliness and bigness and smallness are all relative, then we may just as well think ourselves important as not. 'Important, unimportant—unimportant, important,' as the King of Hearts said, trying to see which sounded best. So, like the Victorians, we shall no doubt compromise—say it is important when we have a magnum opus to present to an admiring creation, and unimportant when it suits our convenience to have our peccadilloes passed over. Forgive me wandering away like this. It's just a sort of talking the thing out with you before I talk it out in the book.[133]

ORIENTED FOR THE JOURNEY

Whilst scientists, and columnists, were considering the nature of space itself, space travel was moving from a wholly speculative realm which science fiction could use to build solely imaginary or satirical worlds, into a scientific possibility. Indeed Lewis himself was part of a generation who wrote sci-fi which was overtaken by science fact during their own lifetimes. His trilogy of space novels, *Out of the Silent Planet*, *Perelandra* and *That Hideous Strength* play with the idea that humans invent space travel, only to discover that the universe resembles medieval cosmological models. In a science-fictional world in which the Fall only happened on Earth, and in which planetary intelligences exist, travelling into space does not render 'traditional' concepts of morality and metaphysics irrelevant. On the contrary, they become the focus of all attention. *The Voyage of the Dawn Treader* can be seen as a book of Narnian space-travel, from this point of view, as its adventurers strike out into the realm beyond the horizon, travelling towards the light of the sun, and even meeting a star on the way. This is where Narnian cosmology and the quest genre share a moral and existential implication: the world has meaning. Everything in it is closer to, or further from, Aslan, and everything is moving in one direction or the other. In depicting the great quest of its characters, the novel shows us that human life can have a shape, and that meaning in the world is not solipsistic or relative. I suggested in the chapters on *Prince Caspian* that the story of the young prince and his Pevensie companions grapples with the question of the past. That book asks how we can believe that metaphysically important things happened in the past, and, even if they did, how it can matter to us in a later age. *Dawn Treader* seems to tackle another question, asking if the universe has any meaning, and, even if it does, whether the shape of our lives can connect us with that meaning. In the story of Caspian, Reepicheep, Lucy, Edmund and Eustace, it answers that question in a dazzling affirmative.

CHAPTER ONE
FRESH AIR AND OTHER FADS

The very beginning of *The Voyage of the Dawn Treader* lets us know that we are not in Narnia any more. Not only are we not in Narnia itself, but we are no longer in the social milieu which the Pevensies inhabited in the previous novels. This is not the big, rambling country house within which they discovered the way into the woods in *The Lion the Witch and the Wardrobe*, nor even the railway station piled with kitbags and school trunks from which they were summoned in *Prince Caspian*. Lucy and Edmund are staying with a cousin, and it is his world which Lewis deftly sketches in the opening pages of the novel.

The family atmosphere, and indeed the social atmosphere, of this household, is markedly different from what we have seen of the Pevensies' own life. Lewis's description of the Scrubb family picks up on details which we assume strike Edmund and Lucy as unusual or unfamiliar.

> He didn't call his Father and Mother 'Father' and 'Mother', but Harold and Alberta. They were very up-to-date and advanced people. They were vegetarians, non-smokers and tee-totallers, and wore a special kind of underclothes. In their house there was very little furniture and very few clothes on beds and the windows were always open.
>
> Eustace Clarence liked animals, especially beetles, if they were dead and pinned on a card. He liked books if they were books of information and had pictures of grain elevators or of fat foreign children doing exercises in model schools.[134]

We are implicitly seeing this from the Pevensies' point of

view, so we might hazard a deduction that they call their parents 'Father' and 'Mother', that they have several sheets on their beds, that they're used to a home atmosphere with less deliberately introduced fresh air and more conventional underwear. We might further speculate that the Pevensie family eats meat at meals, that the parents drink wine, and that Father is fond of a pipe of tobacco. There is more than a dissimilarity between related households here, however, as signalled by the mild irony of '[t]hey were very up-to-date and advanced people'. This has the air of inverted commas surrounding it, as if the narrator is quoting how the Scrubbs would like to be described, or would describe themselves. It is clear that the elements of their lifestyle which are mentioned – vegetarianism, fresh air, lack of clutter – are a major part of how they see themselves. I think it is equally clear that the narrator and reader are assumed to be more like the Pevensies than the Scrubbs. The intervening years may have changed the social implications of vegetarianism or not smoking, but I suspect few readers instinctively identify with Eustace and his parents when reading these early pages.

CRANKERY AND FADDISHNESS

In fact Lewis is producing a social portrait which would be quickly recognisable to most readers of the time. This collection of furnishing preferences, (non-)consumption habits and educational philosophies marks the Scrubbs out as self-conscious progressives of the British mid-century. They are the sort of people whom other people, who did not share their tastes and politics, might call 'faddy' or even 'crankish'. The details which the narrator mentions about them can be found in a range of fiction from the same period; they summon up a 'type' which fitted into a particular niche of the contemporary social imagination. For example, Agatha Christie's short story *The Herb of Death*, which was first published in 1930, involves a character describing the guests at a country house where they once stayed. Amongst the brief accounts she gives of each person, she mentions a Mr Curle, 'one of those elderly stooping men. There are so many of them about, you'd hardly know one from the other' who had come down to discuss rare manuscripts with the owner of the house.[135] When another character suggests that there is more 'flesh' on the 'bones' of the story than she first implied, she recalls some other details about Mr Curle:

> 'Oh! Scheherazade, Scheherazade,' said Sir Henry. 'To think of the way you told us this story at first! Bare bones indeed – and to think of the amount of flesh we're finding on them now.'
>
> 'Don't speak so ghoulishly,' said Mrs Bantry. 'And don't use the word flesh. Vegetarians always do. They say, "I never eat flesh" in a way that puts you right off your little beefsteak. Mr Curle was a vegetarian. He used to eat some peculiar stuff that looked like bran for breakfast. Those elderly stooping men with beards are often faddy. They have patent kinds of underwear, too.'
>
> 'What on earth, Dolly,' said her husband, 'do you know about Mr Curle's underwear?'
>
> 'Nothing,' said Mrs Bantry with dignity. 'I was just making a guess.'
>
> 'I'll amend my former statement,' said Sir Henry. 'I'll say instead that the dramatis personae in your problem are very interesting. I'm beginning to see them all – eh, Miss Marple?'
>
> 'Human nature is always interesting, Sir Henry. And it's curious to see how certain types always tend to act in exactly the same way.'[136]

Miss Marple's comment about human nature underlines the fact that, in typical detective fiction style, a lot of our interest in these characters is not based on who they are,

GOLD ON THE HORIZON

but on what sort of person they are. Mrs Bantry is providing a series of social types, and amongst these is a 'faddy' man with a vegetarian diet and allegedly odd underwear. Christie is by no means the only writer to group these features together. In another genre, Anthony Powell's twelve-volume series *A Dance to the Music of Time*, a sweeping depiction of British social life during the twentieth century, includes a book called *A Buyer's Market*. It was published in 1952, the same year that *The Voyage of the Dawn Treader* appeared, and details the lives of middle- and upper-class characters during the late 1920s. One of the notable figures in this novel is a painter called Edgar Deacon, who later runs an antiques shop, and dies by falling down the steps of a nightclub during his own birthday party. At one point in *A Buyer's Market* the narrator muses upon Deacon's character and habits:

> When travelling on the Continent he commonly went on foot with a haversack on his back, rather than by trains, which he found 'stuffy and infinitely filled with tedious persons'. He was careful, even rather fussy, about his health, especially in relation to personal cleanliness and good sanitation; so that some of the more sordid aspects of these allegedly terre-à-terre excursions abroad must at times have been a trial to him. Perhaps his Continental visits were, in fact, more painful for managers of hotels and restaurants frequented by him; for he was a great believer in insisting absolutely upon the minute observance by others of his own wishes. Such habits of travelling, in so much as they were indeed voluntary and not to some degree enforced by financial consideration, were no doubt also connected in his mind with his own special approach to social behaviour, in which he was guided by an aversion, often expressed, for conduct that might be looked upon either as conventional or conservative.
>
> ...

FRESH AIR AND OTHER FADS

> Mr. Deacon ... was in favour of abolishing, or ignoring, the existing world entirely, with a view to experimenting with one of an entirely different order. He was a student of Esperanto (or, possibly, one of the lesser-known artificial languages), intermittently vegetarian, and an advocate of decimal coinage. At the same time he was strongly opposed to the introduction of 'spelling reform' for the English language (on grounds that for him such changes would mar Paradise Lost), and I can remember it said that he hated 'suffragettes'. [137]

Powell's dry, discursive prose not only outlines the artist's way of life, but also his attitude to the world. The combination of elements is strikingly similar to those displayed by the Scrubbs in their first appearance (though Eustace's attitude to art a few pages on would no doubt have drawn Mr Deacon's ire). He is determinedly progressive, opposed to the way most things are run in the world as it stands, and convinced that things should be put on a more rational footing. His aversion to 'stuffy' trains suggests a fondness for open windows and fresh air which would fit with the Scrubbs' household, as would his insistence on modern hygiene and his bouts of vegetarianism. (Elsewhere in the novel, he mentions that he met one of the other characters when they were staying in the same vegetarian holiday camp.) The narrator mentions two final attitudes – the dislike of spelling reform and organised feminism – as surprising, since these evidently sit at odds with his other views. The reader is expected to realize that a belief in simplifying and rationalising the spelling system of English might be expected to go along with vegetarianism, and that promoting decimal coinage would suit the world-view of many of those sympathetic to the suffragettes. (We might recall Eustace's insistence that if the Pevensies could only hear his mother explain the subject, they would realize that chivalry towards women is an artificial and degrading practice.) There

GOLD ON THE HORIZON

is no mention, in this general exploration of his character, of any special undergarment, but only a few pages later his appearance in an art gallery is described thus:

> He wore a thickish pepper-and-salt suit ... and he carried in his hand a hat, broad-brimmed and furry, the general effect of the whole outfit being, perhaps intentionally, a trifle down-at-heel: together with the additionally disturbing suggestion that his slightly curved torso might be enclosed within some form of imperfectly fitting corset.[138]

Regardless of the critical line he takes on women's enfranchisement, Mr Deacon is clearly in the same category as the Scrubb family (though of an older generation). We might, perhaps, doubt the precise accuracy of this social stereotype. Surely not everyone who refrained from eating meat in the mid-century also wanted to reform the coinage system, and not all those who avoided smoking were fresh-air fanatics with weird nether garments. These traits, nonetheless, make up a recognisable 'type' in the literature and culture of the period. We do not need to be convinced that Lewis is writing entirely objective anthropological observations – indeed, from the air of judgement which hangs over the Scrubbs, we can feel fairly sure he is not – in order to understand this passage. Eustace and his family are self-consciously modern and 'up-to-date' in a way which classes them alongside various forms of faddishness and crankery. This is not mere political or cultural prejudice on Lewis's part, even if he is depicting them in a rather stereotyped way. The three writers I have quoted so far – Lewis, Christie and Powell – could all be described as conservative with a small 'c', to a greater or lesser extent. They have an attachment to traditional ways of doing things, and a mild suspicion of great plans for reform or revolution. However, it is not only those with a conservative turn of mind

FRESH AIR AND OTHER FADS

who associated this cluster of fads together with a progressive outlook. We can find the same theme in one of the most famous leftist writers of the British twentieth century.

George Orwell is not a writer whom one might immediately compare to C. S. Lewis. They differ so widely in literary style, in temperament, in political outlook and hopes for the world. There are, nonetheless, some striking parallels between them. Both wrote symbolic novels in which talking animals fight against totalitarian regimes (*Animal Farm* and *The Lion, the Witch and the Wardrobe*), both wrote futuristic stories in which language is the key to huge moral insights (*Nineteen Eighty-Four* and *Out of the Silent Planet*), both wrote treatises on the need to safeguard the meaning of words in contemporary society ('Politics and the English Language' and *Studies in Words*), and both made fun of vegetarian leftists. Orwell's *The Road to Wigan Pier*, which appeared in the late 1930s, combines a description of the atrocious conditions of working-class life in Northern England, with reflections on the state of the contemporary Socialist movement in Britain. In these later chapters, Orwell is fairly unsparing about what constitutes organized Socialism at the time, remarking that '[a]s with the Christian religion, the worst advertisement for Socialism is its adherents'.[139] One of the major problems with much British Socialism, for Orwell, is that it is not an organized movement of the working classes, but an intellectual interest for the middle classes:

> The first thing that must strike any outside observer is that Socialism, in its developed form, is a theory confined entirely to the middle classes. The typical Socialist is not, as tremulous old ladies imagine, a ferocious-looking working man with greasy overalls and a raucous voice. He is either a youthful snob-Bolshevik who in five years' time will quite probably have made a wealthy marriage and been converted to Roman Catholicism;

or, still more typically, a prim little man with a white-collar job, usually a secret teetotaller and often with vegetarian leanings, with a history of Nonconformity behind him, and, above all, with a social position which he has no intention of forfeiting. [140]

Having identified the mismatch between the image (and perhaps self-image) of the Socialist movement and its actual members, Orwell goes on to complain about the connections between his brand of leftish politics and general crankishness:

In addition to this there is the horrible – the really disquieting – prevalence of cranks wherever Socialists are gathered together. One sometimes gets the impression that the mere words 'Socialism' and 'Communism' draw towards them with magnetic force every fruit-juice drinker, nudist, sandal-wearer, sex-maniac, Quaker, 'Nature Cure' quack, pacifist, and feminist in England.[141]

In an echo of Mr Deacon's vegetarian holiday camp, Orwell goes on to object to the acceptance by Socialists that their movement is mired in a lot of faddishness and irrelevant social attitudes:

And some such notion seems to exist even among Socialists themselves. For instance, I have here a prospectus from another summer school which states its terms per week and then asks me to say 'whether my diet is ordinary or vegetarian'. They take it for granted, you see, that it is necessary to ask this question.[142]

In a conclusion worthy of the novelist who produced *Animal Farm*, the infuriated Orwell goes on to imagine a sort of left-wing bonfire of the vanities:

I do not think the Socialist need make any sacrifice of essentials, but certainly he will have to make a great sacrifice of externals.

> It would help enormously, for instance, if the smell of crankishness which still clings to the Socialist movement could be dispelled. If only the sandals and the pistachio-coloured shirts could be put in a pile and burnt, and every vegetarian, teetotaller, and creeping Jesus sent home to Welwyn Garden City to do his yoga exercises quietly! But that, I am afraid, is not going to happen.[143]

The reference to 'Welwyn Garden City' may need some explanation here; it is not simply that Orwell met several annoying people who lived there. The town was founded in the 1920s as a deliberately-planned new community, intended to provide the ideal combination of rural and urban living. It was a symbol of both a progressive ethos and the potential for future towns to be intentionally designed and planned. As such, it raised the suspicions of a writer like Orwell, who could write so enthusiastically about symbols of traditional England such as the open fire and the local pub. As I suggested above, Lewis and Orwell might have disagreed on a very large number of political, social and religious topics, but they both cast a very sceptical eye at the Utopian schemes of the mid-century 'cranks'.

THE MODEL YOUNGSTER

The mention of Eustace's tastes and education suggest another comparison to a contemporary of Lewis. His fondness for dead insects neatly sums up a worldview which is analytical rather than traditional; he would rather find out how a creature works by killing it and making it into a specimen than by watching a living one. (If nothing else, this suggests he will find it difficult to adjust to Narnia and the connections between humans and talking beasts.) His tastes are similarly analytic, as he prefers books of information, and the mention of grain elevators and foreign children in model schools continues to fill in his mental background. Like his parents, Eustace is consciously international in outlook, but also curiously narrow: he reads books about other children, as if he exists in a carefully-designed social niche, rather than ranging across other kinds of writing and experience. This recalls another depiction of an unlovely young person (though a rather older one), in Evelyn Waugh's novel *Brideshead Revisited*. The protagonist, Charles Ryder is a painter who has become an infantry officer during the Second World War. Most of the novel is about his memories of pre-war life, but the early pages contain a description of his depressing life as an officer. He finds he has lost his enthusiasm for military life, and amongst the dispiriting features of the world is a junior officer called Hooper. In Ryder's account of him, Hooper is a perfect product of the modern world, revealing its narrowness, its lack of vision and its emptiness:

> Hooper had no illusions about the Army – or rather no special illusions distinguishable from the general, enveloping fog from which he observed the universe. He had come to it reluctantly, under compulsion, after he had made every feeble effort in his power to obtain deferment. He accepted it, he said, 'like the measles'. Hooper was no romantic. He had not as a child ridden with Rupert's horse or sat among the camp fires at Xanthus-side; at the age when my eyes were dry to all save poetry ... Hooper had wept often, but never for Henry's speech on St Crispin's day, nor for the epitaph at Thermopylae. The history they taught him had had few battles in it but, instead, a profusion of detail about humane legislation and recent industrial change. Gallipoli, Balaclava, Quebec, Lepanto, Bannockburn, Roncevales, and Marathon – these, and the Battle in the West where Arthur fell, and a hundred such names whose trumpet-notes, even now in my sere and lawless state, called to me irresistibly across the intervening

years with all the clarity and strength of boyhood, sounded in vain to Hooper. [144]

Like Eustace Scrubb, Hooper apparently lacks the imaginative resources to see the world in any other way than technically and analytically. Books about humane legislation and industrial change would no doubt have been the next volumes in the sequence which began with Eustace's agricultural and educational non-fiction. He is not clear-eyed – Ryder describes him as inhabiting a general fogginess – but neither is he stirred by imaginative visions. Hooper also shares with Eustace a misplaced faith in systems and their ability to sort out human life. For Eustace this is the bureaucracy of consulates and the administration of the law overseas which he hopes will save him from Narnian adventures, for Hooper it is business:

> He seldom complained. Though himself a man to whom one could not confidently entrust the simplest duty, he had an overmastering regard for efficiency and, drawing on his modest commercial experience, he would sometimes say of the ways of the Army in pay and supply and the use of 'man-hours': 'They couldn't get away with that in business.'[145]

For Ryder, Hooper becomes both an object of distaste and evidence that the high-sounding abstract terms of progressive ideals will turn out to be pretty tawdry if they have to be translated into people like Hooper:

> He slept sound while I lay awake fretting. In the weeks that we were together Hooper became a symbol to me of Young England, so that whenever I read some public utterance proclaiming what Youth demanded in the Future and what the world owed to Youth, I would test these general statements by substituting 'Hooper' and seeing if they still seemed as

plausible. Thus in the dark hour before reveille I sometimes pondered: 'Hooper Rallies', 'Hooper Hostels', 'International Hooper Cooperation', and 'the Religion of Hooper'. He was the acid test of all these alloys.[146]

The satirical deflation provided by phrases such as 'Hooper Rallies' and 'International Hooper Cooperation' underlines the hollowness which Ryder finds in these ideals, and in the young man who was created by them. Eustace displays many of the same tendencies: he is avowedly un-romantic and scornful of the chivalric world he finds in Narnia, but is not in fact practical or down-to-earth. He is simply in hock to a different set of ideals, which remain misty abstractions for him. Like Hooper, he has also suffered from a lack of heroic and epic literature. The battles of Charlemagne and Arthur which so stirred Ryder, but which were not part of Hooper's mental world, are paralleled by the fantastical books which Eustace has not read. When Eustace is found taking more water than his ration, at a time when the crew are all suffering badly from thirst, his diary records:

Caspian showed up in his true colours as a brutal tyrant and said out loud for everyone to hear that anyone found 'stealing' water in future would 'get two dozen'. I didn't know what this meant till Edmund explained to me. It comes in the sort of books those Pevensie kids read.[147]

Later, when Eustace wanders away from the others when they have landed on an island, and finds himself lost, his lack of suitable reading comes into sharper focus. He sees something moving in a cave:

Something was crawling. Worse still, something was coming out. Edmund or Lucy or you would have recognized it at once, but Eustace had read none of the right books. The

FRESH AIR AND OTHER FADS

> thing that came out of the cave was something he had never even imagined – a long, lead-coloured snout, dull red eyes, no feathers or fur, a long, lithe body that trailed on the ground, legs whose elbows went up higher than its back like a spider's, cruel claws, bat's wings that made a rasping noise on the stone, yards of tail. And the lines of smoke were coming from its two nostrils. He never said the word Dragon to himself. Nor would it have made things any better if he had.[148]

After the dragon dies (without Eustace's involvement), the narrator once again makes the point about inadequate literary experience, and contrasts it with the material which stocks Eustace's mind:

> Most of us know what we should expect to find in a dragon's lair but, as I said before, Eustace had read only the wrong books. They had a lot to say about exports and imports and governments and drains, but they were weak on dragons.[149]

We can have little doubt that the junior officer from *Brideshead Revisited* would have been in an equally bad position if he had stumbled across one of these winged and scaly creatures. He and Eustace apparently read such very similar books. To paraphrase yet another slogan in the style of Charles Ryder, if he had to face a dragon: 'Hooper Is Back On The Menu'.

FELLOW-TRAVELLERS AND OTHER DIRECTIONS

The opening page of *The Voyage of the Dawn Treader* is packed with social and political signals which would have been a great deal more obvious to readers in the 1950s than their early-twenty-first century equivalents. (How clear they would have been for child readers is another matter, and is another point which complicates the Narnia novels' status as children's books.) As the parallels with other writers such as Agatha Christie and Anthony Powell suggest – not to mention George Orwell's furious denunciation – Eustace and his parents do not simply display a bunch of characteristics which Lewis personally disliked. Vegetarianism, fresh air, non-smoking, patent underwear and non-fiction books cluster together to mark them out as a recognisable social type. Even if some elements of the portrait are painted with rather broad brushstrokes, the appearance of similar characters in the work of other authors makes it clear that contemporary readers would recognise the Scrubbs. They are faddish social reformers, with a misplaced confidence in the imminent reordering of the world along strictly rational, hygienic and progressive lines. Eustace is the carefully-nurtured result of that confidence: he has imbibed all his parents' principles and been brought up to enjoy informative and analytical activities. Like a younger Hooper, he is an entirely modern child who does not feel the unsettling pull of irrational or romantic longings, and does not understand why others might.

If the Scrubbs are not constituted by a random set of traits which Lewis disliked, then neither are they simply in the book to be ridiculed and dismissed. Their adherence to progressive social reform, and its connected attitudes to food, health and learning, is not simply introduced into *The Voyage of the Dawn Treader* for the sake of connecting unpleasant characters with views the author found distasteful. On the contrary, they play an important part in the novel's theme. I argued in the introduction that *Dawn Treader* is a book about quests and about the ideals that people seek in their quests. The Scrubbs may be unattractive and joyless, but they possess a specific set of ideals, and they are on their own kind of quest. They are part of a recognisable (if heterogenous) social movement, which does not accept the world in its current state, and which seeks to remake it according to their beliefs.

FRESH AIR AND OTHER FADS

It is extremely fitting that Eustace and Reepicheep clash with each other early in the story, become something like personal enemies, and then eventually develop an odd form of companionship during the dragon episode. They are both, in a sense, the sons of the quest. They are each the other's opposite to such an extent that they sometimes appear to be mirror images. The progressive social ideals of the Scrubbs are not an irrelevant part of the scene-setting, nor do they just impress upon us that the 'real world' is awful and boring whilst we wait for the expected journey into Narnia. (As we have seen in previous books, that would not at all be the 'Narnian' attitude to our world.) They are thoroughly in tune with *The Voyage of the Dawn Treader*'s themes and narrative. It is a book about questing, about following where your ideals lead, and it begins with a suburban family who are doing just that.

Of course, whether a modern reader has more or less sympathy with the narrator's implied attitudes when it comes to lighting up and ordering a steak, it is fairly clear that the novel is not presenting the Scrubbs as people to emulate. Their attitude to the world, as embodied by their young son Eustace, is tested throughout *The Voyage of the Dawn Treader*, and found decidedly wanting. It is not just that he has never read about dragons, and therefore is unprepared to recognise or deal with one when he is faced with one of these creatures. (After all, fantastical fauns and their appropriate handling might be regarded as just another branch of informative non-fiction.) Nor is it solely Eustace's surprise at finding a giant mouse that can talk which condemns him in the early Reepicheep scenes. It is the inflexible and dull cast of his mind which marks him out from the others. When he is unexpectedly dropped into the sea, and fished out onto the deck of a galleon, he regards it as a personal insult rather than an adventure. His instinct is to remedy the situation by demanding curatives which emphasize his distance from the natural world: a patent nerve food which must be made with distilled water. He displays a petulant and ill-founded reliance on bureaucracy, demanding that he be put in contact with the British Consulate and threatening people with vaguely-conceived legal instruments. More troublingly, his rational and progressive principles seem to be rather easy to twist to selfish ends. His complaint that it is unjust Lucy be given the best cabin, on the grounds that advances in gender equality have shown chivalry to be actually degrading to women, is one hint of this. The reader might believe more in Eustace's feminism if this objection had not come amidst a string of other demands for his own comfort and consequence. Later in the novel, the same motif appears in a more unpleasant tone, as Eustace claims that scientific principles have established that the sailors doing hard manual labour do not need as much water to drink as the officer class. (Another moment where the fictional worlds of Lewis and Orwell have a very thin wall between them: Eustace's convictions here would not seem out of place in *Animal Farm*.)

The novel could be criticized for subjecting the Scrubb family's ideals to an unfair test, for setting Eustace up to fail. But novels are not thought experiments, and I think this would be to misunderstand the way the Scrubb ethos is examined. *The Voyage of the Dawn Treader* opens up a world to Eustace where his principles cannot guide him. They falter at precisely the points where they are supposed to be unassailable. For a start, it becomes clear that they are not held out of an individual process of reasoning and personal decision. Eustace holds his ideas not because he arrived at them himself after investigating the possible worldviews and weighing the evidence. He is as much a blind follower of inherited tradition as the stodgy reactionaries whom his parents despise. Nor are they universal and independent of social position: it is telling that when Eustace wishes to express his distaste for Reepicheep, he declares that performing animals are 'silly and vulgar and − sentimental'.[150] This is a major category error which reveals the narrowness of his mind, since he interprets Reepicheep not as an independent being with his own personality and moral qualities, but as something which has been owned and trained by people like himself for their own entertainment. (This moral error will come into sharper focus when the slave-traders treat the talking mouse in exactly the same way.) It is also however, accidentally revealing of his snobbishness. He uses the progressive epithet 'sentimental', bundling up performing animals with Valentine's cards, Dickensian good cheer, melodramatic plays about wronged women, and other things which put emotional self-indulgence in the way of recognising and solving social problems. Calling them 'vulgar', though, suggests that his reason for judgement is social rather than socialist; that they are contemptible because lower-class people like them. Another crack appears in the coherence of the Scrubb's view of the world. As mentioned above, these principles turn out to be neither practical, since Eustace ends up invoking laws he does not understand and mechanisms he cannot explain, nor egalitarian, since they are so easily bent to serve personal advantage. In each of these cases, the Scrubbs' attitude to life is shown to be weakest at the exact points where they would pride themselves on being superior to the Pevensies. Believing themselves to be just, open-minded, unblinded by prejudice or self-interest, un-beholden to tradition or received ideas, practical and down-to-earth, they turn out to be quite otherwise. Eustace is increasingly baffled, furious and lost, even to the point of having his human form twisted into that of a dragon, before he finally arrives at the eerie allegory of baptism when he meets a lion at a well. Lewis takes the Scrubbs' view of the world seriously enough to package it together in the opening pages, present it in terms which we might recognise in the work of Christie, Waugh, Powell, et al, and then ruthlessly unravel it through the subsequent chapters, leading up to the moment when Eustace realizes that he cannot scrape off the scales with his own claws. The Scrubbs are shown to be people on a quest driven by their ideals, but one which is fogged by self-satisfaction, imperilled by heartlessness, and directed towards an end which they can neither articulate nor recognise. Though he does not know it when the novel begins, Eustace is already on a quest. It takes him some time and pain to realize that, and to find a truer one.

CHAPTER TWO
NARNIAN BUREAUCRACY

The voyage is now well underway, and the first serious adventures take place when the *Dawn Treader* puts in at the Lone Islands. The main characters are captured by slavers, though Caspian is bought from them by a nobleman who is struck by something familiar in the young man's air. A small coup results, with Caspian taking the islands back from the corrupt governor's regime using only a small band of men, a cask of wine, and some haughty royal rhetoric. However, the figure of Governor Gumpas is a curious one in Narnia. In a land of high fantasy and medieval romance we are more used to seeing nobles and fantastical creatures than administrators and bureaucrats. The cold, serene air of this world, which helps to turn the Pevensies into their true regal selves, might be thought too rich and fine an atmosphere to support an ignoble parchment-pusher of Gumpas' sort. Admittedly we have encountered some fantastical creatures who are less than epic in their scope, and who seem closer to the atmosphere of our world. In *The Lion, the Witch and the Wardrobe*, Mr Tumnus was rather on the fussy side, with his little bows and his invitation to tea. The Beavers, with their snug kitchen and sewing machine, were not exactly figures of elfin fantasy. However, both of them were domestic rather than bureaucratic; they may have fallen short of heroic stature, but they were not ignoble. (I shall pause here for as long as these parentheses take, because my experience with Narnia Club has taught me that someone will wish to mount an immediate and spirited defence of Mr Tumnus and/or the Beavers.) The Governor of the Lone Islands is in a very different category.

GOLD ON THE HORIZON

In order to explore the significance of Governor Gumpas, I am going to make a rather unusual argument. I shall suggest that Gumpas is a deliberate and personal insult perpetrated by Lewis on a person to whom he felt a strong animosity. By writing the character of Governor Gumpas, he caricatured everything about this person which he found rebarbative and offensive, creating a figure of almost metaphysical repugnance. Admittedly, since this is Lewis we are discussing, Gumpas is not the cover-name of another Oxford don whom the Inklings despised, nor of some bully who had tormented the writer during his miserable schooldays. He is, I would argue, a lurid caricature of Alanus ab Insulis, a poet who had been dead for eight centuries, and whom Lewis absolutely loathed.

The first clue to the Governor's true identity is his name. 'Gumpas' is an eye-catching word, and a search in the best historical dictionaries provides some associations which might come with the name. According to the Oxford English Dictionary, a 'gumpus' is a variant of the word 'gump', a dialect word meaning a foolish person. The OED describes it as Scottish in origin, and a look at the *Dictionars o the Scots Leid* (or *Dictionaries of the Scottish Language*) confirms it, recording various usages in the nineteenth and twentieth centuries. The Victorian poet Hew Ainslie, for example, included lines in his *Pilgrimage to the Land of Burns* which use the simile 'Like some great gumphy o' a fule Wha sticks his carritches at Schule' ('Like some great gumphy of a fool, Who messes up his catechism at school'.)[151] Likewise, the *DSL* quotes a line by the Ulster novelist St John Greer Ervine: 'You great, big gumph! And you that's afeard of a bull want to marry a wife!'[152] The *OED* also notes that the word survives in some regional dialects in the US: Governor Gumpas may share the derivation of his name with a character from modern film, *Forrest Gump*. So 'gumpus' (and its variants) sounds close enough to 'Gumpas' to suggest a connection, especially as we know Lewis was

NARNIAN BUREAUCRACY

himself an Ulsterman with a love of Old Scots literature. From this point of view, the name of the chief official of the Lone Islands is merely an elaborate way of calling the character 'Commissioner Stupidhead' or 'Viceroy Idiotfeatures'.

However, there is another, and rather more obscure, association with the name 'Gumpas'. In two of Lewis's published works he quoted the Latin phrase *gumphis subtilibus*. In both cases he was quoting Alanus ab Insulis, a twelfth-century poet. He comments on this unusual phrase in *The Discarded Image*, Lewis's book describing the worldview of medieval and renaissance writers. It comes in a discussion of the way medieval authors reproduce material from Classical authors:

> In Bernard's successor, Alanus ab Insulis, we find an equally close linkage. In his *Anticlaudian* we are told that the soul is fastened to the body *gumphis subtilibus*, 'with tiny little nails'. We may smile at the (almost 'metaphysical') quaintness of the image, which, if deliberate, would be quite characteristic of Alanus. In reality he is exactly following Chalcidius, who is exactly following Plato, and may not even know very clearly what a gumphus is.[153]

In *The Allegory of Love*, Lewis's study of the dominance of allegorical poetry in the medieval period, he describes the same poem by Alanus ab Insulis at more length. Whilst summarizing the action of the poem, he once again mentions the *gumphis*, which obviously appealed to his imagination as a phrase:

> God then called Noys to bring him an exemplar out of her treasury and impressed its likeness with his seal upon the new soul which he gave to Prudence. She rejoined her sister Reason whom she found waiting at the celestial frontier, and the two returned together to the house of Natura. A perfect body was fashioned and united to the soul *gumphis*

subtilibus and the Virtues in turn endowed the man with their choicest gifts.[154]

These tiny invisible nails appear once again, in a later passage of *The Discarded Image*, when Lewis is explaining the way the medieval worldview saw the connection between the soul and the body. I will quote the passage at a bit more length, since it is worth considering the context. Lewis has already explained in this book that medieval thought saw everything as interconnected, but in hierarchical and orderly ways. In this view of the world, between two separate things there was often a third thing (or 'tertium quid', in Latin) which connected them by partaking of the same nature as both at the same time. (This idea, Lewis elaborates, originates in Plato.) Thus the human and the divine are connected by angels, which can communicate between them and which can exist in both the earthly and celestial realms. On a more prosaic level, the froth and spray at the top of waves would be a third thing, or 'tertium quid', which exists at the frontier between the elements of water and air, and which partakes of both in some way. Here is Lewis's discussion of the 'tertium quid' between body and soul:

> This tertium quid, this phantom liaison-officer between body and soul, was called Spirit or (more often) the spirits. It must be understood that this sense does not at all overlap with the sense which enables us to speak of angels or devils or ghosts as 'spirits'. To pass from the one meaning to the other would be merely to make a pun.
>
> The spirits were supposed to be just sufficiently material for them to act upon the body, but so very fine and attenuated that they could be acted upon by the wholly immaterial soul. They were, putting it bluntly, to be like the aether of nineteenth-century physics, which, for all I could ever learn of it, was to be and not to be matter.

> This doctrine of the spirits seems to me the least reputable feature in the Medieval Model. If the tertium quid is matter at all (what have density and rarity to do with it?) both ends of the bridge rest on one side of the chasm; if not, both rest on the other. Spirits, then, are the 'subtle gumphus' required by Plato and Alanus to keep body and soul together, or as Donne says, 'the subtile knot which makes us man'.[155]

The fact that the 'subtle gumphus' clearly stuck in Lewis's mind does not mean that he liked Alanus ab Insulis' work. On the contrary, other passages of *The Allegory of Love* make clear his low opinion of the poet. He nearly dismisses it with the comparison that the '*Anticlaudianus* of Alanus ab Insulis is a work in every respect inferior to the *De Mundi Universitate*, and may be described as nearly worthless except from the historical point of view', before adding with scholarly scrupulousness that '[f]rom that point of view it is important'.[156] As he continues to describe the poem, Lewis criticizes its failures of style, which include pretentiousness, pomposity and an appallingly verbose style:

> Since the perfect man, at the end of the poem, proves his mettle in combat against the vices, the poem may be described as a Psychomachia with a lengthy introduction; and Alanus, like Prudentius, probably believed himself to be composing an epic. The work is written throughout in hexameters and always couched in the same monotonous rhetoric. It is a principle with Alanus that whatever is worth saying once is worth saying several times. Thus 'she thinks about the way to heaven' becomes 'She thinks, inquires, devises, seeks, elects What way, or path, or road may guide her steps To high heav'n and the Thunderer's secret throne.' 'She bids them make a chariot' becomes 'She bids, commands, orders, enjoins, begs one Of those in Wisdom's train, with hand and heart And faith

and zeal and sweat and toil to effect The carriage into being of her carriage.'[157]

It is worth pointing out, in passing, that the *Anticlaudianus* is entirely in Latin. Thus in the latter sentences of the passage I have quoted, Lewis is paraphrasing the meaning in English and then translating into a lengthy, mannered English style to demonstrate the effect of the lengthy, mannered Latin style.[158] Having done so, the scholar is still concerned that his readers may not appreciate how truly dreadful Alanus' poem is:

> But no quotation can do justice to the effect of the book as a whole. Those who have read it to the end—a small company—and those only, can understand how speedily amused contempt turns into contempt without amusement, and how even contempt at last settles into something not far removed from a rankling personal hatred of the author. Nor are the vices of the style redeemed, as their much more pardonable counterparts were redeemed in Bernardus, by any real profundity or freshness in the matter. Once or twice, when he is describing external nature, the author shows a trace of real feeling; once or twice, in moral passages, he attains a certain dignity; for the rest this book is one of the melancholy kind that claim our attention solely as influences and as examples of a tendency.[159]

The depth of feeling displayed here, with its 'contempt without amusement' and 'something not far removed from a rankling personal hatred for the author' suggests a reason for Governor Gumpas' name. Lewis both detested Alanus' work, and was struck by one particular phrase in it. I believe he borrowed the term 'gumphus' (and probably appreciated its closeness to the Scots 'gumphy') in order to create the unlikeable Governor. Alanus and Gumpas share one obvious

NARNIAN BUREAUCRACY

characteristic: their obsession with words at the expense of meaning. The sheer verbiage of Alanus' poetry which Lewis, as a conscientious scholar, forced himself to slog through, corresponds to the litter of writing equipment which covers Gumpas' table; the 'cascade of letters, dossiers, ink-pots, pens, sealing-wax and documents' which are tipped off when it is overturned.[160] When Caspian makes the declaration that 'I am king of Narnia', the obfuscation continues: 'Nothing about it in the correspondence,' blusters Gumpas, 'Nothing in the minutes. We have not been notified of any such thing. All irregular. Happy to consider any applications—'[161] Gumpas commits the same verbal crime as Alanus: he employs language to obscure and mystify what is going on in the world. In his hands written texts do not become secure repositories of knowledge, but rather ways of ensuring no-one ever finds out what is happening. This tendency continues as Caspian raises a very straightforward point, demanding why the tribute owed to Narnia has not been paid by the Lone Islands:

> 'That would be a question to raise at the Council next month,' said Gumpas. 'If anyone moves that a commission of enquiry be set up to report on the financial history of the islands at the first meeting next year, why then ...'[162]

The terrible implications of this Gumpas' determined career of dislocating words from the real world become clearer when Caspian continues his indictment, demanding why the Lone Islands permit trading in slaves: 'Necessary, unavoidable,' said his Sufficiency. 'An essential part of the economic development of the islands, I assure you. Our present burst of prosperity depends on it.'[163] When he attempts to persuade Caspian against abolishing the slave trade, he does not put forward an argument, but declares he has more documents: 'Your Majesty's tender years ... hardly make it possible that you should understand the economic problem involved. I have statistics, I have graphs, I have—'[164] Gumpas has allowed himself to substitute words for things so continually, and has thrived so well as governor whilst doing so, that he has come to substitute words for people. There is no suggestion in the novel that the Governor is violent or sadistic, but he has presided over a trade which involves the abuse and dehumanisation of people who are made into commodities. He has produced a wall of paperwork and procedure which cuts him off from the misery and degradation which the slave trade involves. He justifies it to himself and others as 'unavoidable' and part of 'economic development', putting verbiage in place of moral reasoning or human empathy. I do not think Lewis was attempting to accuse Alanus ab Insulis of profiting from the trading of slaves, but the way the scene of Caspian and Gumpas continues does show some outworkings of the abuse of language.

Lewis's concern for the accuracy of language, and the moral risks of sloppy usage, chime with another imaginative novelist of this era. In an earlier chapter I suggested that the portrayal of the Scrubbs was recognisably a picture of progressive 'cranks' in the mid-century, as memorably denounced by George Orwell. I think Orwell can also highlight what Gumpas is doing in his defence of the slave trade. The essay 'Politics and the English Language' was published in the mid-1940s, and offers a manifesto for clear and unambiguous political writing, as well as a warning against vagueness and humbug. It was to become a classic, if a controversial one, in the annals of journalism and public writing. In it Orwell rails against the way abstraction and stock phrases prevent people from recognising what is actually being discussed in political speeches and articles. He gives an entertainingly satirical paraphrase of a passage from the biblical book of Ecclesiastes, as it might be rewritten by a contemporary politician:

NARNIAN BUREAUCRACY

> I returned and saw under the sun, that the race is not to the swift, nor the battle to the strong, neither yet bread to the wise, nor yet riches to men of understanding, nor yet favour to men of skill; but time and chance happeneth to them all.
>
> Objective consideration of contemporary phenomena compels the conclusion that success or failure in competitive activities exhibits no tendency to be commensurate with innate capacity, but that a considerable element of the unpredictable must invariably be taken into account.[165]

His point is not only that the language of the second passage is threadbare and complicated, but that its lack of concrete images prevents the reader from grasping clearly what is being said. Though the biblical passage might sound at first more grandiose or high-flown, it is in fact more 'matter-of-fact' since it conveys the meaning more immediately. One part of the argument between the King and the Governor almost mimics this comparison:

> 'I want to know why you have permitted this abominable and unnatural traffic in slaves to grow up here, contrary to the ancient custom and usage of our dominions.'
>
> 'Necessary, unavoidable,' said his Sufficiency. 'An essential part of the economic development of the islands, I assure you. Our present burst of prosperity depends on it.'[166]

Caspian's moral clarity does not prevent him using a high register, with his 'abominable' and his 'ancient custom and usage', but it is evident that he is trying to reveal meaning, whilst Gumpas is trying to hide it. Gumpas sounds as if he is doing exactly what Orwell condemned:

> modern writing at its worst does not consist in picking out words for the sake of their meaning and inventing images in order to

make the meaning clearer. It consists in gumming together long strips of words which have already been set in order by someone else, and making the results presentable by sheer humbug.

When Gumpas brings up 'economic necessity' and later demands of Caspian 'Have you no idea of progress, of development?', it recalls Orwell's criticism of euphemism:

> Thus political language has to consist largely of euphemism, question-begging and sheer cloudy vagueness. Defenceless villages are bombarded from the air, the inhabitants driven out into the countryside, the cattle machine-gunned, the huts set on fire with incendiary bullets: this is called *pacification*. Millions of peasants are robbed of their farms and sent trudging along the roads with no more than they can carry: this is called *transfer of population* or *rectification of frontiers*. People are imprisoned for years without trial, or shot in the back of the neck or sent to die of scurvy in Arctic lumber camps: this is called *elimination of unreliable elements*. Such phraseology is needed if one wants to name things without calling up mental pictures of them.[167]

Part of Orwell's energy in this essay comes, as the passage above suggests, from his horror in seeing fellow left-wing intellectuals defend atrocities carried out by leftists in other parts of the world. I suspect he would immediately recognise the image Lewis has created, of an avowedly 'progressive' Governor allowing fellow humans to be bought and sold, under the name of 'economic development'. Lewis and Orwell would have disagreed on many political, social and literary points, but they had a very similar eye for the lethal hypocrisy which surrounded them in public speech. The scene of Caspian calling Gumpas to account reads as if it was written as a practical demonstration of Orwell's arguments in 'Politics and the English Language'.

NARNIAN BUREAUCRACY
EVERYTHING IN ITS PLACE

Having argued that Gumpas is a vivid caricature of everything which Lewis found objectionable about Alanus ab Insulis, I am forced to ask why. There is, no doubt, some emotional relief to be found in pillorying real people in fiction. Mid-century English literature produced some remarkable literature which drew more or less visibly on public personages. George Orwell, whom I quoted above, appears in Anthony Powell's *A Dance to the Music of Time* as a mildly satirical sketch under the name of Lord Erridge, an aristocrat who prefers to be called 'Alf' by his left-wing cronies. Agatha Christie apparently put herself into her own later novels as the scatter-brained detective novelist Ariadne Oliver. Sally Bowles, the main character of *Cabaret*, originated in the fiction of Christopher Isherwood and was based on a nightclub singer called Jean Ross. It is possible that Lewis indulged the same instinct, and presumably it is more satisfying to lampoon a person one detests in fiction than to produce an adoring portrait of a beloved. (It certainly seems to happen more frequently.) Lewis would be taking an unusual approach by working off his feelings in this way, since his target was not a personal enemy but a long-dead poet. But Lewis was a man with admittedly unusual feelings, particularly when it came to literature.

However, I think there is something more going on in the throne-room of the Lone Islands. Alanus ab Insulis is not simply someone Lewis found tiresome and verbose. The poet stands for a whole attitude to the world which made Lewis uneasy at times, precisely because he approved of it in general. Some of the scholar's best work was done in explicating the literature of the past, and insisting that we should read it on its own terms rather than rushing to assimilate it to our own world. In works like *The Discarded Image*, *Studies in Words* and 'De Audiendis Poetis', Lewis insisted on a disciplined reading of historical poetry, with scrupulous attention to changes in the meanings of words and the way people looked at the world. This was not, however, because he thought literature should stay as a historical curiosity. On the contrary, Lewis was so concerned to understand and appreciate past literature in its own time because he was convinced it could have an effect on the present. In his view, it was reading which looked too quickly for a modern use or meaning to a text which rendered it incapable of speaking to the present. Doing so smoothed out its strangeness, and simply reflected our own world back to us. In *The Discarded Image*, a book which I've quoted elsewhere in this volume, he attempts to give readers of medieval and renaissance literature an appreciation of what he calls 'the medieval model', the image of the world which is assumed behind the literature. In doing so, he tries to correct some misunderstandings of the era by modern readers. A major error, Lewis believed, was to see medieval culture as dreamy, elusive and mysterious. I suspect he had in mind the medievalism of the Pre-Raphaelite painters, and of Tennyson's *Idylls of the King*, which depict the medieval world as full of yearning and a nameless melancholy. (I also suspect he might diagnose that form of medievalism as accidentally using medieval art and literature to reflect back the attitudes and emotions of the modern era. Modern people know little about the medieval world, so it was a time of mystery and magic. Modern people like to feel yearning and melancholy when looking at pictures of knights and ladies, so medieval people must have spent their time feeling like that.) In contrast to this misty, plangent mood, Lewis asserts that:

> At his most characteristic, medieval man was not a dreamer nor a wanderer. He was an organiser, a codifier, a builder of systems. He wanted 'a place for everything and everything in the right place'. Distinction, definition, tabulation were his delight. Though full of turbulent activities, he was equally

> full of the impulse to formalise them. War was (in intention) formalised by the art of heraldry and the rules of chivalry; sexual passion (in intention), by an elaborate code of love. Highly original and soaring philosophical speculation squeezes itself into a rigid dialectical pattern copied from Aristotle. Studies like Law and Moral Theology, which demand the ordering of very diverse particulars, especially flourish. Every way in which a poet can write (including some in which he had much better not) is classified in the Arts of Rhetoric. [168]

This is a very different image of the medieval world than the Romantic landscape of knights palely loitering, or of turrets in which ladies sighed and wove some eldritch weft. It is also, incidentally, rather different from another popular conception of the medieval era (which has become even more widespread in recent years) as chaotic, brutal, grimy and riven by meaningless factional power struggles. Both those images emphasize a lack of order, of system and comprehensibility, whether in misty vagueness or psychotic violence. Lewis insists that the reverse is true: the salient characteristic of the medieval mind was its love of order and formal structure. He goes on to assert that:

> There was nothing which medieval people liked better, or did better, than sorting out and tidying up. Of all our modern inventions I suspect that they would most have admired the card index. This impulse is equally at work in what seem to us their silliest pedantries and in their most sublime achievements. In the latter we see the tranquil, indefatigable, exultant energy of passionately systematic minds bringing huge masses of heterogeneous material into unity. The perfect examples are the *Summa* of Aquinas and Dante's *Divine Comedy*; as unified and ordered as the Parthenon or the Oedipus Rex, as crowded and varied as a London terminus on a bank holiday.[169]

GOLD ON THE HORIZON

To these two, Lewis adds a third example of the 'passionately systematic' quality of the medieval era: their image of the universe itself. Where a modern mind might see superstition and unreason in medieval belief about the stars, for example, Lewis saw a densely-packed system of correspondences and connections which collected what was known about the heavens and the earth and then synthesized them into an interdependent whole. That question of 'what was known' brings in another element which Lewis considered essential about the period, and hugely misunderstood by people in his own time:

> the overwhelmingly bookish or clerkly character of medieval culture. When we speak of the Middle Ages as the ages of authority we are usually thinking about the authority of the Church. But they were the age not only of her authority, but of authorities. If their culture is regarded as a response to environment, then the elements in that environment to which it responded most vigorously were manuscripts. Every writer, if he possibly can, bases himself on an earlier writer, follows an *auctour*: preferably a Latin one.[170]

Where many modern people might see 'ignorance' as the defining characteristic of the medieval period, and the arrival of the printing press as a defining change in eras, Lewis argues that this would be to misunderstand the difference between them. For him, the spread of literacy did not make modern culture inherently more 'bookish', nor did it prevent modern people from depending on what experts told them (though that expertise might be derived in different ways):

> This is one of the things that differentiate the period almost equally from savagery and from our modern civilisation. In a savage community you absorb your culture, in part

unconsciously, from participation in the immemorial pattern of behaviour, and in part by word of mouth, from the old men of the tribe. In our own society most knowledge depends, in the last resort, on observation. But the Middle Ages depended predominantly on books. Though literacy was of course far rarer then than now, reading was in one way a more important ingredient of the total culture.[171]

With these two characteristics in mind – systematic thinking and bookishness – I think we can start to see more of what Governor Gumpas stands for in this novel, and what connects him to Alanus ab Insulis. As we have seen above, he looks like a thoroughly modern bureaucrat or politician, with his insistence on only arranging meetings through the proper (though nearly impossible) channels, and on answering awkward questions by setting up a formal enquiry. Indeed, he is so modern that he is precisely the figure whom Eustace has apparently been hoping to meet throughout the novel so far. As soon as the Pevensies' cousin recovered sufficiently from his sea-sickness to look about him and start talking, he put his faith in paperwork and bureaucracy:

> he began demanding to be put ashore and said that at the first port he would 'lodge a disposition' against them all with the British Consul. But when Reepicheep asked what a disposition was and how you lodged it (Reepicheep thought it was some new way of arranging a single combat) Eustace could only reply, 'Fancy not knowing that.'[172]

When he is captured by the slavers, Eustace once again tries to invoke this system, in hopes that it will save him:

> 'Where will you take us?' asked Lucy, getting the words out with some difficulty.

> 'Over to Narrowhaven,' said the slaver. 'For market day tomorrow.'
>
> 'Is there a British Consul there?' asked Eustace.
>
> 'Is there a which?' said the man. But long before Eustace was tired of trying to explain, the slaver simply said, 'Well, I've had enough of this jabber. The Mouse is a fair treat but this one would talk the hind leg off a donkey. Off we go, mates.'[173]

He even raises the topic when Caspian comes to rescue them, commenting sulkily that he expects the Prince has been having fun adventuring and not even bothered to discover whether there was a Consulate. Of course by this time the reader has seen the spectre of all Eustace's hopes in the figure of Gumpas (and it is only by Caspian's banishing of him that Eustace has been freed).

This all shows that Eustace's faith in paperwork on its own merits is misplaced, and that he has been rescued on the basis of values which he would deplore, such as monarchy, chivalry and derring-do. It focuses our attention on the way Gumpas apparently represents the part of the medieval attitude to the world which Lewis found troubling; or at least those parts which could be taken to dangerous extremes. The fondness for order and system could become an obsessive bureaucratisation of the world, in which the system became more important than the things which were understood and arranged via its framework. The delight in the copiousness of the world, and the elaboration of it in words, could turn into a deranged verbosity (like that of Alanus) which is not content until everything has been said and then rephrased in all possible ways. The trust in a rational investigation of the universe could slip into an attitude which was satisfied with clever formulae which sounded as if they had solved a problem but actually only shuffled terms around; like the *tertium quid* of the spirits linking soul and body which Lewis found so unconvincing. If I am

NARNIAN BUREAUCRACY

right in this suggestion, and 'Governor Gumpas' is indeed name borrowed from Alanus' own poetry in order to satirize him as a monster of meaningless bloviating and administrative solipsism, then this is a striking moment in Lewis's fantasy world-building. He is usually delighted and inspired, in his literary scholarship and his fiction, by the imaginative power of the medieval world. The scholar Michael Ward has made a persuasive case, in his book *Planet Narnia: The Seven Heavens in the Imagination of C. S. Lewis*, that medieval cosmological lore is the system which underpins much of the Narnia books' imagery. Ward further argues that Lewis believed that this medieval symbolism could help his modern readers to reconceive the world around them in healthier and more holy ways. As the passages I quoted above show, Lewis was fascinated by the medieval way of looking at the world, and thought their 'model' of the universe was itself a work of great beauty and creativity. However, in the figure of Governor Gumpas, he seems to be picking out elements which could tarnish or corrupt that great edifice. Gumpas is the medieval virtues gone sour, those mental skills of order and elaboration turned away from good ends and practised for their own sake until they become vices. The fact that he is perhaps the most modern-looking character in the book, besides Eustace, suggests that the medieval vices have something to say about the contemporary world, as well as the medieval virtues. Just as the Pevensies can inhabit two worlds, taking their regal Narnian selves back into the world of trains and school holidays, so Eustace can be tinged by the defects which are so visible in Gumpas. The Lone Islands do not stage a Narnian rejection of the medieval world-view – far from it – but I believe they show that the roots of banal, bureaucratic wickedness run deep.

Twelfth-century French poetry is not the only source text which can be felt in the adventure on the Lone Islands. Caspian's bloodless conquest of the islands produces some odd resonances with another king making himself known: Jesus of

GOLD ON THE HORIZON

Nazareth. The second chapter of John's Gospel presents two episodes in Jesus' ministry which are worth placing next to the Narnian adventurers. Firstly the wedding at Cana, where Jesus was told the wine had run out, and where he performed a miracle:

> Jesus saith unto them, Fill the waterpots with water. And they filled them up to the brim. And he saith unto them, Draw out now, and bear unto the governor of the feast. And they bare it. When the ruler of the feast had tasted the water that was made wine, and knew not whence it was: (but the servants which drew the water knew;) the governor of the feast called the bridegroom, and saith unto him, Every man at the beginning doth set forth good wine; and when men have well drunk, then that which is worse: but thou hast kept the good wine until now.
>
> (John 2:7-10)

Immediately after this passage in John's Gospel comes the episode known as the 'cleansing of the Temple'. (In fact this sequence does not take place in the same way in all the Gospels, but in the narrative according to John, Jesus goes to Jerusalem immediately after Cana.) In an equally famous passage, Jesus visits the Temple in Jerusalem, and is horrified at the commercial exploitation of the faithful. He reacts drastically to the sight of people making money by selling animals for the sacrifices and by changing money for the Temple donations:

> After this he went down to Capernaum, he, and his mother, and his brethren, and his disciples: and they continued there not many days. And the Jews' passover was at hand, and Jesus went up to Jerusalem, and found in the temple those that sold oxen and sheep and doves, and the changers of money sitting:

NARNIAN BUREAUCRACY

and when he had made a scourge of small cords, he drove them all out of the temple, and the sheep, and the oxen; and poured out the changers' money, and overthrew the tables; and said unto them that sold doves, Take these things hence; make not my Father's house an house of merchandise. And his disciples remembered that it was written, The zeal of thine house hath eaten me up.

(John 2:12-17)

These are not perhaps the most obvious intertexts for Caspian's reclaiming of the Lone Islands, but there are some distinctive echoes. The one which first caught my eye (or gave me a sense that there was another text hovering around the scene) was the way Governor Gumpas is turned out of his office. There is a deliberate and almost ceremonial overthrowing of the table upon which he has been doing business (since one can hardly call what he does 'ruling'):

He glanced up as the strangers entered and then looked down at his papers saying automatically, 'No interviews without appointments except between nine and ten p.m. on second Saturdays.'

Caspian nodded to Bern and then stood aside. Bern and Drinian took a step forward and each seized one end of the table. They lifted it, and flung it on one side of the hall where it rolled over, scattering a cascade of letters, dossiers, inkpots, pens, sealing-wax and documents. Then, not roughly but as firmly as if their hands were pincers of steel, they plucked Gumpas out of his chair and deposited him, facing it, about four feet away.

Caspian at once sat down in the chair and laid his naked sword across his knees. 'My Lord,' said he, fixing his eyes on Gumpas, 'you have not given us quite the welcome we expected. I am the King of Narnia.'[174]

The deliberate turning over of the table of a dishonest and exploitative merchant, especially in a world like Narnia which is soaked with biblical imagery, is an unusual enough gesture to suggest the cleansing of the Temple in the background. Once the connection has been made, the question of wine and celebration also comes into focus. Just as Jesus made wine freely available at Cana in the passage of the Gospel immediately before he overturned the tables, Caspian insisted on an issue of wine to the Governor's men:

> 'It is our wish,' said Caspian, 'that our royal visitation to our realm of the Lone Islands should, if possible, be an occasion of joy and not of terror to our loyal subjects. If it were not for that, I should have something to say about the state of your men's armour and weapons. As it is, you are pardoned. Command a cask of wine to be opened that your men may drink our health. But at noon tomorrow I wish to see them here in this courtyard looking like men-at-arms and not like vagabonds. See to it on pain of our extreme displeasure.'
>
> The captain gaped but Bern immediately cried, 'Three cheers for the King,' and the soldiers, who had understood about the cask of wine even if they understood nothing else, joined in. Caspian then ordered most of his own men to remain in the courtyard.[175]

In context this is more like a piece of realpolitik rather than a demonstration of hospitality and noblesse oblige. Caspian needs to get past the sentries to Gumpas, and needs to avoid anyone on the Lone Islands realizing that he does not have the military strength to take the lands back. Acting as if everyone naturally admits his sovereignty, and declaring an issue of wine to the troops, is essentially a bold bluff. It is very different from the miracle at the wedding. Nonetheless, Caspian is a king demonstrating the beneficence of his kingship, giving gifts

NARNIAN BUREAUCRACY

to his subjects and calling to account those who have misused authority. The move from a wine cask in the courtyard to the overturning of Gumpas' trestle does have a touch of the same themes as the Gospel passages: magnificence and judgement. There is even an odd verbal parallel in the fact that the wedding at Cana, in the words of the Authorized Version, involves a 'governor' of the feast. This portion of John's Gospel seems to have been in the back of Lewis's mind when he sketched out the return of the king of Narnia to the Lone Islands. This does not, of course, mean that Caspian is to be read as an allegory of Jesus, or that we should see him as a Messiah in the novel as a whole. Rather, the themes of joy and judgement of the Gospel shed some light on his figure as he strides through the chapter. In a novel so concerned with light, it is as if Caspian is gilded for a moment as the sun catches the edge of his armour.

CHAPTER THREE
OF DRAGONS AND SOLAR HEROES

A storm drives the *Dawn Treader*, causing damage to the ship's mast and revealing dissent amongst some of those onboard. It does not immediately seem important that we get to hear Eustace's inner thoughts, via passages from his diary. When the ship manages to make it to an unknown island to find stores and wood for repairs, however, young Scrubb becomes the centre of the story. His transformation into a dragon, and his even stranger return from that form, take us deep into the fantastical and allegorical landscape of the novel. Tales of knights, dragons and mysterious quests have a deep history in English literature. The medieval (and Renaissance) texts which detail them were some of Lewis's favourite works, and in this chapter I will be tracing the way he wove these images into *Dawn Treader*. The first appearance of medieval romance comes in a comparison between the Pevensie children and one of the figures who defines the genre. It is an apparently throwaway comment made during an explanation of Narnian time, but signals the novel's concern with this form of story:

> He called Edmund and Lucy their Majesties because they and Peter and Susan had all been Kings and Queens of Narnia long before his time. Narnian time flows differently from ours. If you spent a hundred years in Narnia, you would still come back to our world at the very same hour of the very same day on which you left. And then, if you went back to Narnia after spending a week here, you might find that a thousand Narnian years had passed, or only a day, or no time at all. You never know till you get there. Consequently, when the Pevensie

children had returned to Narnia last time for their second visit, it was (for the Narnians) as if King Arthur came back to Britain, as some people say he will. And I say the sooner the better.[176]

In fact the equivalent passage in *Prince Caspian* does not mention *Queen Lucia, regina quondam, regina futura*. When they work out the difference in time (and how Cair Paravel could now be a ruin on an apparent island) Peter comments that 'now we're coming back to Narnia just as if we were Crusaders or Anglo-Saxons or Ancient Britons or someone coming back to modern England!'[177] This does not, of course, mean that the Narnians did not feel the way Lewis described here, but it is striking that in this novel he reaches for a comparison from Arthurian legend. At the other end of the novel there is another simile which might alert us to the presence of medieval romance. As the voyagers discuss the way their quest might end, Reepicheep uses a noticeable phrase:

> 'H'm,' said Edmund. 'That's not so nice if the World really has an edge and we're getting near it.'
> 'You mean,' said Caspian, 'that we might be just – well, poured over it?'
> 'Yes, yes,' cried Reepicheep, clapping his paws together. 'That's how I've always imagined it – the World like a great round table and the waters of all the oceans endlessly pouring over the edge. The ship will tip up – stand on her head – for one moment we shall see over the edge – and then, down, down, the rush, the speed—'[178]

The most adventurous and chivalric member of the party, the Mouse himself, instinctively uses the phrase 'a great round table' and is thrilled by the image it presents. As with the

OF DRAGONS AND SOLAR HEROES

reference to King Arthur above, this is a comparison in dialogue rather than anything actually existing in Narnia, but it might tune our ear to Arthurian echoes in the novel.

When Caspian and Drinian tell the story of what has happened so far on the sea voyage, they describe another characteristic episode from medieval romance: a tournament where royalty and nobility jousted against each other:

> 'We had a fair wind from Cair Paravel and stood a little north for Galma, which we made on the next day. We were in port for a week, for the Duke of Galma made a great tournament for His Majesty and there he unhorsed many knights—'
>
> 'And got a few nasty falls myself, Drinian. Some of the bruises are there still,' put in Caspian.
>
> '—and unhorsed many knights,' repeated Drinian with a grin. 'We thought the Duke would have been pleased if the King's Majesty would have married his daughter, but nothing came of that—'
>
> 'Squints, and has freckles,' said Caspian.
>
> 'Oh, poor girl,' said Lucy.[179]

There are several elements here which bring medieval chivalry to mind. Drinian uses a ringingly heroic phrase to describe his master's exploits at Galma – 'there he unhorsed many knights' – whose archaism contrasts with the practical interjection made by Caspian himself about bruises. The term 'unhorse', used to mean one combatant knocking the other off his mount, can be found in Thomas Malory's Le Morte D'Arthur. In this particular passage it appears when jousting is being discussed:

> And then Sir Launcelot and Sir Palomides rushed together with two spears strongly, but Sir Launcelot smote Sir Palomides so hard that he went quite out of his saddle, and had a great fall.

> When Sir Tristram saw Sir Palomides have that fall, he said to Sir Launcelot: Sir knight, keep thee, for I must joust with thee. As for to joust with me, said Sir Launcelot, I will not fail you, for no dread I have of you; but I am loath to have ado with you an I might choose, for I will that ye wit that I must revenge my special lord that was unhorsed unwarly and unknightly.[180]

I am not suggesting that Malory was Lewis's only source when thinking about medieval knights. However, we do know Lewis was intimately familiar with the text (he reviewed Vinaver's edition published in the 1940s, based on the discovery of a new manuscript) and it provides a useful compendium of Arthurian material. Drinian's attempt at framing Caspian's deeds in high knightly style is again undercut when he refers to the Duke of Galma's wish that his daughter might be a suitable bride for the king, and the potential bridegroom remarks that she 'squints, and has freckles'. It rather sounds as if the Duke (and perhaps his daughter) were hoping that jousting and declaration of love would go together as they do in this episode from Malory:

> Sir Pelleas[...]loveth a great lady in this country and her name is Ettard. And so when he loved her there was cried in this country a great jousts three days, and all the knights of this country were there and gentlewomen, and who that proved him the best knight should have a passing good sword and a circlet of gold, and the circlet the knight should give it to the fairest lady that was at the jousts. And this knight Sir Pelleas was the best knight that was there, and there were five hundred knights, but there was never man that ever Sir Pelleas met withal but he struck him down, or else from his horse; and every day of three days he struck down twenty knights, therefore they gave him the prize, and forthwithal he went thereas the Lady Ettard was, and gave her the circlet, and said

OF DRAGONS AND SOLAR HEROES

openly she was the fairest lady that there was, and that would he prove upon any knight that would say nay.[181]

Unfortunately for them, Caspian did not play his part. Indeed, it is tempting to wonder if this briefly sketched scene owes something to another moment in Malory when a lady's personal attractions are bound up with the prowess of knights in a tournament. When Sir Gareth is about to enter a jousting contest, Dame Lionesse lends him a ring which will both disguise him and protect him against bloodshed. As she explains, however, the loan is not without some temporary cost to herself:

> Then Dame Lionesse said unto Sir Gareth: Sir, I will lend you a ring, but I would pray you as you love me heartily let me have it again when the tournament is done, for that ring increaseth my beauty much more than it is of himself. And the virtue of my ring is that, that is green it will turn to red, and that is red it will turn in likeness to green, and that is blue it will turn to likeness of white, and that is white it will turn in likeness to blue, and so it will do of all manner of colours. Also who that beareth my ring shall lose no blood, and for great love I will give you this ring. Gramercy, said Sir Gareth, mine own lady, for this ring is passing meet for me, for it will turn all manner of likeness that I am in, and that shall cause me that I shall not be known.[182]

If this episode was at the back of Lewis's mind during the discussion of the tournament at Galma, it might have produced the idea of a valiantly-fought joust, a noble champion, and a lady whose looks were a little less alluring than they might otherwise have been. Even if Dame Lionesse and the magic ring were not part of the Arthurian influence on this conversation, the remarks on the personal attractiveness of the young aristocrat of Galma still evoke a world of knightly prowess and virtuous damosels. The high tone is undercut by Caspian's mention of bruises and freckles, but it has nonetheless been evoked for the reader. This is not an obvious thing to do, since Arthurian knights did not spend their time island-hopping, and the Narnian voyagers are not going to meet many knights errant on their travels. Nonetheless this theme is established; Lewis seems to almost deliberately add a knightly-sounding episode at the outset, to place the idea in a reader's mind.

As the *Dawn Treader* continues its way into unknown waters, images of medieval romance appear at various points. The appearance of a dragon suggests that we are still in this territory. There are a few mentions of dragons in Malory, and the most significant involves a dream which Arthur himself dreamt:

> And as the king lay in his cabin in the ship, he fell in a slumbering and dreamed a marvellous dream: him seemed that a dreadful dragon did drown much of his people, and he came flying out of the west, and his head was enamelled with azure, and his shoulders shone as gold, his belly like mails of a marvellous hue, his tail full of tatters, his feet full of fine sable, and his claws like fine gold; and an hideous flame of fire flew out of his mouth, like as the land and water had flamed all of fire.[183]

The dream continues, with a boar appearing out of the east, and a battle ensuing between them which the dragon wins. On waking, Arthur is understandably keen to have his dream interpreted.

> And therewith the king awoke anon, and was sore abashed of this dream, and sent anon for a wise philosopher, commanding to tell him the signification of his dream. Sir, said the philosopher, the dragon that thou dreamedst of betokeneth thine own person that sailest here, and the colours of his

OF DRAGONS AND SOLAR HEROES

wings be thy realms that thou hast won, and his tail which is all to-tattered signifieth the noble knights of the Round Table; and the boar that the dragon slew coming from the clouds betokeneth some tyrant that tormenteth the people, or else thou art like to fight with some giant thyself, being horrible and abominable, whose peer ye saw never in your days, wherefore of this dreadful dream doubt thee nothing, but as a conqueror come forth thyself.[184]

It seems resonant for Eustace's adventures that the most important dragon in the *Morte D'Arthur* is one which Arthur comes to realize is himself. The episode is not loaded with the same kind of moral emphasis or self-examination which occurs in *Dawn Treader*, but a similar idea is present in both texts.

Arthurian elements cluster again near the end of the narrative, as the voyagers come close to the goal of their quest. The sleepers at the feast evoke in passing one of the mysterious symbols of the Arthurian stories: the Dolorous Stroke. In the legends, this is a blow struck during the quest for the Holy Grail. During a fight at a feast, Sir Balin's sword is broken, and is chased through the castle by his adversary, until he suddenly finds a weapon in another room:

And at the last he entered into a chamber that was marvellously well dight and richly, and a bed arrayed with cloth of gold, the richest that might be thought, and one lying therein, and thereby stood a table of clean gold with four pillars of silver that bare up the table, and upon the table stood a marvellous spear strangely wrought. And when Balin saw that spear, he gat it in his hand and turned him to King Pellam, and smote him passingly sore with that spear, that King Pellam fell down in a swoon, and therewith the castle roof and walls brake and fell to the earth, and Balin fell down so that he might not stir foot nor hand. And so the most part of the castle, that was fallen down through that dolorous stroke, lay upon Pellam and Balin three days.[185]

Unknown to Balin, the weapon he picked up and used to attack Pellam was the Lance of Longinus. This was the name given to a legendary relic in medieval Christian tradition; the spear with which Christ's side was pierced by a Roman solider as he hung on the cross. Its Narnia equivalent, also seized at a feast, but with less disastrous consequences, appears on Ramandu's island: 'Lucy now noticed something lying lengthwise on the table which had escaped her attention before. It was a knife of stone, sharp as steel, a cruel-looking, ancient-looking thing'.[186] Lucy asks Ramandu's daughter what happened to the sleeping men, and she explains that they arrived here and quarrelled over whether they should stay there forever, return to Narnia in the hope that Miraz was no longer king or travel further into the west:

> 'And as they quarrelled [one] caught up the Knife of Stone which lies there on the table and would have fought with his comrades. But it is a thing not right for him to touch. And as his fingers closed upon the hilt, deep sleep fell upon all the three. And till the enchantment is undone they will never wake.'
> 'What is this Knife of Stone?' asked Eustace.
> 'Do none of you know it?' said the girl.
> 'I – I think,' said Lucy, 'I've seen something like it before. It was a knife like it that the White Witch used when she killed Aslan at the Stone Table long ago.'
> 'It was the same,' said the girl, 'and it was brought here to be kept in honour while the world lasts.'[187]

The Arthurian narrative involves a wasteland which is created around the castle by the Dolorous Stroke and a terrible wound

OF DRAGONS AND SOLAR HEROES

in King Pellam. In Narnia the results are less disastrous, but the parallel is very clear. It strongly associates Ramandu's island with the Grail Castle, and brings to the fore the connection between Arthurian legends and the Christian tradition. When Reepicheep comes to depart into the east, the echoes of King Arthur become stronger once again:

> At that moment, with a crunch, the boat ran aground. The water was too shallow now for it. 'This,' said Reepicheep, 'is where I go on alone.' They did not even try to stop him, for everything now felt as if it had been fated or had happened before. They helped him to lower his little coracle. Then he took off his sword ('I shall need it no more,' he said) and flung it far away across the lilied sea. Where it fell it stood upright with the hilt above the surface.

The casting of a sword into the water, where it remains upright, evokes the death of Arthur, and the return of Excalibur to the lake. As Arthur lies dying, he orders Sir Bedivere to throw his sword into the water and tell him what he sees. Twice Bedivere lies and hides Excalibur, but Arthur knows he is lying because Bedivere does not say anything marvellous happened as he threw the sword. On the third time he carries out his king's orders:

> Then Sir Bedivere departed, and went to the sword, and lightly took it up, and went to the water side; and there he bound the girdle about the hilts, and then he threw the sword as far into the water as he might; and there came an arm and an hand above the water and met it, and caught it, and so shook it thrice and brandished, and then vanished away the hand with the sword in the water. So Sir Bedivere came again to the king, and told him what he saw.[188]

GOLD ON THE HORIZON

The image of the upright sword in the water renews the associations between Reepicheep which began with his suggestion that the end of the world was like a round table. The narrator's comments on the mouse, as he departs (like Arthur) in a boat, bring those associations to a higher pitch:

> Then it vanished, and since that moment no one can truly claim to have seen Reepicheep the Mouse. But my belief is that he came safe to Aslan's country and is alive there to this day. As the sun rose, the sight of those mountains outside the world faded away. The wave remained but there was only blue sky behind it.[189]

This narrative caution, in which the author admits he does not know exactly what happened, is characteristic of various medieval writers including Malory. He is prone to hesitancy over some details, remarking that his sources do not specify a particular matter, or that there are different tales about the subject. In both tone and content the departure of Reepicheep evokes several lines in Malory's account of Arthur's end:

> Thus of Arthur I find never more written in books that be authorised, nor more of the very certainty of his death heard I never read, but thus was he led away in a ship wherein were three queens
>
> [...]
>
> Yet some men say in many parts of England that King Arthur is not dead, but had by the will of our Lord Jesu into another place; and men say that he shall come again, and he shall win the holy cross. I will not say it shall be so, but rather I will say: here in this world he changed his life. But many men say that there is written upon his tomb this verse: Hic jacet Arthurus, Rex quondam, Rexque futurus.[190]

OF DRAGONS AND SOLAR HEROES

As with other elements of the Arthurian material, Lewis has transposed the departure of King Arthur into a more celebratory key. Reepicheep's departure has its heart-rending side, but Lewis borrows the mystery rather than the melancholy of the episode. It is worth noticing that characters are not particularly identified with specific Arthurian knights or kings: Arthur's dream of being a dragon is given to Eustace, whilst his departure is given to Reepicheep. There is more a diffuse borrowing of images and episodes which enrich the symbolism of the novel.

SWELLING SAILS IN CASPIAN SEA ...

To explore the influence of knightly romance on *The Voyage of the Dawn Treader* further, I would like to turn to a later writer of chivalric tales. Edmund Spenser lived in Elizabeth's reign, but his genre and style deliberately evokes medieval romance. His multi-part (and unfinished) epic *The Faerie Queene* sets up a deeply intricate set of interlocking allegories which use the machinery of questing knights, wizards, strange beasts and distressed damsels to explore the spiritual, moral, religious and courtly virtues. Lewis wrote on Spenser in various of his critical works, and *The Voyage of the Dawn Treader* seems to have been influenced by Spenser's combination of episodic questing and moral allegory. One rather striking example can be found in *The Faerie Queene* when the knight Sir Guyon finds the allegorical figure Mammon in his lair. Mammon extols the power and glory of gold, but he is rebuked by the knight. Guyon describes the horrors and treasons which gold has caused, and mentions a notable sea in the process:

> Ne thine be kingdomes, ne the scepters thine;
> But realmes and rulers thou doest both confound,
> And loyall truth to treason doest incline;
> Witnesse the guiltlesse bloud pourd oft on ground,
> The crowned often slaine, the slayer cround,

GOLD ON THE HORIZON

> The sacred Diademe in peeces rent,
> And purple robe gored with many a wound;
> Castles surprizd, great cities sackt and brent:
> So mak'st thou kings, & gaynest wrongfull gouernement.
>
> Long were to tell the troublous stormes, that tosse
> The priuate state, and make the life vnsweet:
> Who swelling sayles in Caspian sea doth crosse,
> And in frayle wood on Adrian gulfe doth fleet,
> Doth not, I weene, so many euils meet.
> Then Mammon wexing wroth, And why then, said,
> Are mortall men so fond and vndiscreet,
> So euill thing to seeke vnto their ayd,
> And hauing not complaine, and hauing it vpbraid?[191]

The image of sails swelling to cross the Caspian Sea, connected with the way the desire for gold can cause treason and set people against each other, strongly suggests that Spenser is a key text for *Dawn Treader*. Elsewhere in the poem, a dragon flying down to do battle with a knight is described with an extended simile:

> His flaggy wings when forth he did display,
> Were like two sayles, in which the hollow wynd
> Is gathered full, and worketh speedy way:
> And eke the pennes, that did his pineons bynd,
> Were like mayne-yards, with flying canuas lynd,
> With which whenas him list the ayre to beat,
> And there by force vnwonted passage find,
> The cloudes before him fled for terrour great,
> And all the heauens stood still amazed with his threat.[192]

A dragon whose body is detailed in terms of sails, main-yards and canvas finds an echo in the *Dawn Treader* herself, a ship which possesses sails and yards but is shaped like a dragon. This is an imaginative trick which happens in a number of places in Narnia, when Lewis takes a metaphor and turns it inside out. Christ is accorded the title 'Lion of Judah' and Aslan is an actual lion; Eli addresses Samuel as 'my son' and says he didn't call him, whilst Lucy thinks she hears her father's voice. Here a dragon which looks like a ship becomes a ship which looks like a dragon. This way of making metaphors real and real things metaphorical is one of the characteristics of fantastical writing, according to the literary theorist Tveztan Todorov.[193] It is also extremely apt for the way these novels move the reader between our world and Narnia, unsettling their assumptions about what is real and what is fantastical.

Dragons provide another connection between *The Faerie Queene* and Lewis's novel when Spenser describes the sorcerer Archimago preparing to use magic to change his own shape:

> He then deuisde himselfe how to disguise;
> For by his mightie science he could take
> As many formes and shapes in seeming wise,
> As euer Proteus to himselfe could make:
> Sometime a fowle, sometime a fish in lake,
> Now like a foxe, now like a dragon fell,
> That of himselfe he oft for feare would quake,
> And oft would flie away. O who can tell
> The hidden power of herbes, and might of Magicke spell?[194]

This finds an echo in Eustace's predicament:

> But there was no good crying. He must try to crawl out from between the two dragons. He began extending his right arm. The dragon's fore-leg and claw on his right went through exactly the same motion. Then he thought he would try his left. The dragon limb on that side moved too.

GOLD ON THE HORIZON

> Two dragons, one on each side, mimicking whatever he did! His nerve broke and he simply made a bolt for it.
>
> There was such a clatter and rasping, and clinking of gold, and grinding of stones, as he rushed out of the cave that he thought they were both following him. He daren't look back. He rushed to the pool.[195]

The passing mention of a wizard who ran away from himself when he changed into a dragon is developed into part of the narrative in Lewis's novel. It also takes on a moral function, as part of Eustace's symbolic failure to recognise himself. The end of the youngster's sojourn as a dragon also has connections with the first book of *The Faerie Queene*. In Spenser's poem the climax of the first set of adventures involves a multi-day fight between the Redcrosse knight and the dragon. At one point the knight is struck backwards by his reptilian foe, but falls backwards into a well. This well, as the poem explains, has remarkable physical and spiritual powers:

> It fortuned (as faire it then befell)
> Behind his backe vnweeting, where he stood,
> Of aunciient time there was a springing well,
> From which fast trickled forth a siluer flood,
> Full of great vertues, and for med'cine good.
> Whylome, before that cursed Dragon got
> That happie land, and all with innocent blood
> Defyld those sacred waues, it rightly hot
> The well of life, ne yet his vertues had forgot.
>
> For vnto life the dead it could restore,
> And guilt of sinfull crimes cleane wash away,
> Those that with sicknesse were infected sore,
> It could recure, and aged long decay
> Renew, as one were borne that very day.

OF DRAGONS AND SOLAR HEROES

> Both Silo this, and Iordan did excell,
> And th'English Bath, and eke the german Spau,
> Ne can Cephise, nor Hebrus match this well:
> Into the same the knight backe ouerthrowen, fell.[196]

When the battle is rejoined the next morning, the dragon sees his enemy rising out of the well with his strength renewed:

> Out of the well, wherein he drenched lay;
> As Eagle fresh out of the Ocean waue,
> Where he hath left his plumes all hoary gray,
> And deckt himselfe with feathers youthly gay,
> Like Eyas hauke vp mounts vnto the skies,
> His newly budded pineons to assay,
> And marueiles at himselfe, still as he flies:
> So new this new-borne knight to battell new did rise.[197]

With this new vigour, the Redcrosse knight fights so powerfully that the narrator of the poem himself remarks that he is not sure exactly what made him so deadly:

> I wote not, whether the reuenging steele
> Were hardned with that holy water dew,
> Wherein he fell, or sharper edge did feele,
> Or his baptized hands now greater grew;
> Or other secret vertue did ensew;[198]

Once again there are remarkable parallels here which have been rearranged in the Narnian story. Eustace is also taken to a well, in his dragon form, and is renewed by his immersion in it. The metaphorical reference to the knight's 'baptized hands' in Spenser becomes more elaborate in Lewis's work, as his character is immersed in the water and has his dragonish elements stripped away. In *The Faerie Queene* the well clearly represents baptism as one aspect of its symbolism, but this becomes more focused in the story of Eustace. It also become more internal: Redcrosse rises from the water in order to kill the dragon in battle, whilst young Scrubb descends into the water in order to kill the dragon within himself.

These individual borrowings from *The Faerie Queene* point to a larger similarity between Spenser's epic and *The Voyage of the Dawn Treader*. The Elizabethan poet was very consciously using the images and episodes of medieval romance to produce an allegorical narrative. The book is entitled *The Faerie Queene, Disposed into Twelve Books, Fashioning Twelve Moral Virtues*, and a letter printed at the beginning referred to it as a 'continual Allegory, or dark Conceit' which was intended

> to fashion a gentleman or noble person in virtuous and gentle discipline: which for that I conceived should be most plausible and pleasing, being coloured with an historical fiction, the which the most part of men delight to read, rather for variety of matter than for profit of the ensample, I chose the History of King Arthur, as most fit for the excellency of his person, being made famous by many men's former works, and also farthest from the danger of envy and suspicion of present time.[199]

Spenser's work is layered with moral, religious, national and political allegories. To take one example: the first episodes concern a Redcrosse Knight, who battles a loathsome creature called Error and a dragon, and who undertakes a quest for a lady called Una but is separated from her after Archimago sends a spirit to him in a dream which appears to be Una but is full of lascivious suggestions. In this brief collection of elements, we might read Redcrosse as the human soul seeking after holiness and failing when it does not stay alongside the One Truth (Una). It could also be seen, however, as a religious allegory about the struggle of the Protestant Church against supposedly heretical other Churches, and as a national allegory about St George as a symbol of England battling against foreign powers. The episode involving the dream could even be read as a psychological allegory in which a nobleman has morally troubling thoughts about a courtly lady, and imputes his own guilt to her. Lewis writes extensively about Spenser in *The Allegory of Love*, and traces out different forms of symbol and allegory in *The Faerie Queene*. I believe that Spenser provided more than dragon metaphors and the Caspian sea for *Dawn Treader*: he furnished a symbolic world in which forms of allegory could cluster around heroic quests, and where moral, spiritual and psychological meaning could be dramatized at different moments. The quarrel at Deathwater Island, the ship's journey into the Darkness and Eustace's vision of Aslan, are all forms of allegory, but they emphasize different aspects of the mental, moral and spiritual worlds. The way *The Voyage of the Dawn Treader* shapes the world into a quest seem to owe a great deal to the 'dark Conceit' which Spenser wove amidst his knights and ladies.

THE RISING OF THE SUN

I have traced some moments when Arthurian romance, in its Malorian and Spenserian forms, seems to be strongly invoked by *The Voyage of the Dawn Treader*. Lewis's novel tends to take particular elements from each of them. Malory provides mysterious symbols and a particularly Arthurian flavour, whilst Spenser offers an allegorical method, telling metaphors and overlapping images. On a larger scale, the whole project of weaving Arthurian romance in a Narnian novel can also be read in the intellectual and literary context of the mid-twentieth century. The medieval romances are explicitly Christian in content; the Arthurian court are regularly mentioned as attending mass, celebrating Christian feasts and praying to the Christian God, whilst one of the greatest cycles of adventures concerns the quest for the Holy Grail. However, the interest in myth and comparative religion which developed in British and American culture in the nineteenth century produced a conviction that the chivalric romances were originally pagan. Or at least, that they contained the traces of pagan beliefs and practices. As the historian Ronald Hutton notes, '[a] major scholarly industry was developed to detect possible traces of paganism in the medieval Arthurian legend', with the scholar Edward Davies 'declaring that Arthur himself had been a sun-god' and 'between the mid nineteenth and the mid twentieth centuries first-rank academic authors on both sides of the Atlantic... devoted much energy to finding other such connections.[200] Hutton cites works like Davies' *The Mythology and Rites of the British Druids*, Sharman Loomis' *Celtic Myth and Arthurian Romance*, Alfred Nutt's *Studies in the Legend of the Holy Grail* and Jessie Laidlay Weston's *From Ritual to Romance* as classics in this niche of finding pagan material 'behind' the resolutely Christian narratives of the Arthurian tales. An example of this approach, in a very sophisticated form, can be found in Weston's exploration of the Grail legend. For her this cannot be simply a story about knights searching for one of the holiest relics in the Christian imagination, the cup at which Christ and his disciples drank at the Last Supper. For Weston, the answer to the Grail question involves three intermingled strands. An original set of mystical rituals, preserved as a story, which was taken over by Christianity, and later blended with elements of Celtic folk-tale. Her insistence that not everything in the Grail legends is traceable to Celtic sources is part of a conviction that it is not simply 'fairy tales' which have been 'Christianised', but the traces of a mystical union with the divine, and the rituals which that union involved.

OF DRAGONS AND SOLAR HEROES

At its root lies the record, more or less distorted, of an ancient Ritual, having for its ultimate object the initiation into the secret of the sources of Life, physical and spiritual. This ritual, in its lower, exoteric, form, as affecting the processes of Nature, and physical life, survives to-day, and can be traced all over the world, in Folk ceremonies, which, however widely separated the countries in which they are found, show a surprising identity of detail and intention. In its esoteric 'Mystery' form it was freely utilized for the imparting of high spiritual teaching concerning the relation of Man to the Divine Source of his being, and the possibility of a sensible union between Man, and God. The recognition of the cosmic activities of the Logos appears to have been a characteristic feature of this teaching, and when Christianity came upon the scene it did not hesitate to utilize the already existing medium of instruction, but boldly identified the Deity of Vegetation, regarded as Life Principle, with the God of the Christian Faith. Thus, to certain of the early Christians, Attis was but an earlier manifestation of the Logos, Whom they held identical with Christ.[201]

This passage displays several of the classic features of such theories about medieval romance. It asserts that narrative aspects of the texts are dim memories of religious rituals, and that those rituals can also be traced in the ceremonies and folk-dances of rural people. It believes that these rituals are evidence of a very ancient religious system which was once practised across the world, and that Christianity later imposed its own beliefs on this system. It also deduces that this religion involved a secret and mystical union with the divine, which was known to educated initiates, as well as an external set of rituals which were familiar to the less elevated. It has an emphasis on ritual and mystical experience, over theology or history, which is characteristic of many writers on paganism from this period.

GOLD ON THE HORIZON

Lewis took issue with this approach to medieval romance, most fully in a literary essay entitled 'The Anthropological Approach'. He criticized it as an inadequate way of reading texts, but one which also displayed mistaken assumptions about the nature and role of literature. He does admit that, if it is true, this method may be useful on the surface:

> It is clear that an anthropological statement (supposing it to be a true one) can often explain some detail in a text. Thus Gawain's property of growing stronger as the sun ascends can be explained as the last vestige of a myth about the sun-god.[202]

However, for Lewis this 'explanation' is only a technical fact about literary history. It cannot carry the freight of meaning and belief which he sees other critics attributing to it:

> The causal explanation of Gawain's peculiarity 'explains', in this other sense, nothing whatever. That peculiarity remains, in Malory's book, a complete irrelevance. Nothing leads up to it; nothing of any importance depends on it. Apart from it there is nothing divine and nothing solar about Gawain. All that he does, suffers, or says elsewhere would have exactly the same value if this odd detail had been omitted. The anthropological explanation may be true and it may have an interest of its own; but it cannot increase our understanding or enjoyment of one single sentence in the Morte.[203]

The particular literary critic he has in mind, named Speirs, made a case that mythical and pagan sources produced a general effect on the narrative:

> Mr Speirs maintains the literary relevance of such origins on two grounds. One is that they affect the poet; the other, that a knowledge of them affects the reader. After quoting the place

about the perilous fountain from Ywain and Gawain, he connects it conjecturally with a rain-making ritual. He then very properly asks what difference this makes to the poetry; especially since the poets may have known nothing about the ritual origin. Part of his answer is that, whether they knew the origin or not, 'they surely inherited with such episodes something of the traditional attitude of reverence towards them, a sense of their mystery, a sense too of the mystery of all life'.[204]

I have noted above the use which Lewis made of a mysterious fountain in a chivalric text, and the spiritual atmosphere which he used it to conjure. He is, however, unimpressed by Speirs' argument:

> But where is the evidence that ritual origins are the only or commonest source of such feelings or that such feelings always result from (even a forgotten) ritual origin? Might not the poet equally well be awed and mystified by a mere unexplained magic fountain such as this purports to be? Might he not have believed in such things? Is it not more probable he believed in them than that he cared about rain-rituals? Or, even without belief, might not the idea of perilous adventures in enchanted forests have moved him deeply? [205]

Lewis objects that this 'type of criticism ... always takes us away from the actual poem and the individual poet to seek the sources of their power in something earlier and less known' and claims that it has received a 'dolorous stroke' from the work of Professor Vinaver on Malory. For Lewis, all this deducing of pagan rituals which are residually present in stories of Christian knights cannot tell us anything meaningful about the text as we have it. It does, he speculates, have one major use: it apparently induces a feeling of awe and mystery in some modern people:

GOLD ON THE HORIZON

> At a great price (in the way of anthropological study) Mr Speirs obtains his freedom to respond deeply and solemnly to the romances; but earlier generations, including my own, were free born. We never thought of responding—never had power to respond—in any other way. The ferlies, simply for what they are shown to be in the texts, conquered us at once and have never released us. We stand amazed when our juniors think to interest us in the Grail by connecting it with a cauldron of plenty or a prehistoric burning glass, for the Grail as Chrétien or Malory presents it seems to us twenty times more interesting than the cauldron or the glass. [206]

In a twist of argument, Lewis suggests that literary critics like Speirs have not found a problem in the medieval romances which can only be explained by pagan rituals. They have found a problem in themselves which means they can only read medieval romances in the right spirit by inventing such rituals. Thus, the anthropological approach may serve a paradoxical purpose, if it is not mistaken for a genuine theory about the history of these texts, but instead treated as a means to recapture a spirit of mystery in some modern literary critics who cannot respond normally to chivalric romance:

> Now all these sensations are in my opinion pretty like those the authors meant to give you. The romancers create a world where everything may, and most things do, have a deeper meaning and a longer history than the errant knight would have expected; a world of endless forest, quest, hint, prophecy. Almost every male stranger wears armour; not only that there may be jousts but because visors hide faces. Any lady may prove a fay or devil; every castle conceal a holy or unholy mystery. The hero is a sort of intruder or trespasser; always, unawares, stumbling on to forbidden ground. Hermits

and voices explain just enough to let us know how completely he is out of his depth, but not enough to dissipate the overall mystery.[207]

In *The Voyage of the Dawn Treader* this process is reversed. Lewis picks up on images like the dolorous stroke and a mysterious fountain, but not in order to suggest that ancient pagan mysteries lie behind them. On the contrary, he does so in order to elaborate the Christian symbolism which the original texts insist upon. He even expands on the 'solar hero' imagery which supposedly pointed to pagan myth; as Michael Ward has pointed out at length, *Dawn Treader* is an extremely 'solar' novel. It is suffused with sun imagery; the sun catches Caspian's armour, Aslan appears as if the sun is shining on him, and the sun flashes on Octesian's arm-ring at Deathwater, amongst many other moments. Lewis has taken that favourite 'proof' that medieval romances are pagan, and made it a dominating image for his Christian quest story.

CHAPTER FOUR
THE QUEEN'S HONOUR

Once Eustace is back again in human form, the ship sails on. The voyagers encounter a vast but rather foolish sea serpent and an island with a pool which turns anything to gold (including people). They next arrive at a place which might either be called the island of the Dufflepuds, or the island of the magician, depending on how you look at things. Lucy faces tests of her outward courage, and of her inward integrity. I would like to highlight a thread which runs through *The Voyage of the Dawn Treader*, and which will be the topic of this chapter. Lucy's status as a queen is emphasized at various points in the novel, as is her heroism. It is Lucy who prevents the fight breaking out at the island where water turns things to gold, Lucy who prays to Aslan when they are lost in the darkness, and Lucy who undertakes the eerie journey to the magician's room to free the Dufflepuds. The fact that Lucy is a young queen in a book about a ship sailing to discover new worlds sets up resonances with part of the cultural imagination of Britain in the middle of the twentieth century: the so-called 'New Elizabethanism'. The tone for this chapter is set by an exchange which the talking mouse has with the invisible chief:

> 'We want something that little girl can do for us,' said the Chief Voice'
>
> [...]
>
> Little girl!' said Reepicheep. 'The lady is a queen.'
> 'We don't know about queens,' said the Chief Voice.[208]

During the early 1950s, when the first three Narnia novels

were published, many people in Britain found their imagination fired by the Elizabethan period. The nation had faced a long war, post-war economic austerity and a marked reduction in its position in the world. In this situation the young Princess Elizabeth became a focus for future hopes. The reigning monarch, King George VI, was growing older and seemed increasingly ill. During the late 1940s, his daughter Elizabeth undertook more and more of the public duties of the royal family. The British people began to turn their attention to what seemed inevitable: within the next few years the king would succumb to illness and Elizabeth would become queen whilst still in her mid-twenties. The fact that she would ascend the throne at such a relatively young age, and that she would become Queen Elizabeth II, provided a symbol for national aspirations. Many British people regarded the Elizabethan Age as a golden one: it was the era of Shakespeare, of the Book of Common Prayer, of the naval triumph against the Spanish Armada and the voyages of exploration undertaken by Walter Raleigh. The idea that there might be a young queen presiding over a second Elizabethan era encouraged people to hope that the same spirit of daring and achievement might emerge from Britain's post-war drabness. The newspapers of the early 1950s provide plenty of examples of this imagery. A record-breaking flight in a Canberra aeroplane was greeted as a 'Whirlaway Start To A New Elizabethan Age' by the *Daily Mirror*.[209] 'Where are the swashbucklers and daredevils, the men of Drake's calibre which will make the new Elizabethan Age as glorious as the old?' demanded the article, 'Are there any? Certainly. Two have already gone sailing across the sky to prove that Britain can still show the world how things are done'. It concluded triumphantly that the flight by Squadron-Leader L.C. De Vigne and Flight-Lieutenant Paul Hunt was proof that the pilots of British aeroplanes 'will see to it that the new Elizabethans are worthy of the old'. The analogy between the sailing expeditions of the sixteenth century and the air travel of the twentieth was a common one. Other writers compared the voyages of discovery in Elizabeth's reign to the first confirmed ascent of the summit of Mount Everest, which was made in 1953 by Edmund Hillary and Tenzing Norgay.

When George IV died in 1952, and Elizabeth became queen, this language of a New Elizabethan era echoed around the public square. It was probably even more powerful since people had been expecting it to happen, and already had the imagery and ideas to hand. The journalist and writer Philip Gibbs produced a book called *The New Elizabethans*, which gives a good flavour of this feeling:

> We look back to the Elizabethan era of the sixteenth century as our flowering time of genius, high adventure, and national spirit, and now that there is a second Queen Elizabeth beginning her reign many of us are inclined to take stock of ourselves and to compare our own character, conditions, manners, morals, and chances of a new blossoming, with those of our Elizabethan ancestors.[210]

In comparing the two periods, Gibbs stressed what seemed to him odd similarities between the sixteenth and twentieth centuries. For him, the Victorian era was a cultural and historical monument which obscured the continuities between the two Elizabethan periods:

> How do we compare, then, with our ancestors in the first Elizabethan era? Are we less cruel? What about all these young men with coshes who bash out the brains of old women? Are we less coarse? Some of our novelists are frank enough in their choice of words. Have we lost the spirit of our forefathers? The Battle of Britain and the little ships at Dunkirk, and the civilians in cities under air bombardment, answer that, though

they are now getting middle-aged. What of the younger crowd, those who for good or bad will carry on our history through the reign of the second Elizabeth – the boys and girls of sixteen to twenty-five or so?

It is this 'younger crowd' whom Gibbs writes about in the rest of his book, and in whom he places his hopes for Britain's return to greatness. There are, however, forces which seem to threaten the resurgence of this national spirit:

> What of our social conditions with their austerities – the meagre rations, the shortages in the shops, the tightness of money, the deliberate policy of liquidating the nobility and gentry of this land by ruthless taxation and the levelling down of all classes to one common mould? Are we losing our individualism and independence of character, asking to be pap-fed by a benevolent State? Are these the first steps to Communism and police control? Is our old quality of the spirit dying down into the white ash of a tired decrepitude? Or is the spirit of adventure still with us? Have we other dreams and visions to lead us on to new achievement? Can we save our souls, our songs, our humour, our laughter, even if we lose our Empire and our former wealth?[211]

This worry, from a conservative-leaning writer, that Britain was becoming too bureaucratic and quiescent has echoes in the plot of *Dawn Treader*. The socially progressive outlook, which I discussed in an earlier chapter, expressed itself in Eustace via his harping on about the British consulate and the legal writs he will issue to everyone when he gets a chance. It takes an even more sinister form in the bureaucratic slovenliness which rules in the Lone Islands. Governor Gumpas has an intricate system of forms and meetings, which prevents anything from actually happening and allows him to rule without any accountability or any benefit to the Lone Islanders. Indeed, it is this complex system of regulations and conventions which allows the slave trade to flourish in the absence of strong moral leadership.

The New Elizabethans provides an illuminating sense of how British culture was discussing the new era (or what it hoped was a new era.) As well as concentrating on the possibilities implicit in the young people of the nation, Gibbs emphasizes one particular group: young women. This is perhaps unsurprisingly, since the person who made New Elizabethanism possible as an idea was herself a young woman. Nonetheless, the book indulges in a remarkable rhapsody on young British womanhood:

> What of the women of today compared with those of the first Elizabethan age? An immediate thought might be that they have more freedom of speech and action, and that may well be; but it was only in a later and Puritanical time, and then later again, in the Victorian era, that the women of England were not supposed to be capable of saying 'Bo!' to a goose, and were assumed to be delicate and meek little creatures with dainty appetites, angelic souls, and a tendency to become hysterical if their sensibilities were affected.[212]

On the contrary, Gibbs insists, the 'first Elizabethan girls' can be found in Shakespeare's plays, such as Audrey in *As You Like It* who was 'a typical country wench who would return a slap for a stolen kiss', and Rosalind in the same play 'dressed as a boy in the Forest of Arden was a young lady of spirit whom one might meet in any Tudor hall'. Beatrice from *Much Ado About Nothing* shows off the 'keen wit' and 'sharp tongue' of Elizabethan women, whilst Juliet's nurse shows that they could be 'pretty coarse in their speech' lower down the social scale. The plays of Ben Jonson show the women of the 'markets, and fairs, and taverns' who were 'lusty, ribald, quick-tongued, laughter loving, hands-on-hip lasses and the counterparts of the Elizabethan men in their coarseness and good humour'.[213]

This strength of character and realistic outlook is paralleled, for Gibbs, in the women of the second Elizabethan era:

> In the last war, during the Blitz over London and many of our cities, the courage of the young girls, as often I saw, was equal if not superior to that of the men. I believe many of them were braver than men. I used to watch little typists and shop girls taking their lunch in the parks when the 'doodle bugs' came over ... They hardly turned their heads ... It is for the women and girls who went home from their job to the much-bombed suburbs for whom one's admiration goes out first. There they were in little rows of houses one brick thick, with slate or tiled roofs, useless as a shield against high explosives or incendiary bombs. There year after year, they defied the demons of the night with handbags packed by their bedsides in case they had to 'hop it' ... Some were afraid, no doubt. They weren't all heroines, I guess. But generally the women in wartime showed a super-natural courage which had to last a long time.
>
> ... So what now? Has that spirit died? Who can say so? The girls of this new Elizabethan era are the same young women only a little older, and their younger sisters are coming along merry and bright, ready to go anywhere and do anything, fighting their way down the tubes in rush-hour, or looking very tired but laughing when they are jolted together in a mass of home-going humanity.[214]

This account of the New Elizabethan girls, whether it was strictly historically accurate or not, throws light on several elements of *Dawn Treader*. It is striking that when Gibbs talks about girls in Elizabethan times, his first point of reference

THE QUEEN'S HONOUR

is Shakespeare, where he finds girls being adventurous and girls dressed in boys' clothes. Lucy slips into both these 'Shakespearean' roles as soon as she arrives in Narnia. The novel shows her being afforded every courtesy and honour as a queen of Narnia, but as Caspian remarks 'I'm afraid we have no women's clothes on board. You'll have to make do with some of mine'.[215] Lucy finds that the king's boots and shoes are too big for her, but she happily pulls on some baggy garments and decides to go barefoot on the planks.[216] She is in the same situation as the Rosalind mentioned by Gibbs, or Viola in *Twelfth Night*: the characteristically Shakespearean heroine dressed as a boy and setting out on an adventure.

The emphasis in *The New Elizabethans* on the personal bravery of the young women also finds an echo in Lucy's adventures on the island of the Dufflepuds. When she arrives at the magician's room and finds his spell book, she will face a number of moral trials, but on first undertaking the quest she needs physical courage. After all, the invisible Dufflepuds demand that she undertake a risky venture into the magician's house, which none of them are willing to ask of their wives or daughters, and they threaten to kill all the Narnians if she refuses. When she declares she will do it, support comes from Reepicheep. This might seem surprising, given how protective he is of his queen, but he explains:

> 'Her Majesty is in the right,' said Reepicheep. 'If we had any assurance of saving her by battle, our duty would be very plain. It appears to me that we have none. And the service they ask of her is in no way contrary to her Majesty's honour, but a noble and heroical act. If the Queen's heart moves her to risk the magician, I will not speak against it.'
>
> As no one had ever known Reepicheep to be afraid of anything, he could say this without feeling at all awkward. But the boys, who had all been afraid quite often, grew very red.[217]

Lucy's adventurous valour, at her own personal risk, chimes with the image Gibbs presents of British girls enduring the dangers of bombing with 'super-natural courage'. As a girl from 1950s Britain undertaking quests on a sailing ship in unknown waters, she seems to span the two eras which *The New Elizabethans* brings together.

IF HE WANTED TO SINGE THE KING OF SPANE'S BERD

The idea of the 'New Elizabethan Age' became so thoroughly part of public culture in the 1950s that many writers could refer to it casually or satirically, in the expectation that readers would know what they meant. In this decade the comic writer Geoffrey Willans wrote a series of columns, which were collected in books, known as the 'Molesworth' series. These purport to be the diaries, letters and opinions of a schoolboy called Nigel Molesworth, who attends a comically awful school called St Custard's. Tellingly, they were first published in a publication called *The New Elizabethan*. They provide a brilliant (and, to a certain sense of humour, unspeakably amusing) glimpse into British culture in the 1950s. In the process, they highlight the idea of the 'New Elizabethans'. Molesworth mentions the idea of New Elizabethanism in the first collection, *Down with Skool!*, where it appears during a discussion of science. An interest in scientific matters is clearly a distinctive feature, and he lists the ingenious inventions which the schoolboys have dreamed up. These include a space-ship, the 'plunket radio-controlled germ beam to atack all masters', a thermometer which can be used to simulate illness and a 'jet bowling attachment for criketers' which 'Fits on arm and delivers ball at mach 8'.[218] A later book, *How To Be Topp*, continues the theme of science as the hallmark of the New Elizabethan mind, declaring that conkers is played too conservatively and needs a modern approach:

THE QUEEN'S HONOUR

> As new elizabethans we must adventure with science i.e. select a new conker bombard it with uranium 238 (element 92) folow it with a beam of nitrogen atoms fired from a 60 inch cyclotron. If it stands this all the neutrons will hav gummed together in a nucleus. If it do not, turn the cyclotron on molesworth 2 or fotherington-tomas and see wot it do to them.[219]

This vision of the New Elizabethans as science-minded, future-looking heroes, as parodied in the image of schoolboys producing elaborately pointless inventions, takes a striking turn in the next Molesworth book, *Whizz For Atoms*. In one of its chapters, the schoolboy narrator imagines himself transported back in time and he sees what the world (and the school) was like in the first Elizabethan era. Rather than science, it is exploration and conquest which fires his imagination this time, as Molesworth comments that 'Aktually Drake was pritty tuough and did more or less as he liked espueshully if there were Spaniards about. Good Queen Bess was very keen on him in spite of the remonstrances of the king of spane who had a lisp like all Spaniards'.[220] There follows a vignette in which the King of Spain lisps and Queen Elizabethan pronounces the letter 's' as it is spelled in Elizabethan manuscripts:

> THE KING OF SPANE: I tha, beth, that thcoundrel drake hath thinged my berd agane.
> ELIZABETH: (wiping her fhoes on his cloke) La coz you furprise me you fimply fake me rigid.
> THE KING OF SPANE: Tith twithe thith week. Ith abtholutely off-thide.
> ELIZABETH: Off-fide? Where are your fectaclef? He was on-fide by fix yardf.
> THE KING OF SPANE: Yar-boo. Thend him off.
> ELIZABETH: Upon my foul tif clear you do not kno the rules of foccer.

> (Raleigh, the earl of essex, john and sebastian cabot join in the brawl with vulgar cries. Which match are you looking at? Pla the game, ruff it up ha-ha etc.)
> DON SEBASTIAN ORSINO JERETH DE LA FRONTERA (a courtier): How common![221]

The harking back to Drake as the quintessential Old Elizabethan strikes a distinct note of mid-century anxiety, given the implicit comparison with contemporary Britain and its reduced role in the world. Molesworth then imagines his hero brought into the Britain of the 1950s:

> They were certainly swashbukling adventurers in those days and life in general was tuougher than an end of term rag at skool. But it is all very well it is not the same today – I mean what would happen to Drake if he wanted to singe the king of spane's berd today?
> LOUDSPEAKER: Passengers by Golden Hind for Cadiz please report to the customs.
> OFICIAL: Hav you read this card? Hav you anything to declare?
> DRAKE (trembling): No.
> OFICIAL: No buble gum no spangles no malteaser? nothing in the nature of a weapon –
> DRAKE: Just this pike –
> OFICIAL: Did you buy that pike in Britain, Mr Drake? Hav you an export license? Hav you filled in form 3 stroke D stroke 907? Are you Mr Mrs or Miss? Do you possess a dog license?
> DRAKE (on his knees): Hav mercie.
> OFICIAL: Folow the blue lights to the place of execution.
> (A gold ingot fall from Drake's pocket and he crawls away blubbing. Oficial takes up the ingot. He is lawffing triumphantly the skool dog howls a skool sossage stands on its head.)
> THE CURTAIN FALLS SLOWLY[222]

Here Molesworth imagines a clash between the spirit of the Old Elizabethans and the bureaucratic modern world, in which the latter triumphs. *The Voyage of the Dawn Treader* stages something rather similar, in the person of Eustace. I mentioned above his demands that he be put ashore at the next suitable port, that the British consulate be informed of his situation, and his threats to embark on legal action against everyone. Then there is Governor Gumpas, who represents the bureaucratic impulse at its most extreme. Of course, neither of these characters succeed in their attempts to bring Narnia under a regime of forms and regulations. They would dearly like to do to Caspian and his comrades what the customs official does to Sir Francis Drake in Molesworth's daydream, but Gumpas has his tables overturned and Eustace is transformed into a dragon. Lewis and Willans are both dramatizing, in their different ways, an acutely-felt tension between the worlds of the two queens.

THE QUEEN AND HER COURTIER

Perhaps the most famous example of 'New Elizabethanism' in the arts was Benjamin Britten's opera *Gloriana*. It was commissioned to mark the coronation of the second Queen Elizabeth, and was performed for the first time at Covent Garden, at a special gala night which the royal family and numerous other dignitaries attended. As the composer Christopher Palmer commented, 'the intention [was] that the *first* Elizabethan era would be assisting at the birth of what was confidently expected to be the *second*'.[223] There is some debate over how the opera was received: many people claim it was a terrible failure at first, whilst others insist it was appreciated warmly. Whatever the response of those first audiences, it is certainly true that *Gloriana* was an unexpected opera to be presented to a newly-crowned queen. Peter Pears, who was the composer's partner and who took the male lead in the opera, remarked that 'what was hoped for by many was a kind of superior *Merrie England*. This story about an ageing monarch was considered quite unsuitable for the young Queen at the start of her reign'.[224] *Gloriana* dramatizes the relationship between Elizabeth I and the Earl of Essex, focusing on their stormy emotional relationship, his attempted rebellion and her signing of his death warrant for treason. Elizabeth appears as a complex and conflicted woman, possessed by personal desires and public duty. The (frustrated and unconsummated) love story between Elizabeth and Essex which appears in *Gloriana* was a major part of the public memory of the queen in the mid-twentieth century. William Plomer's libretto for Britten's opera was based upon an imaginative biography by Lytton Strachey entitled *Elizabeth and Essex: A Tragic History*. In 1952 there was a radio adaptation of the American playwright Maxwell Anderson's work *Elizabeth the Queen*, which also centred on the relationship between these two characters (in 1939 it had been adapted into a film as *The Private Lives of Elizabeth and Essex*).

Given the enthusiasm for things Elizabethan in this era, and the focus on the relationship between Elizabeth and Essex in works like Strachey's biography and Britten's opera, I would like to make one more speculation. It is not central to the connection between *The Voyage of the Dawn Treader* and the New Elizabethanism, but I would like to suggest that there is a distant echo of the queen and Essex in Lucy and Reepicheep. The first time the mouse is described, a great deal of stress is laid on his noble and courteous qualities, but this is combined with an odd emotional reaction in Lucy:

> You might call it – and indeed it was – a Mouse. But then it was a Mouse on its hind legs and stood about two feet high. A thin band of gold passed round its head under one ear and over

THE QUEEN'S HONOUR

> the other and in this was stuck a long crimson feather. (As the Mouse's fur was very dark, almost black, the effect was bold and striking.) Its left paw rested on the hilt of a sword very nearly as long as its tail. Its balance, as it paced gravely along the swaying deck, was perfect, and its manners courtly. Lucy and Edmund recognized it at once – Reepicheep, the most valiant of all the Talking Beasts of Narnia, and the Chief Mouse. It had won undying glory in the second Battle of Beruna. Lucy longed, as she had always done, to take Reepicheep up in her arms and cuddle him. But this, as she well knew, was a pleasure she could never have: it would have offended him deeply.[225]

The description here would fit portraits of Essex, with its feather, left hand on the hilt of a long sword, and gravely balanced pose. There is a portrait of the Earl, attributed to Nicholas Hillard or his school, in which he stands with his left hand on the hilt of a remarkably long sword whilst two horses display plumes in the background, and another one by Marcus Gheeraerts the Younger, in which he wears a startlingly scarlet suit of clothes, has his hand on his sword hilt, and has a feather in his hat. This is probably coincidence, though, since many figures of the time, such as Sir Philip Sidney and John Donne, were painted in a similar pose. The account of Reepicheep here does not so much recall a particular image as show the mouse as the quintessence of an Elizabethan gallant. As an aside, Lewis's use of the word 'courtly' is probably a pun which has lost almost all of its force in the decades between the publication of *Dawn Treader* and the present day. Describing someone as possessing 'courtly' manners in mid-century Britain meant that they were very polite and perhaps slightly old-fashioned in the way they behaved. It was not a consciously archaic term, but one which could reasonably be applied to modern people, even if it indicated they were a bit Victorian in their attitudes. Indeed, the Miss Marple short stories from which I quoted in a previous chapter include a moment when a doctor makes 'a courtly bow' in the direction of a guest, and another character is described as having 'charming manners – courtly – that's the word that describes him best. You never saw him ruffled or upset'.[226] Since 'courtly' is no longer generally in use to describe manners in this way, we would probably use the term 'formal' to indicate the kind of attitude and bearing it implies. This means that a potential slippage of meaning has been lost: I suspect in this passage, 'courtly' means 'formal in manners' but also contains its much older, literal meaning, 'belonging to the royal court'. It is an outward description of the Chief Mouse as a polite person which also smuggles in a more archaic significance, that he is a member of the Narnian court. This would bolster the feeling that here we have a queen encountering a favourite courtier. However, since both meanings of 'courtly' probably seem entirely archaic to most modern readers, the play on words is now inert.

It is Lucy's reaction to this figure from the court which goes further and potentially evokes Essex. We are told that as soon as she sees him, she wishes to take him in her arms; that she always feels this way but knows that 'it was a pleasure she could never have'. This is not to suggest that there is anything romantic between Lucy and Reepicheep, of course, but to note that she experiences an emotional pang because as a girl she longs to cuddle him, but as a queen she knows she cannot. It is striking that the intense devotion which the Chief Mouse shows to the queen (rather more so than to the kings at times) in the subsequent chapters of the novel, is requited here in another emotional key. Lucy has a strong emotional longing for Reepicheep, and quells it because it would be unsuitable to their positions and his dignity. At the very last moment, when they are saying farewell and it can have no further effect on either of them, she allows herself one liberty:

THE QUEEN'S HONOUR

> Then he took off his sword ('I shall need it no more,' he said) and flung it far away across the lilied sea. Where it fell it stood upright with the hilt above the surface. Then he bade them goodbye, trying to be sad for their sakes; but he was quivering with happiness. Lucy, for the first and last time, did what she had always wanted to do, taking him in her arms and caressing him. Then hastily he got into his coracle and took his paddle, and the current caught it and away he went, very black against the lilies.[227]

In a later chapter I will argue that the relationship between Caspian and Ramandu's daughter owes something to the courtship of Jason and Medea. There is no sorcery and infanticide in the Narnian version, though: it gestures towards the Greek prince and the witch, and then presents a happier echo of them. I would read Lucy and Reepicheep as carrying out the same kind of allusion: their intense emotional connection, some of which is inappropriate given their positions in Narnia, is acknowledged and then taken in another direction. Recognising the potential echo does make some sense of the way Reepicheep and Lucy are reframed in this novel, as the venturesome Queen and the dashing favourite courtier. It is difficult to ignore the fact that the first thing Lucy does on seeing Reepicheep is stop herself throwing her arms around him, and the second thing she does is get in the way of his fighting a duel, as happens in the opening scene of *Gloriana*. The version of Elizabeth and Essex presented in *The Voyage of the Dawn Treader* resolves the angst and tragedy presented by Strachey, Britten and others. Reepicheep only wants to protect the queen's honour, and Lucy is able to let him go as he seeks something greater than the glory of any queen.

Thus in this novel it seems that Lewis gives another twist to Lucy's character. She is always a major character – if not the main character – whenever she appears in a Narnia story, but she plays a number of different roles. In *The Lion, the Witch and the Wardrobe* she is a Daughter of Eve, in *Prince Caspian* she is a prophet and in *The Voyage of the Dawn Treader* she is a queenly adventurer. As a queen of a voyaging nation, attended by an infatuated rapier-wielding courtier on the deck of a sailing ship, she echoes the first Queen Elizabeth. As an English girl taking on the mantle of a monarch with pluck and daring, she echoes the hopes for the second Queen Elizabeth. Lucy stands between these two queens, reflecting the excitement and anxiety felt in Britain about how possible it might be to recover the 'Elizabethan' spirit in the modern world.

CHAPTER FIVE
OF WITCHES, FLEECES AND THE WINE-BRIGHT SEA

The *Dawn Treader* begins to glide oddly across the seas, once it has passed through a mysterious and terrifying darkness (which held memories of Coleridge's *Rime of the Ancient Mariner*.) New stars appear in the sky, and it seems at times as if they are sailing in a realm of fire. When they make landfall, the adventurers find a magnificent ruin with a feast laid out, but the only guests have been asleep for years. It is here that they meet Ramandu and his daughter, marking what the novel calls 'the beginning of the end of the world'.[228] Beyond this island is the last sea, the merpeople, the departure of Reepicheep in the direction of Aslan's country, and a meeting with a lamb. These last chapters show a blending of two ancient traditions. In a previous chapter I have discussed *The Voyage of the Dawn Treader* as a medieval romance; a narrative of adventure in which heroes make vows, follow quests and seek the holiest symbols of the Christian tradition. It is certainly useful to see the traces of Arthurian literature in the book. At first sight, however, a reader might easily see another form of adventure story in a novel about a group of friends who sail a boat from island to island, encountering strange creatures and magical challenges. These elements would very reasonably put a reader in mind of the Classical voyages

Sea voyages are part of the 'Elizabethan' air of parts of the novel, since amongst the most famous of Elizabeth's subjects were sea-farers like Francis Drake and Walter Raleigh. They are also characteristic of the Classical world, partly for geographical reasons; roaming and adventuring done in the Mediterranean region eventually ends up at the sea, and travel by boat is often the quickest way to connect two points (not to mention the quickest way to part characters in a shipwreck or introduce pirates to the story). The Classical tales of adventure and romance such as Longus' *Daphnis and Chloe* and Heliodorus' *Aethopica* involve copious sea-journeys. Indeed voyaging across the ocean is built into the literary DNA of Greek and Roman culture, since both looked back to the epics of Homer. *The Odyssey* is an account of a voyage home, and even though *The Iliad* takes place on land, much of it happens in a military encampment by the sea, and ships are a significant presence in the poem.

There are several moments at which *The Voyage of the Dawn Treader* seems to invoke a Homeric mood. The title of the novel (and the ship's name) sound like a kenning from Anglo-Saxon poetry. The word 'dawn', however, is also part of the one of the most famous Homeric formulae. These short phrases, often used as epithets for famous people or things, form one of the building blocks of oral epic poetry. The Ancient Greek phrase usually translated as 'rosy-fingered dawn' appears repeatedly in *The Odyssey*, as a way of referring to the rising of the sun. Lewis uses a very similar phrase when Eustace tells Edmund about the baptismal experience which turned him back into a human, and Edmund says it sounds as if he has met Aslan:

> 'But who is Aslan? Do you know him?'
>
> 'Well – he knows me,' said Edmund. 'He is the great Lion, the son of the Emperor-beyond-the-Sea, who saved me and saved Narnia. We've all seen him. Lucy sees him most often. And it may be Aslan's country we are sailing to.' Neither said anything for a while. The last bright star had vanished and though they could not see the sunrise because of the mountains on their right, they knew it was going on because the sky above them and the bay before them turned the colour of roses. Then some bird of the parrot kind screamed in the

> wood behind them, and they heard movements among the trees, and finally a blast on Caspian's horn. The camp was astir.
>
> Great was the rejoicing when Edmund and the restored Eustace walked into the breakfast circle round the camp fire.[229]

The sun is vital in *Dawn Treader*, as I have discussed in an earlier chapter, and here there is a striking moment of Classical and religious imagery. Edmund makes what would be called a Christological confession in our world, naming Aslan as saviour, and they do not see the sun rising, but they see its effects in the 'colour of roses' in front of them. In fact their first arrival on the island had a decidedly Homeric atmosphere, though it is less textually explicit than the roses of the dawn. After Eustace has sneaked off in order to avoid contributing to the work going on, the others complete their tasks and settle down to a meal:

> At that very moment the others were washing hands and faces in the river and generally getting ready for dinner and a rest. The three best archers had gone up into the hills north of the bay and returned laden with a pair of wild goats which were now roasting over a fire. Caspian had ordered a cask of wine ashore, strong wine of Archenland which had to be mixed with water before you drank it, so there would be plenty for all. The work had gone well so far and it was a merry meal.[230]

Goats are a staple food in *The Odyssey*, and wine which needs to be mixed with water is characteristic of the Classical world, rather than medieval or Renaissance feasts. The scene when Odysseus and his companions land on the Cyclopes' island includes rosy dawn, shooting goats and wine brought from the ship:

> As soon as Dawn appeared, fresh and rosy-fingered, we were delighted with what we saw of the island, and set out to

explore it. Presently the Nymphs, those children of Zeus, set the mountain goats on the move to ensure my companions a meal. Directly we saw them we fetched our curved bows and our long spears from the ships, separated into three parties, and began shooting at the goats; and in a short time the god had sent us plenty of game. When it was shared out, nine goats were allotted to each of the twelve ships under my command, but to me alone they made an allotment of ten.

So the whole day long till the sun set we sat down to rich supplies of meat and mellow wine, since the ships had not yet run dry of our red vintage. There was still some in the holds, for when we took the sacred citadel of the Cicones, every member of the company had drawn off a generous supply in jars.[231]

The *Odyssey* elements repeated in the *Dawn Treader*'s visit to the island suggest that even if Lewis did not have this particular scene in mind, he was producing a Homeric atmosphere. (It is even tempting to suggest a small joke, since the next line of the poem says that the Greek heroes could see the smoke rising from the Cyclopes' fires, and wisps of smoke are soon going to prove important for the Narnians ...)

A SHINING FLEECE

Having suggested a Homeric source for some details, I would like to point to another Classical epic of sea-voyaging: Apollonius' *Argonautica*. (I must acknowledge, with gratitude, that Emily Williams suggested to me a connection between the two texts. Indeed, she did more than suggest it, she raised the point week after week in meetings of Narnia Club, and made a persuasive case for it.) This is a much later poem than Homer's, written in Latin in the third century. As the title suggests, it tells the story of Jason and the Argonauts, on their quest for the

OF WITCHES, FLEECES AND THE WINE-BRIGHT SEA

Golden Fleece. The first suggestion that the Argonauts might be significant for *Dawn Treader* comes as soon as Caspian explains why they are at sea:

> I swore an oath that, if once I established peace in Narnia, I would sail east myself for a year and a day to find my father's friends or to learn of their deaths and avenge them if I could. These were their names – the Lord Revilian, the Lord Bern, the Lord Argoz, the Lord Mavramorn, the Lord Octesian, the Lord Restimar, and – oh, that other one who's so hard to remember.'
>
> 'The Lord Rhoop, Sire,' said Drinian.[232]

Any such list of exotic-sounding names in a Narnia novel is bound to set the reader wondering about their potential meanings. In a book called *The Voyage of the Dawn Treader* the name 'Lord Revilian' jumps out, since 'réveiller' is the French for 'to wake up', and the 'reveille' is the English word for a signal used to wake soldiers and tell them to begin their duties in the morning. (In true English fashion, it is almost always pronounced 'revalley' or 'reevelly'.) Thus Lord Revilian sounds like a lord who would be found around the time of dawn, or who might need waking. The Lord Mavramorn sounds as if he might also have something to do with rising suns, and a deeply speculative dive into etymology might connect his name with 'maverick-morn' and interpret his name as 'cattle of the sun', which is the name of an episode in *The Odyssey*. The Lord Bern's name is the same word as an Anglo-Saxon term for 'hero', which Tolkien used in a variant form for his character Beorn. The Lord Restimar might send a reader back to French again, since 'rester' means to stay and 'mer' is the sea; he may be a lord who enjoys sailing, or alternatively a lord who will never be brought back from his voyage. 'Octesian' could recall 'octo', the Latin word for

GOLD ON THE HORIZON

'eight'. The Roman system of time divided up the day and night into numbered 'hours', referring to times as 'the fourth hour' or 'the tenth hour' and so on. The eighth hour was around noon or one o'clock (depending on the time of the year), so the point at which the sun was at its height and most visible. In such a solar novel as *The Voyage of the Dawn Treader* the Lord Octesian might be named for the sunniest hour of the day. The name of Lord Rhoop suggests the poop deck, where the captain and naval officers would often stand. This rather speculative trawl through the potential meanings of the aristocratic Narnians whom Caspian is seeking – and some readers may feel they have just watched the scholarly equivalent of a drowning man clutching at straws – at least indicates that many of the elements which make up these names have some significance for the story. Taken as a whole they conjure an atmosphere of naval voyages and the sun on the sea. (Indeed, some readers may feel that this is the better way of interpreting the list of names; noting a syllable here and a sound there, which all add up to a general tone, rather than trying to analyse what individual names mean.) The last name is perhaps the most obvious: the Lord Argoz seems to be a direct reference to the Argo, the ship which gave its name to the Argonauts and the *Argonautica*.

The 'z' at the end suggests that there is also an echo of the renaissance term 'argosy', which meant a large merchant ship. This appears in two of Shakespeare's plays. One, unsurprisingly, is *The Merchant of Venice*:

> Antonio, you are welcome;
> And I have better news in store for you
> Than you expect: unseal this letter soon;
> There you shall find three of your argosies
> Are richly come to harbour suddenly[233]

OF WITCHES, FLEECES AND THE WINE-BRIGHT SEA

The other is *The Taming of the Shrew*:

> Two thousand ducats by the year of land!
> [Aside] My land amounts not to so much in all.-
> That she shall have, besides an argosy
> That now is lying in Marseilles road.
> What, have I chok'd you with an argosy?[234]

Thus the Lord Argoz has a renaissance, as well as a Classical, sound to his name. In both cases the word suggests voyaging and venturing. It signals from the first chapter that we might keep Jason and his companions in mind as the *Dawn Treader* continues her explorations. *The Argonautica* is most strongly recalled at the other end of the novel, in the closing chapters. When the adventurers arrive at Ramandu's island, a particular detail about him stands out:

> Slowly the door opened again and out there came a figure as tall and straight as the girl's but not so slender. It carried no light but light seemed to come from it. As it came nearer, Lucy saw that it was like an old man. His silver beard came down to his bare feet in front and his silver hair hung down to his heels behind and his robe appeared to be made from the fleece of silver sheep. He looked so mild and grave that once more all the travellers rose to their feet and stood in silence.[235]

Amidst all the light and the shining, the narrator mentions that Ramandu's garment looks as if it is made from silver fleece. Caspian and his companions have met the equivalent of Aeëtes, the king who possessed the Golden Fleece which was the entire purpose of the Argonauts' quest. Any mention of shining fleece reignites the association which started with the name of Lord Argoz, and continued more mutedly through the shape of the island-hopping narrative. Ramandu's daughter also provides echoes of the *Argonautica*, since her appearance is so impressive, but Edmund retains some suspicions about her:

> Edmund, who had been looking more and more uncomfortable for the last few minutes, now spoke.
>
> 'Look here,' he said, 'I hope I'm not a coward – about eating this food, I mean – and I'm sure I don't mean to be rude. But we have had a lot of queer adventures on this voyage of ours and things aren't always what they seem. When I look in your face I can't help believing all you say; but then that's just what might happen with a witch too. How are we to know you're a friend?'
>
> 'You can't know,' said the girl. 'You can only believe – or not.' [236]

The reference to a witch could be Edmund's uneasy memories from his first adventures in Narnia. *The Lion, the Witch and the Wardrobe* tells how he was beguiled by the White Witch, and betrayed his siblings to her, after she gave him magical food to eat. Since he has just seen the knife used to kill Aslan on the Stone Table, heard a story about betrayal and is being offered apparently enchanted food, it might not be unreasonable for him to feel he has fallen into this trap before. However, the reference to witches has a Classical echo as well. When the Argonauts arrived at their destination, Colchis, they were faced with the task of persuading King Aeëtes to give Jason the Golden Fleece. They were helped in their plans by the king's daughter Medea, who had fallen in love with their leader. The love story of Jason and Medea is extremely bleak and angst-ridden, since it involves her betraying her father for Jason's sake and killing her brother to help him escape. It culminates in him abandoning her for another princess, and her killing their children in revenge. Medea was also famous for being

OF WITCHES, FLEECES AND THE WINE-BRIGHT SEA

a witch and priestess of Hecate, a goddess associated with sorcery. Apollonius refers repeatedly to this aspect of her character, at one point depicting her in mid-spell casting:

> with such beguiling words she scattered to the air and the breezes her witching charms, which even from afar would have drawn down the savage beast from the steep mountain-height.[237]

At another, the adventurers discuss the possibility of bringing her over to their side, specifically mentioning her magical abilities:

> then Argus addressed Jason with these words: 'Son of Aeson, thou wilt despise the counsel which I will tell thee, but, though in evil plight, it is not fitting to forbear from the trial. Ere now thou hast heard me tell of a maiden that uses sorcery under the guidance of Hecate, Perses' daughter. If we could win her aid there will be no dread, methinks, of thy defeat in the contest.[238]

This seems to set up another connection with the *Argonautica*, as the voyagers meet a young woman whose father possesses a shining cloak of fleece, and who is herself momentarily suspected of witchcraft. Of course Ramandu's daughter is not a witch, as Reepicheep proves by tucking into the banquet without any ill effects. The mention of sorcery has the double effect of recalling Medea to the mind of a reader who has been following the connections with the Argonauts, and of marking how distinctly different this young woman will turn out to be. Her story continues to develop in parallel with Medea, since she too falls in love with the leader of the sea-adventurers, but once again it has a happier tone, as we are told parenthetically:

GOLD ON THE HORIZON

Only two more things need to be told. One is that Caspian and his men all came safely back to Ramandu's Island. And the three lords woke from their sleep. Caspian married Ramandu's daughter and they all reached Narnia in the end, and she became a great queen and the mother and grandmother of great kings.[239]

MILK AND WOOL

These allusions to the *Argonautica* are combined, in a typically Lewisian way, with a strand of Biblical imagery. Just as the romp across Narnia with Aslan and the Classical divinities in *Prince Caspian* combines imagery from the Gospels and Ovid, the episodes here layer symbolism across each other. As ever with Lewis, the differences are as interesting as the similarities, once a literary echo is recognized. Ramandu does not bear a Golden Fleece, but a silver one. I suspect that he does so in order to emphasize that he is not the final goal of their quest. Silver is extremely valuable and shiny, but it is almost always ranked as second to gold. (The exception that springs to mind is in dealing with werewolves, and Caspian might have found a silver weapon more useful than a golden one beneath Aslan's How, but that matter is dealt with in another tale.) I suspect that Ramandu's fleece is silver to allow the adventurers, and readers, to marvel at him, but still retain a sense that this is not the most glorious light possible. The moon provides an analogy, as a celestial body which shines with silver light, but which is actually reflecting the light from the sun. After all, the adventurers are going to encounter another character who bears a fleece, though the narrator never mentions that word again:

> But between them and the foot of the sky there was something so white on the green grass that even with their eagles' eyes they could hardly look at it. They came on and saw that it was a Lamb.

OF WITCHES, FLEECES AND THE WINE-BRIGHT SEA

> 'Come and have breakfast,' said the Lamb in its sweet, milky voice. Then they noticed for the first time that there was a fire lit on the grass and fish roasting on it. They sat down and ate the fish, hungry now for the first time for many days. And it was the most delicious food they had ever tasted.[240]

The appearance of the silver fleece (or something which looks like it) on Ramandu's back prepares the way for the arrival of the Lamb. Lewis is dovetailing two similar image systems into each other within Narnia: the Classical myth of Jason and the Golden Fleece, and the Christian tradition of describing Jesus as the Lamb of God. The capital letter used for the Lamb's name in the texts indicates that this is no ordinary pastoral creature, and the way the companions meet the Lamb echoes another meal of fish on a shore. One of Jesus' appearances to his disciples after the resurrection involved a stranger telling them to cast their fishing nets on the other side of the boat. When they had done so, and the net was bursting full of fish, they brought the boat to shore:

> As soon then as they were come to land, they saw a fire of coals there, and fish laid thereon, and bread. Jesus saith unto them, Bring of the fish which ye have now caught. Simon Peter went up, and drew the net to land full of great fishes, an hundred and fifty and three: and for all there were so many, yet was not the net broken.
> Jesus saith unto them, Come and dine. And none of the disciples durst ask him, Who art thou? knowing that it was the Lord. Jesus then cometh, and taketh bread, and giveth them, and fish likewise. This is now the third time that Jesus shewed himself to his disciples, after that he was risen from the dead.
> (John 21:9-14)

The details of fire and fish, and the invitation to come and have a meal, establish the parallels between these scenes.

GOLD ON THE HORIZON

Even here, Lewis is swapping imagery around, since Jesus is not referred to by the title of Lamb in this passage. It is a title which appears strikingly in the first chapter of John's Gospel, when John the Baptist uses it to describe Jesus:

> The next day John seeth Jesus coming unto him, and saith, Behold the Lamb of God, which taketh away the sin of the world.
>
> This is he of whom I said, After me cometh a man which is preferred before me: for he was before me.
>
> (John 1:29-30)

Jesus' identity as 'lamb' is a crucial part of the way John's Gospel presents him, linking him to the temple sacrifices and the killing of lambs at Passover. It is in the book of Revelation, though, at the end of the Bible, that a character called 'the Lamb' appears, who is clearly Christ. This figure is glorified by everyone in heaven:

> And I beheld, and I heard the voice of many angels round about the throne and the beasts and the elders: and the number of them was ten thousand times ten thousand, and thousands of thousands; Saying with a loud voice, Worthy is the Lamb that was slain to receive power, and riches, and wisdom, and strength, and honour, and glory, and blessing. And every creature which is in heaven, and on the earth, and under the earth, and such as are in the sea, and all that are in them, heard I saying, Blessing, and honour, and glory, and power, be unto him that sitteth upon the throne, and unto the Lamb for ever and ever. And the four beasts said, Amen. And the four and twenty elders fell down and worshipped him that liveth for ever and ever.
>
> (Rev. 5:11-14)

Thus the Narnian Lamb both appears in a similar situation to Jesus in the Gospel episode (and speaks similar words), he also occupies a similar position to the biblical Lamb. He is a figure who appears at the end of the world. The reference to the Lamb's 'sweet, milky voice' draws in other biblical images. The promised land is referred to in the Hebrew Bible as a land of milk and honey; 'If the Lord delight in us, then he will bring us into this land, and give it us; a land which floweth with milk and honey' (Num. 14:8). This suggests the spot they have reached might be the goal of the journey, the place that Aslan has promised them. Sweetness and milkiness would identify the Lamb as the end of their quest. At the same time, the milky voice gestures towards another quest which the Pevensies will have to undertake. In the Epistle to the Hebrews, milk is a symbol of those who have not yet come to maturity:

> [Christ] became the author of eternal salvation unto all them that obey him; called of God an high priest after the order of Melchisedec.
> Of whom we have many things to say, and hard to be uttered, seeing ye are dull of hearing. For when for the time ye ought to be teachers, ye have need that one teach you again which be the first principles of the oracles of God; and are become such as have need of milk, and not of strong meat. For every one that useth milk is unskilful in the word of righteousness: for he is a babe. But strong meat belongeth to them that are of full age, even those who by reason of use have their senses exercised to discern both good and evil.
>
> (Heb. 5: 9-14)

Yet another scriptural echo is suggested by the presence of a lion and a lamb in one person: Isaiah's prophecies that at the end of the world fierce and gentle creatures will lie down together. When the Lamb reveals itself as Aslan, the lion tells them that this is not how they will reach his country. They

GOLD ON THE HORIZON

must return to our world, and they will not come back to Narnia.

> 'You are too old, children,' said Aslan, 'and you must begin to come close to your own world now.'
>
> 'It isn't Narnia, you know,' sobbed Lucy. 'It's you. We shan't meet you there. And how can we live, never meeting you?'
>
> 'But you shall meet me, dear one,' said Aslan.
>
> 'Are – are you there too, Sir?' said Edmund.
>
> 'I am,' said Aslan. 'But there I have another name. You must learn to know me by that name. This was the very reason why you were brought to Narnia, that by knowing me here for a little, you may know me better there.'[241]

The lamb with the 'milky voice' becomes the lion who tells them they are nearing maturity, and must seek him in another way. They must give up milk for strong meat. As elsewhere in Narnia, Lewis layers sets of symbols over each other. Here the Classical voyages of the *Odyssey* and the *Argonautica* are brought together with the Christian seeking of God. The shining fleece which the Argonauts set out to find becomes a sign which points to Christ as Lamb of God. What the voyagers gain is not a powerful magic item or a collection of treasure, but a glimpse of the glory beyond the world itself. If the delving of *Prince Caspian* kept suggesting to the readers that there was something deeper and more ancient beneath the stone circles and the barrows, then the voyaging of *Dawn Treader* suggests to them that there is something further and brighter beyond the horizon. For Lucy and Edmund that quest will take them in another direction, and here the echoes of Odysseus have a quiet irony. As they beached their ship on unknown islands, as they ate goats hunted with well-strung bows, as they mixed wine with water and watched the roses

OF WITCHES, FLEECES AND THE WINE-BRIGHT SEA

of the dawn give a sign that some bright god was near; as they carried out all these Homeric actions, they did not ever quite realize the story they were in. For the whole tale of *The Odyssey* is a voyage home.

ENDNOTES

1. Richard W. Schoch *Shakespeare's Victorian Stage* (Cambridge University Press, 1998) P.1; Robin Gilmour, *The Victorian Period: The Intellectual and Cultural Context of English Literature, 1830-1890* (Routledge, 1993) p. 1, 25
2. Lewis, *Caspian*, p. 23
3. Farah Mendleson and Edward James, *A Short History of Fantasy* (Middlesex University Press, 2009, repr. 2012, ebook) p.95
4. Enid Blyton, *Third Year at Malory Towers*, p. 35
5. Blyton, *Third Year*, pp.89-90
6. The texts of 'The Ruin' and 'The Wanderer' in this chapter are excerpted from the edition provided in *A Choice of Anglo-Saxon verse* by Richard Hamer (Faber, 1970). The translations are based on Hamer, but modified from other versions consulted over the years, and by my own much less skilful word-choices.
7. Lewis, *Caspian*, p. 21-2
8. Lewis, *Caspian*, p. 28
9. Lewis, *Caspian*, p. 18
10. Lewis, *Caspian*, p. 28-9
11. Lewis, *Caspian*, p. 30
12. Lewis, *Caspian*, p. 30-1
13. Lewis, *Caspian*, p. 82-3
14. Lewis, *Caspian*, p. 137
15. Lewis, *Caspian*, p. 137
16. *Hull Daily Mail*, 31st July, 1939
17. The text of *Beowulf* quoted here is from Michael Swanton's edition (1978, rev. 1997), though, as with the elegies, the translation is based on Swanton's prose translation with modifications from other sources and my own meddling.
18. Kenneth Grahame, *The Wind in the Willows* (1908, repr. Harper Perennial 2010, ebook), pp. 54-55
19. *Willows*, p. 55
20. Lewis, *Caspian*, p. 149
21. See Ronald Hutton, *The Triumph of the Moon*, p. 39
22. In this book I will quote from the Authorized Version of the Bible (or AV, also known as the King James Bible), unless noted otherwise. This is not because I advance the AV as the best version, or because Lewis was himself a proponent of it above later translations, but because it was the version which Lewis and his contemporaries would have been steeped in. For better or worse, it is the AV which provided the Biblical text as it

GOLD ON THE HORIZON

existed in the mind of Jane Austen, Anthony Trollope and Agatha Christie, and the majority of literary allusions to the Bible in Lewis's era use its wording.

23 As I understand I, this is an identity which rests similarly on a distinction between national groups in the past, and which prides itself on a hard-bitten, stalwart character which might equally express itself in poaching and military service. We might imagine an extra couplet on this topic: 'Don't hinder their fiddles or banjos, a wise Norman lets bluegrass thrive/ If ever the hollows fall silent, you'll never leave Harlan alive.'
24 *Gloucester Citizen*, 12th January 1922
25 See *Gloucestershire Echo*, 21st July 1933, and *Cheltenham Chronicle*, 18th August, 1934.
26 C. S. Lewis, *Prince Caspian* (Geoffrey Bles, 1951, repr. Lion, 1987), p. 50
27 Lewis, *Caspian*, p.56-7
28 Shakespeare, *Hamlet*, 1.5.796-813
29 Lewis, *Caspian*, p. 36-7
30 Lewis, *Caspian*, p. 137
31 Lewis, *Caspian*, pp. 48-9
32 Shakespeare, *Hamlet*, 1.1.34-9
33 Shakespeare, *Hamlet*, 1.1.111-24
34 Lewis, *Caspian*, p.71-2
35 Shakespeare, *Hamlet*, 2.2.114, 2.2.138
36 Lewis, *Caspian*, p. 11
37 Alan Jacobs, 'The Chronicles of Narnia', p.274
38 C. S. Lewis, *Mere Christianity* (1952, repr. 2007, ebook), p.47
39 Lewis, *Caspian*, pp.120-1
40 Lewis, *Caspian*, p.126
41 Lewis, *Caspian*, p. 122
42 Lewis, *Caspian*, p. 121
43 Cecil Sharp, *The English Country Dance Book* (1909), available online at https://round.soc.srcf.net/dances/cdb, n.pag
44 Sharp, *Dance*, n.pag.
45 Elsie J. Oxenham, *Two Joans at the Abbey* (1945, repr. 1950), p.217-8.
46 Lewis, *Caspian*, p. 122
47 Hugh Stewart, *The Elements of English Country Dance* (1998), online at https://round.soc.srcf.net/dances/elements, n.pag.
48 E. M. W. Tillyard, *The Elizabethan World Picture* (1943, repr. 1998), pp. 33-4
49 Tillyard, *Picture*, pp. 35-6
50 Tillyard, *Picture* p. 36
51 Lewis, *Caspian*, p. 121
52 Lewis, *Caspian*, p. 122
53 Lewis, *Caspian*, p. 122
54 Lewis, *Caspian*, p. 124
55 Tillyard, *Picture*, pp. 109-10
56 Tillyard, *Picture*, p .111
57 Tillyard, *Picture* pp. 112-3
58 Lewis, *Caspian*, p. 124
59 Lewis, *Caspian*, p. 125
60 Lewis, *Caspian*, pp. 27-8

ENDNOTES

61 Henry Rider Haggard, *King Solomon's Mines* (1885, repr. ebook), p.173
62 Lewis, *Caspian*, p.26
63 Lewis, *Caspian*, p.28
64 Rider Haggard, *Mines*, p.162-3
65 Rider Haggard, *Mines*, p.163-4
66 1 Kings, 10: 18-23
67 Lewis, *The Lion, the Witch and the Wardrobe*, p.97
68 Lewis, *Caspian*, p.146
69 Rider Haggard, *Mines*, pp. 178-9
70 Rider Haggard, *Mines*, pp. 91-2
71 Lewis, *Caspian*, pp. 82-3
72 Lewis, *Caspian*, p. 139
73 Rider Haggard, *Mines*, p. 91
74 Lewis, *Caspian*, p.143
75 Rider Haggard, *Mines*, p. 72
76 Rider Haggard, *Mines*, pp. 106-7
77 Rider Haggard, *Mines*, p. 113
78 Rider Haggard, *Mines*, p. 113
79 Rider Haggard, *Mines*, p. 113
80 Rider Haggard, *Mines*, pp. 113-4
81 Rider Haggard, *Mines*, p .91
82 Lewis, *Caspian*, p. 148
83 Rider Haggard, *Mines*, p. 7
84 Rider Haggard, *Mines*, p. 34
85 Rider Haggard, *Mines*,p. 121
86 Lewis, *Caspian*, pp. 26-7
87 Lewis, *Caspian*, p. 30
88 Lewis, *Caspian*, pp. 30, 32
89 Lewis, *Caspian*, p. 93
90 Lewis, *Caspian*, p. 162
91 Thomas Hughes, *Tom Brown's School Days* (1857, repr. Penguin 2004), p. 239
92 Hughes, *School Days*, p. 240
93 Lewis, *Caspian*, p. 165
94 Lewis, *Caspian*, p. 166
95 Hughes, *School Days*, p. 240
96 Lewis, *Caspian* p. 165
97 Hughes, *School Days,* pp. 124-5
98 Hughes, *School Days* pp. 125-6
99 Hughes, *School Days* pp. 67-8
100 Lewis, *Caspian*, p. 11
101 Lewis, *Caspian*, p. 50
102 Hughes, *School Days* pp. 21-2
103 Hughes, *School Days*, p. 22
104 Hughes, *School Days*, p. 24-5
105 Hughes, *School Days*, p. 27
106 Hughes, *School Days*, p. 27-8
107 Hughes, *School Days*, p. 28
108 Hughes, *School Days*, p. 28

GOLD ON THE HORIZON

109 Lewis, *Caspian*, pp. 173-4
110 Lewis, *Caspian*, pp. 172-3
111 Ovid, *Metamorphoses*, tr. Mary Innes (1955, repr Penguin 1995), p. 319
112 Lewis, *Caspian*, p. 171
113 Ovid, *Metamorphoses*, p. 47
114 Ovid, *Metamorphoses*, p. 43
115 K. Sarah-Jane Murray and Matthew Boyd, *The Medieval French Ovid Moralisé: An English Translation* (2023), p. 187
116 Murray and Boyd, *Ovid*, pp. 175-6
117 Murray and Boyd, *Ovid*, p. 176
118 Murray and Boyd, *Ovid*, p. 176
119 Murray and Boyd, *Ovid*, p. 176
120 The text of Henryson here is taken from David J. Parkinson's edition of the complete works (2010, ebook), with translation my own, drawing on Parkinson and other editions.
121 C. S. Lewis, *The Discarded Image* (1964, repr. 2013, ebook), p. 11
122 Lewis, *Discarded*, p. 11
123 C. S. Lewis, *The Voyage of the Dawn Treader* (1952, repr. HarperCollins 2013, ebook), pp. 9-10
124 Lewis, *Treader*, p. 10
125 Lewis, *Lion*, p. 97
126 Lewis, *Lion*, p. 41
127 Lewis, *Lion*, p. 66
128 Lewis, *Lion*, p. 66
129 Lewis, *Lion*, p. 85
130 Lewis, *Caspian*, p. 52
131 Lewis, *Caspian*, p. 64
132 Lewis, *Caspian*, pp. 64-5
133 Dorothy L. Sayers and Robert Eustace, *The Documents in the Case* (1930), p.29-30
134 Lewis, *Treader*, p. 1
135 Agatha Christie, *Miss Marple and Mystery: The Complete Short Stories* (various repr. 2008, ebook), p.473
136 Christie, *Marple*, p. 476
137 Anthony Powell, *A Dance to the Music of Time: Spring* (1952, repr. In collected ed. 1997, ebook), pp. 246-7
138 Powell, *Dance*, p.250
139 George Orwell, *The Road to Wigan Pier* (1937, repr. 2005, ebook), p. 114
140 Orwell, *Wigan*, p. 114
141 Orwell, *Wigan*, p. 114
142 Orwell, *Wigan*, p. 114-5
143 Orwell, *Wigan*, p. 145
144 Evelyn Waugh, *Brideshead Revisited* (1945, repr. 2016, ebook) p. 6
145 Waugh, *Brideshead*, p. 7
146 Waugh, *Brideshead*, p. 7
147 Lewis, *Treader*, p. 36
148 Lewis, *Treader* p. 41
149 Lewis, *Treader* p. 42
150 Lewis, *Treader* p. 7

ENDNOTES

151 *The Oxford English Dictionary*, oed.com, 'gumph'
152 Dictionaries of the Scots Language/ Dictionars o the Scots Leid, dsl.ac.uk, 'gumphy'
153 C. S. Lewis, *The Discarded Image* (Cambridge University Press, 1964, repr. 2012, ebook), p.34
154 Lewis, *The Allegory of Love*, p. 127
155 Lewis, *Image*, p. 86-7
156 C. S. Lewis, *The Allegory of Love* (Cambridge University Press, 1961, repr. 2012, ebook), p.123
157 Lewis, *Allegory*, p.124
158 As a footnote, given the fact that Lewis is translating Alanus to give the correct literary impression – one of empty verbosity – I cannot avoid speculating that the use of 'carriage' in his translation might be an echo of *Hamlet*. When the courtier Oaric comes to discuss the arrangements for the fatal fencing match at the end of the play, Hamlet complains that he is so wordy and elaborate that his speech cannot be understood. Their dialogue involves a quibble over the meaning of the very word 'carriage':

> OSRIC The King, sir, hath wagered with him six Barbary
> horses, against the which he has impawned, as I
> take it, six French rapiers and poniards, with their
> assigns, as girdle, hangers, and so. Three of the
> carriages, in faith, are very dear to fancy, very
> responsive to the hilts, most delicate carriages, and
> of very liberal conceit.
> HAMLET What call you the 'carriages'?
> HORATIO I knew you must be edified by the margent
> ere you had done.
> OSRIC The carriages, sir, are the hangers.
> HAMLET The phrase would be more germane to the
> matter if we could carry a cannon by our sides. I
> would it might be 'hangers' till then. But on. Six
> Barbary horses against six French swords, their
> assigns, and three liberal-conceited carriages—
> that's the French bet against the Danish.

159 Lewis, *Allegory*, p. 125
160 p. 28
161 Lewis, *Treader*, p. 28
162 Lewis, *Treader*, p. 28
163 Lewis, *Treader*, p. 29
164 Lewis, *Treader*, p. 29
165 George Orwell, 'Politics and the English Language', repr. online by the Orwell Foundation, https://www.orwellfoundation.com/the-orwell-foundation/orwell/essays-and-other-works/politics-and-the-english-language/, n.pag.
166 Lewis, *Treader*, p. 29
167 Orwell, 'Politics', n.pag.
168 Lewis, *Discarded*, p. 11

169 Lewis, *Discarded*, p. 11
170 Lewis, *Discarded*, p. 9
171 Lewis, *Discarded*, p. 9
172 Lewis, *Treader*, pp . 13-4
173 Lewis, *Treader*, p. 21
174 Lewis, *Treader*, pp. 27-8
175 Lewis, *Treader*, p. 27
176 Lewis, *Treader*, p. 6
177 Lewis, *Caspian*, p. 34
178 Lewis, *Treader*, p.120
179 Lewis, *Treader*, p. 11
180 Sir Thomas Malory, *Le Morte D'arthur*, ed. and modernized A.W. Pollard (1921, repr. 2020, ebook) p. 813
181 Malory, *Morte*, p. 208
182 Malory, *Morte*, p. 318
183 Malory, *Morte*, p. 237
184 Malory, *Morte*, p.237-8
185 Malory, *Morte*, p.114
186 Lewis, *Treader*, p.104
187 Lewis, *Treader*, p. 104-5
188 Malory, *Morte*, p. 1291
189 Lewis, *Treader*, p. 128
190 Malory, *Morte*, p. 1293-4; p. 1295
191 Edmund Spenser, *The Faerie Queene*, eds. Abraham Stoll and Erik Gray (2008), p.102
192 Spenser, *Faerie*, p. 177
193 See Tveztan Todorov, *The Fantastic: A Structural Account of a Literary Genre*, for a fuller account
194 Spenser, *Faerie*, p. 26
195 Lewis, *Treader*, p. 44
196 Spenser, *Faerie*, p. 183
197 Spenser, *Faerie*, p. 184
198 Spenser, *Faerie*, p. 185
199 Spenser, *Faerie*, p. 205
200 Ronald Hutton, *Pagan Britain* (Yale University Press) pp. 533-4
201 Jessie Laidlay Weston, *From Ritual to Romance* (Cambridge University Press, 1920), 191-2
202 C. S. Lewis, 'The Anthropological Approach', in *Selected Literary Essays* (Cambridge University Press, 1961, repr. Canto 2012, ebook), p. 399
203 Lewis, *Selected*, pp. 399-400
204 Lewis, *Selected*, p. 404
205 Lewis, *Selected*, pp. 404-5
206 Lewis, *Selected*, p. 407
207 Lewis, *Selected*, p. 409
208 Lewis, *Treader*, p. 71
209 *The Daily Mirror*, 20th February, 1952
210 Philip Gibbs, *The New Elizabethans* (London: Hutchinson and Co, 1953), p. 13
211 Gibbs, *Elizabethans*, pp. 18-9

ENDNOTES

212 Gibbs, *Elizabethans*, p. 19
213 Gibbs, *Elizabethans*, p. 19
214 Gibbs, *Elizabethans*, p. 20-1.
215 Lewis, *Treader*, p. 7
216 In fact, if I may be a little self-indulgent here, I would mention that when I came to look up this passage again, I found I had misremembered it. I was certain the novel mentioned her feet standing on the boards of the cabin, dressed in Caspian's clothes. In fact, it does not mention boards, planks or the cabin floor at all. I had been remembering the illustration by Pauline Baynes, which appeared in the original edition and lots of reprintings, which depicts Lucy carefully tying a belt (presumably to cinch in Caspian's tunic so it fits her a little better), amidst the greens and browns of the cabin. Looking at this picture, the eye is drawn to the lightest patch of it, where the light coming through the porthole falls in a pool on the floor. This spot shows Lucy's feet standing on the planks of the deck. This is no doubt where I had got the idea that the text itself mentions Lucy treading on the planks, which itself has a distinctly Shakespearean flavour. A girl putting on boys' clothing, ready to set out on the adventure, whilst her feet stand on the planks of the floor, could be a picture of a Shakespearean heroine standing on the famous planks of the stage at the Globe theatre. (Theatrical slang still sometimes uses the rather arch phrase 'treading the boards' to refer to performing in a play.) This is probably just memory playing tricks, but I am tempted to wonder whether Pauline Baynes also picked up the Shakespearean flavour of the scene and drew a Lucy who could be standing on the boards of the Globe in her disguise.
217 Lewis, *Treader*, p. 74
218 Geoffrey Willans and Ronald Searle, *Molesworth* (collected Penguin, 1999, repr. 2000), p. 59
219 Willans and Searle, *Molesworth*, p. 169
220 Willans and Searle, *Molesworth*, p. 216
221 Willans and Searle, *Molesworth*, pp. 216-7
222 Willans and Searle, *Molesworth*, pp. 217-8
223 In Nicholas John, ed. *Opera Guides: Peter Grimes/ Gloriana* (London: John Calder, 1983), p.87
224 In John, ed. *Grimes/ Gloriana*, p.66
225 Lewis, *Treader*, pp. 6-7
226 Christie, *Marple*, pp. 472, 307
227 Lewis, *Treader*, p. 128
228 Lewis, *Treader*, p. 107
229 Lewis, *Treader*, p. 55
230 Lewis, *Treader* p. 40
231 E. V. Rieu, tr., rev. D. C. H. Rieu, *The Odyssey* (1946, rev. 1991, ebook), 196-7
232 Lewis, *Treader*, p. 10
233 Shakespeare, *The Merchant of Venice*, 5.1. 280-4
234 Shakespeare, *The Taming of the Shrew*. 2.1.388-91
235 Lewis, *Treader*, p. 107
236 Lewis, *Treader*, p. 105

237 R. C. Seaton., ed. and tr., Apollonius of Rhodes, *Argonautica* (Harvard University press, 1912), p. 127
238 Seaton, *Argonautica*, p. 91
239 Lewis, *Treader*, p. 130
240 Lewis, *Treader*, p. 129
241 Lewis, *Treader*, p. 130